THE
JOURNEY OF GRACE

THE
JOURNEY OF GRACE

Dr Lisa Guinness

They dress the wound of my people as though it were not serious.
'Peace, peace,' they say, when there is no peace

(JEREMIAH 6:14)

Who is among you who reverently fears the Lord
yet has no shining splendour in his heart?

(ISAIAH 50:10) (AMP)

Jesus came and dwelt among us full of grace...
even grace upon grace...

(JOHN 1:14,16)

CONTENTS

THE
JOURNEY OF GRACE

Jesus promises to be the Way for each of us, wherever our starting point. He enables us to set off again on the next phase of our journey. The Journey of Grace is the journey back to the Father to receive His heart of love for us and to reclaim our full status as beloved sons and daughters – co-heirs with Christ.

During the course, we will look at our relationship with God, our relationship with our mother and father, and also our relationships with our peers and siblings. We will acknowledge all that was good and helpful from them, but also seek to identify what may have been missing, as well as those things that were not the best for us. After all, the people in our lives were born into and live in a fallen world, and therefore they could not always give us all that God intended.

On The Journey of Grace we will consider these relationships in the context of the Cross and the basic spiritual disciplines, such as seeking God's face, confessing our sins, forgiving others and practising His presence. We will acknowledge any defences we have put up and any coping mechanisms that are unhelpful or sinful and block our relationships with God and each other.

One key area in which God's glory is evident through us is in our being made in His image: male and female. We will explore what this means for us in our culture, and in the church.

During the course, each session will include worship to come into God's presence; teaching from a chapter that you will have prepared in advance, and time before the Holy Spirit. Each session ends with listening prayer in small groups under the guidance of trained leaders. Participants are encouraged to pour out their hearts to God and to listen for His healing word. You are encouraged to approach the material with your heart, as well as your head, taking note of any emotions or memories that arise and allowing yourself to feel them again in your adult body, in God's presence. From here God will lead us into a time of healing, revelation, confession or consolation and comfort – whatever He sees we need.

This course is an expression of many people's journeys back to the Father.

Enjoy – He is ready and waiting.

Dr Lisa Guinness

SECTION 1 – IN THE BEGINNING GOD...

In the Beginning God...

(GENESIS 1:1)

CHAPTER 1 – CREATION

Have you ever asked someone the way, only to hear the reply, "Well, I wouldn't start from here..."? For some of us, life has surpassed our expectations, but for many more it has turned out to be such a disappointment. Maybe we thought we would be somewhere else by now. Maybe we have deep regrets or sinful patterns of behaviour that we try to hide. We may have walled ourselves off and be living in survival mode. Perhaps we have decided to grit our teeth until the end of time. If there are problems in our close relationships or we feel particularly 'heavy laden', we can want the world to revolve around us. We may then find ourselves making excuses for the sin or chaos in our life.

But God doesn't think like this. He just wants us to know Him and love Him with all our heart, mind, soul and strength, and to feel the same way about ourselves and those with whom we live.

So, we are going to start with Him: *"In the beginning God..."*

What is the context in which we are to live? As Christians, we know that we live in the context of eternity. But few of us can imagine the infinite and the eternal. It is worth contemplating that there is far more reality in the unseen part of our world than there is in the seen.

Living in the world, we cannot see history, nor can we see heaven where God the Trinity enjoy their relationship together. We cannot see Satan or all the angelic beings. But our inability to see does not make them less real.

Jesus, the Lamb, was slain before the foundation of our world. He was ready to bear our sins and sorrows. The Bible tells us that God has always been in existence and always will be, and that His kingdom is glorious beyond measure. We are to live in the light of this eternal glory.

We take our rightful place on an awesome stage.

Do I live in the light of eternity and the unseen part of our world?

Am I awed by the glory of who God is and that He has revealed this to me?

God the Trinity has set us in a carefully planned physical world. There are many theories and theologies of creation, yet however you read the opening chapters of Genesis they give us some obvious parameters for life.

Day one gives us energy and time, divided into days and weeks. Ignoring this rhythm creates problems for us.

Day two gives us earth, rather than heaven, as our present environment.

Day three gives us a sense of place; we are rooted here as opposed to there. We cannot be in more than one place at once.

Day four gives us a sense of perspective and wonder as we admire the vastness of the skies.

Day five begins to give us the splendour of living creatures.

Day six gives us livestock, wild and domestic, to enjoy and rule over. Then God created **us** human beings, fearfully and wonderfully made in His own image – male and female. He blessed us and gave us authority over, and stewardship of, His creation.

Day seven gives us the Sabbath, when we stop work and give all our responsibilities back to God. In the Sabbath we find real rest for our souls and bodies (ie our whole beings). The Sabbath is not simply a day off when we clear a space to worship, because our whole lives are to be lived as worship to the Lord. This Sabbath rest is not just about a day in the week, snatching a rest when we can, as if we know ourselves better than God. It is about living in the ongoing Sabbath rest of God, in the rhythms of grace and recreation.

The theologian Dr Marva Dawn, author of two excellent books on the Sabbath[1], reminds us that the Sabbath always started the evening before. She invites us to join God in ceasing, resting, embracing and feasting. From this place of letting go and allowing God into our lives we keep our rightful place as creatures who are created by God. We can also recharge our batteries and allow them to be recharged in Him and by Him, for the week ahead.

Every aspect of creation that was put in place by God, such as time and place, is there for our benefit. We are not slaves to creation and the Sabbath is there to help us – not to mock or condemn us. We fight this when our lifestyle needs more hours in the day, or when we have the feeling that we need to be in more than one place at once. When we are lax in our stewardship of our resources (including our time) or our areas of responsibility, something is fundamentally wrong: we set ourselves at odds with creation, and therefore with the Creator. Living without the rhythm of God's rest and restoration in the Sabbath will not work and someone will pay the price.

---

1. Marva J. Dawn, *Keeping the Sabbath Wholly: Ceasing, Resting, Embracing, Feasting* (William. B. Eerdmans Publishing Company, Grand Rapids, Michigan, 1989).

The Genesis accounts of creation tell us that we, as human beings, are the grand finale. The whole epic of creation is for us.

Sadly, we can fail to appreciate the full impact of the creation account because of its poetic style. The account describes how the Lord makes Adam, as a human being, from the *adamah* (the Hebrew term for earth) and breathes His own life into him. The Lord plants a garden and causes water to spring up for the garden to grow and to provide food. Adam is given a guided tour of the garden and the Lord points out the different species of trees with a clear warning of the consequences of eating of the tree of the knowledge of good and evil.

We are then made aware that Adam is alone – a helper is needed. The Hebrew term for 'helper', *ezer kenegdo*, means 'one corresponding to him', not subservient to him. It is used of a greater, e.g. God, helping a lesser, e.g. man, in Psalm 121. So God makes Adam a helper: the *isha* (woman), made from the flesh and bone of *ish* (man). Adam begins by naming Eve. Man and woman are made *for* each other and *from* each other, ensuring their equality, mutuality and their intimate relationship with the substance of creation.

As God's creations we are made in the image of the Trinity: majestic; full of grace and truth towards each other; kind; courageous; lovers of justice and mercy; longing to see each other blessed; created for satisfying and intimate relationships with God, ourselves and each other.

We have authority to name and call out the good, setting boundaries and bringing order. God invites us to participate in the unfolding of creation and, using our gift of free will, co-author the ongoing story with Him.

We are blessed into the ideal environment where we can thrive and live out our lives in open relationship with the Trinity. We take our rightful place as glorious creatures dependant on their Creator.

Do I know 'full well' that I am 'fearfully and wonderfully made' by God? (Psalm 139:14)
If not, why not?

Do I live within the framework of creation, or is my lifestyle at odds with it? Why?

Our being in God

As God starts to reveal Himself in the Genesis story we discover that He is called 'I AM'. This means He is first and foremost about *being* not *doing*. As we are made in God's image we too should value being over doing.

Each and every one of God's actions is an expression of who He is. He is creative so He makes a world. He is love so He makes us for relationship. He is eternal and passionate so He plans the redemption of our mortality and gives us back our eternal life. Because He loves life He sets us in a glorious and fun-filled creation.

Can I just 'be'? Do I live out of this? Do I have rest in my soul?

How much is my life an expression of who I am in God?

Do I live with a need to justify my very existence, to find acceptance or purpose or to stave off criticism? If so, why?

What are the most satisfying areas of my life?

God as Trinity

God is three-in-one, with the Father, Son and Holy Spirit all being essential expressions of His being: a Trinity of three equal persons in one being. He invites us to know Him as these three beings, as far as our human minds will allow us to. The Trinity is relational – they each love, bless and prefer each other. Some theologians describe this dynamic as the 'dance' of the Trinity, the *perichoresis*, drawing us in to share the eternal celebration of life with each person. So, as we are in Christ and become partakers of His divine nature, we share His capacity to love and obey the Father as He leads us to Him and we see Him through new eyes. We also need to remember that

God embodies all the characteristics of both male and female. We are made in His image, yet He is beyond human gender and loves us with all the varying kinds of love that we need (for example, as a mother and a father).

It is through the Father, Jesus and the Holy Spirit's relationships with each other that we come to know just who God is in all His glory. He is love, life, the authority, the truth, all knowing and all-powerful. He is eternal, holy, just, merciful, creative, ordered, majestic, decisive, compassionate and involved.

The Father upholds the universe; I cannot sustain my own world. The Son redeems the universe; I cannot save others, nor myself. The Holy Spirit comforts and heals the universe; I cannot comfort and heal myself, nor heal my broken heart.

The truth of God enables me to understand what makes me 'me', and what my rightful place is in creation. After all, in Him everything holds together.

Write down your own description of God.

Which attributes of God do I know in my heart and appreciate the most? Which are the hardest for me to accept or understand?

Do I have a preferred member of the Trinity whom I relate to more easily than the others? If so, why might this be?

God created all the laws of physics and chemistry. He created every living creature – whether they have been discovered yet or not! He built creation around the system of mathematics. He gave our bodies the ability to laugh, cry, touch and speak. He did it all in colour.

At different times in our lives we will be prompted to sit in awe at God's creation. It is important that we take time to admire and notice the world God has created.

The truth that we are made in God's image can often explain both the potential we feel within ourselves: to live on a bigger canvas or express ourselves in new ways, and the frustration we feel when this seems unattainable.

If we are made in the image of God, which aspects of His character do we recognise most easily in ourselves? Which aspects do we see and appreciate in others?

Who has God made me to be?

How do I convey the image of God to those with whom I live, work, play and worship? What hinders this?

Over the coming weeks we will be seeking God as Saviour and Redeemer in very specific ways.

A prayer

Thank you, Lord God, that You have revealed yourself to us as our Creator and Saviour, our Redeemer and the one in whom our souls can rest secure. We ask You to forgive us when we have tried to live outside Your framework for us and when we have doubted Your integrity and goodness because of our experiences of the Fall.

We ask You now, to help us trust in You more, as we bring You the detail of our lives, and may You bless us with understanding and with Your favour and peace as You restore who we really are to us.

Amen

Scriptures for worship and prayer

GENESIS 1–2:2

PSALM 95

ISAIAH 42:5–9

PSALM 62

PSALM 96

MARK 2:23–27

PSALM 93

PSALM 139

EPHESIANS 2:18–22

NOTES

CHAPTER 2 – MY STORY

In oral cultures family history is passed down through storytelling. Members of the family hear their stories over and over and have the opportunity to ask questions and express themselves aloud. This process of hearing and questioning enables an individual to join up the dots in the story and find their own place in it. Most of us have not experienced this. We have rarely pieced our story together, nor heard it told.

Through the Journey of Grace course, we will look at themes such as faith, shame, money and stability, and consider what place they took in our family. Doing so will help us make sense of many of our attitudes and reactions as adults.

At the beginning of the course we asked you to write out your mother's and father's stories and your siblings' stories. Writing our story reminds us that life is not a mystery to be solved but an opportunity for God's redemption and creativity to be expressed even in the most unpromising situations!

Today, in the small groups we will have space to tell our story to our small group in whatever way we like. The story will be offered to and received by the group without judgement or giving advice. In doing so, we allow each person the dignity to speak out their story and be heard. It is each person's holy ground.

As we tell our story, we can start to separate what is ours and appreciate it and take responsibility for it, while leaving others to take responsibility for their part in our journey. We can offer God the suffering that we have experienced and the suffering we have brought to others. We can offer God those occasions that are too deep for words. We can see the patterns and make fresh choices, asking God to give us a right perspective on our lives that puts Him at the centre, rather than us or anyone else. We can speak out what may have gone unspoken for years, and we can also ask God to tell us our story from His point of view and practise tuning into His voice. He longs to dialogue with us.

We need to consider how much choice we have been able to exercise in the writing of our story. Some of us may have felt like a lone author with too little input from anyone else. Others of us may now see that other people have exercised too much influence over our lives and have been writing our story for us. We will have the opportunity to be grateful for all that is right and good in our story, but also to forgive and leave with God all that was inappropriate. We can take up our full authority and choose to write our own adult story now with God as we make our journey of grace with Him.

NOTES

CHAPTER 3 – THE FALL

All of creation has been ruined in the Fall. The only one to escape is God; the Father, Son and Holy Spirit are holy, majestic, perfect and loving for ever. Since the Fall everything else is intrinsically flawed and damaged; we have never seen or known anything as God intended it to be. We have lost both our trust and our relationship with God, meaning that we approach Him with suspicion and antipathy. Yet, we have a latent memory of what we have missed. Romans 8:23 reminds us that we long to become God's sons and daughters again, and that we groan as we feel the pain of this orphaned state physically. Redemption is defined for us as adoption back into son/daughter-ship with God the Father. In our fallen state, we want to be independent and determine our own future, yet we are ashamed of our inability to do so. Until God intervenes we spiral into more and more chaos within ourselves, with each other and within the physical world and no one cares for our soul (Psalm 142:4).

This explains why we have been hurt so much simply from living in a fallen world, why we mismanage things as we do and why we sometimes feel so alone in it all.

> *Let us make man in our image, after our likeness.*
> *And let them have dominion over all the earth. And God blessed them*
>
> *(GENESIS 1:26, 28)*

Before the Fall, we knew God's nature, God's authority and God's blessing. After the Fall, we become carnal, impotent and alone.

Genesis chapter 1

We have God's nature

Genesis 1:26 tell us that we have been made in God's likeness, fully integrated with body, mind and spirit tuned into the Father's will – flowing with each other and creation. We were created with real wisdom, peace and understanding. We enjoyed the presence of God, we enjoyed (not tolerated) full communication and communion with Him and each other, and our lives were relaxed and perfectly balanced. We trusted. Like God, we worked and were productive (Genesis 2:15) but it was not futile, nor was work Adam's identity. We were family, children on into eternity with no expectation of death or change.

Because we are made in God's image we have a memory of being satisfied, of being kind and generous to each other, confident but not proud, assertive but not strident, and of living in tune with God's Spirit.

Do I include myself as part of the glory of God?

Can I enjoy His presence? How do I see God? How do I approach Him?
(e.g. with fear, dread, contempt, joy?)

Our God-given nature ⇒ carnal

Since the Fall, life may feel like labour under a huge sense of failure and shame, even self-hatred. We can spend our time looking for new ways to ease our inner pain, rather than humbling ourselves and admitting our need of a saviour to God.

With the Fall, the ability and desire to live in tune with God's spirit was lost. Our spirit became cut off from God meaning that:

- Our spirit is damaged and adrift from God so that the body (flesh) and the head (mind) start to dominate. We become cut off from our hearts and from God

- We no longer enjoy God's presence. We are no longer comfortable in His presence, nor are we awed by Him or feel natural in worship. Instead of being God-conscious we become self-conscious and ashamed, even ashamed of our relationship with Him. Knowing God can feel like an unattractive or restrictive option

- Instead of seeking God we hide from Him and become fearful and doubting or cynical

- Instead of connecting with God we detach

- This severing from our life source leaves us alone with a huge vacuum inside instead of a solid sense of ourselves and ongoing life

- We are at war inside with the old memory of how good it was to do God's will being challenged by the flesh and the mind

- We can't 'do' love, joy or peace naturally anymore, these things may feel forced

- We are out of sync with everything and everyone: a helpmeet becomes the adversary. Our joining together with others disintegrates into misunderstanding and blame-shifting

- We want the rules to be bent for us. Although we know God's boundaries, we want to rewrite the rules and be the exception without facing the consequences of our choices. We feel we deserve a treat

- We do not even keep our own, inner, rules and deep down we know that we lack real integrity.

How am I living? What am I contending with?

In what ways are my body or mind running the show? Is it just a show?

Do I take care of myself – body, mind and spirit?

Do I have real feelings that I allow myself to feel physically or are feelings just something I deal with using my mind?

Am I open to God's image being formed and refined in me?

Scripture speaks many times and in varying ways about the Fall. Despite this, we tend to hold back from articulating our wounds and disappointments clearly; often we would rather shrug our shoulders and blame God. Yet He is as holy and righteous as ever. It is creation and our human nature that are thoroughly fallen.

In the Bible Jesus describes us as orphans, the broken hearted, captives, those needing comfort and as lost sheep. The Old Testament says we have been robbed, plundered and devastated through the generations, leaving us as wanderers who are hungry, thirsty and heavy-laden.

Compared with God's creation and His provision for us, we have deeply hurt and maimed each other and chosen to go our own way again and again. Scripture is right.

We have authority (Genesis 1:26)

Genesis 1:26 describes us, humanity, in God's kingdom with Him as the King, and we were at the pinnacle of creation. We managed this kingdom with justice, peace, love and joy. We sensed the appropriateness of the level of authority we had, and exercised it effortlessly as part of creation order and as a privilege. We were not underachieving, nor had we been promoted beyond our capacity.

BUT after the Fall: our God given authority ⇒ oppression

The place God gave us, at the pinnacle of creation, suited exactly who He had made us to be: like God, but without the responsibility of upholding the universe on into eternity. Suddenly it didn't seem enough. We wanted more, hence the phrasing of the serpent's temptation: "Did God say?"

When we disobeyed:

- We gave away all our authority. This has left us yearning for power or being ashamed of our powerlessness, often swinging between the two
- We exchanged being benevolent (well-intentioned and kind) rulers for slavery. There wasn't even the prospect of amnesty or early release for good behaviour
- We became vulnerable to false expressions of power such as sex and money
- We are now contending with God instead of always doing His will. We have unintentionally become participants in Satan's revenge on God, doing his dirty work for him
- Our glory (beauty, wisdom, creativity, initiative etc), can now be used to maim, kill, steal and destroy each other and ourselves – further marring God's image in every one of us
- We live as victims instead of from a true place of authority.

In what ways do I feel powerless? And in what ways do I seek power?

Where do I exercise good authority and where am I a victim?

We are blessed (Genesis 1:28)

Creation was exactly the right environment for us. Everything we needed was found in abundance. Creation worked for us and we managed it with ease. As we thrived, we shared the very life of God with each other and it gave us so many ways to bless each other. Once we could make decisions based on the best for everyone, but in our fallen state so many of our decisions are selfish and reactive, intent on hurting others or controlled by money or need.

BUT after the Fall: our God given blessing ⇒ toil

Now, after the Fall:

- The things we once managed and the blessings we once knew begin to contend with us and rule us
- We become further enslaved by the common things of life – those things that should be easy, such as getting food, deciding what to wear, how to be affirmed, work, the ability to take a holiday or rest. These things become idols: subconsciously we ask them to give us significance and comfort
- We use others for our own ends and take from them, rather than give
- We become competitive rather than wanting to bless each other
- Our perception of reality is skewed so we get caught in performance, duty, living in a spiritual/secular divide (believing there are areas of life in which God is not interested or sovereign), or living in a head/heart divide
- Our imagination, which, because it is unfettered by reason, should take us beyond ourselves into the kingdom of God, also becomes a liability. We can become captive to obsession and fantasy, to sexual addiction and envy until we lose the capacity to practise God's presence at all
- Fantasy becomes equivalent to reality, as we see in our culture, although we find this very difficult to acknowledge.

Where do I flourish and feel God's delight? What are my deepest desires?

Where is life toil for me and how do I react to this?

Sadly, Adam and Eve did not live happily ever after. A third party was present and he insinuated himself into the heart of their relationship using subtle manipulation. Adam forgot his guided tour of the trees and watched his wife as she doubted God's goodness and ate from the tree of knowledge. Their intimacy is lost. Adam then hides from God and when he shifts the blame on to Eve he confirms this fatal breakdown. Not only did they cause the Fall which impacted themselves, they also cause creation itself to be fallen and subject to a curse. Instead of productively farming the earth, Adam is now subject to futile toil as he contends with the plants he once loved. Because of the Fall, Eve now has multiplied difficulty in her productivity through pain in childbirth, and instead of being a true and upright soul mate for Adam she now bends into him in frustration and neediness. Both of them feel ashamed, alone and at odds. Our gender has become a liability and a point of contention, rather than complementarity; the intimacy we long for is lost. God's only remedy is to bring their agony to an end in death and expel them from the garden. He knows that the Lamb was slain even before the foundation of the world. In Jesus, His precious creation is not lost forever – there is a way back to His heart through the Son at the Cross.

So, the Fall is comprehensive and has marred the image of God in us beyond recognition and this is why life often hurts so much. We have all been conceived, born, brought up, educated and have worked and worshipped in a fallen world.

Being made in His image, we expected to receive love and mercy, to be allowed to be an individual, to be heard and affirmed, blessed for who we are not for what we do. We longed to take our place in a secure and ordered environment, without fear or anxiety clouding our joy or peace. But again and again, this has not been so. Our hearts will have been disappointed or crushed, and we may not have understood why. The value of disappointment, however, is that it can give definition to our hopes and needs. All is not well with our world.

What circumstances, or people, in my life have hurt or disappointed me and so affected my relationship with God and caused me to question His character?

How can I bring this to God? Do I want to clear the way back to Him?

In our humanity we may be able to ease much of the difficulty and suffering that we encounter, but we cannot save ourselves. We cannot cleanse our consciences, forgive sin or redeem its damage. We cannot heal our broken hearts. We are creatures who need our Creator God also to be our Comforter, our Saviour and our Redeemer. After all, we take the car to the garage or the cat to the vet without any shame, so why do we feel ashamed of needing God as Father or Jesus as Saviour?

In what ways have I allowed myself to need a Saviour?

In what ways am I ashamed of needing a Saviour? Have I tried to save myself or deny there is anything wrong? Why?

In what ways do I allow myself to receive God as Father, both loving and strong?

Hope vs despair

Sometimes, the sheer intensity of sin and fallen human nature (both ours and other people's) can eclipse the presence of God in our lives. We become more aware of the Fall than we are of God's presence, and as a result we can lose hope.

This can make us bitter and detached and it is often easier to place the blame on to God, who is Spirit, than on to those around us. But God invites us to look "to the Rock from which we were hewn" (Isaiah 51:1). He is our key source of objectivity and redemption. So, before anything else, we need to swallow our pride and independence and start to dialogue with Him. It is vital that we stay open to God when things are tough so that we can find grace at our point of need, and not just when everything is going well and we are effectively saving ourselves.

If we feel 'acedia', which is sorrow unto death, we will need to acknowledge that we wish we were dead, or that we feel as good as dead. Also, if we are stuck in a place of resignation – that nothing is ever going to change, or the change is too big to imagine and we don't want to/can't move on – we will need to bring this to God. This may need a deep time of repentance and pouring out our hearts to God. Just as long as it takes to become open to God again!

As we reclaim our rightful identity, as those who are fearfully and wonderfully made in the image of God, we recover our significance and purpose. Hope, love, joy, peace and justice become available to us again. If we allow it, this connection can root us into a truth that transcends our circumstances. Isaiah 51 invites us to receive God's comfort and presence right into our ruined places.

Hope comes as we humbly rest in God again and give Him the weight of our struggles. We can then take our rightful place in creation – within the constraints of a fallen world, but without self-pity or bargaining with God. Only then can we recover the inner truth, that our place in God's kingdom transcends the external and the transient.

Glory vs shame

We will explore shame later on in the course. But at this point we need to acknowledge that we live with the sense of not quite measuring up, and of missing out. We can only oppose this with God's words of redemption – He tells us that we share in His glory; we are not left without comfort and in shame. Many of us are living our lives in a place of shame and defensiveness, sometimes even apologising for our very existence.

What would I be like if the Fall had not happened? - Do this in any way you find helpful, e.g. describe it using words, draw a picture, or make a collage.

NOTES

NOTES

CHAPTER 4 – GOD THE FATHER

God is passionate about being our Father and we need to know, in our heart as well as our head, that He is very different from our earthly fathers. He wants us to seek Him, get to know Him, trust Him and pour out our hearts to Him. As we learn to recognise and welcome His voice, we can dialogue with Him and live out our lives as His beloved sons and daughters.

Before we go any further, we need to check out how we see God by writing down what we know of His character and fatherhood in practice. What do we know in our hearts, and what is actually remote or difficult about Him for us?

Questioning God – His goodness and His being Father

In Jewish culture, after every Sabbath meal, the father of the household would take each child on to his knee, or into his embrace, and bless him or her for something he had seen in them that week. The Father would end with a specific prayer of blessing from God the Father. The words of blessing and prayer would be said in front of all their siblings. God the Father intended this blessing to be an integral part of our upbringing. How we have missed out.

For some of us, the total, or effective, absence of our earthly father is too painful to bear. As a result we can hardly allow God the Father into our lives. We may believe deep down that we are too much of a disappointment for Him to include us in any plans for good. We may be projecting all our hurt on to God the Father. Every broken promise that we have experienced will feel as if it included God. We may put up defenses against His love. Yet He knows this only too well; He simply wants to meet us with His understanding and compassion. We may resist the grace He offers us because it is easier for us to live in a place of control than in His freedom.

Our ability or desire to accept God as Father will depend on our early experiences. Many of us have experienced intense moments in our lives when we cried out to God to come to us. Perhaps we called out to ask Him to stop something or someone, or to help us or rescue us. Our perception is that He didn't. Somewhere inside, our hearts are holding this against Him and wondering if He is really as trustworthy as He says.

Our hearts want to challenge Him and say:

- *If* you are such a good father where were you when?
- How could you have let... happen?
- Why didn't you part the heavens and come down?

God's answer is that He *did* part the heavens and come down – in Jesus.

God the Father knows the conflict in our hearts. He wants to clear the way back to Himself as Father. He wants to hear from us, in our own words and we can approach Him without fear or shame. We need to pour out our hearts to Him with any 'ifs' or 'buts' we are carrying. Jesus said again and again that our heavenly Father *knows* – He knows what we need before we ask, even if our earthly father never did.

Scriptures that say it all

JOB 13:3 (AMP)

> *Surely I wish to speak to the Almighty, and I desire to argue and reason
> my case with God* [that He may explain the conflict between what
> I believe of Him and what I see of Him].

JOB 40:6 –10

> *Then the Lord answered Job out of the whirlwind saying:*
> *Gird up your loins now like a man, I will demand of you and you answer me:*
> *Will you set aside and render void my judgement?*
> *Will you condemn me, your God, that you may appear righteous and justified?*
> *Have you an arm like God? Or can you thunder with a voice like his?*
> *Since you question the manner of the Almighty's rule, deck yourself now with the*
> *excellency and dignity of the Supreme Ruler, and yourself undertake the government*
> *of the world, if you are so wise; and array yourself with honour and majesty.*

JOEL 3:1, 4

> *For behold in those days and at that time, when I restore the fortunes of Judah*
> *and Jerusalem: Are you paying me back for something? If you are paying me back*
> *then I will return your payment on your own head swiftly and speedily?*

JOHN 10:10 (AMP)

> *The thief comes to rob and kill and destroy; but I have come that you may have*
> *life and have it abundantly.* [Rob us of our inheritance as sons and daughters,
> kill off our belief in the father's goodness and desire to bless us, cut us off from
> the life source of the father, rob us of blessing and the belief/receipt of blessing.]

What is missing in my life? How have I been robbed?

God calls Himself Father

The words used to describe the different parts of the God-head are relational. They speak of a family with a Father, a Son and a Spirit who is the Comforter. We could even say that God calls Himself Father for our benefit, so that we can see ourselves in relationship to Him as children, precious sons and daughters. This is especially important as He ordained the family to be the primary unit for human life. As Paul describes in Ephesians 3:15, the Father, "from whom all fatherhood takes its title and derives its name".

At the moment of conception a particular man became our father for life. But, the name 'father' should not merely describe someone who has physically fathered a child, but someone who is committed to that child; someone who is delighted to bless the child into adulthood and be in relationship with the child for the rest of his life. In calling Himself the Eternal Father, God is signifying His desire to be in a similarly committed and loving relationship with us, for all eternity. As He is infinite, He has the capacity to father all who come to Him. He is Father to each one of us as if we were His only precious child. His will is that no one should miss out on His delight in us and our relationship with Him as Father.

Because we live in a fallen world, our experience of our own families and our own father can eclipse the goodness of God, and the goodness of this relationship for us. Later on we will consider how fatherless we *all* are and how much we need the heavenly Father as a result. Despite this deep need, our instinct is to deny it and to try to father ourselves.

Why Jesus came

Jesus' arrival on earth, with great celebration, as God's only Son, shows us just how much the Father wants to reveal Himself to us. God the Father allows Jesus to begin his life like us – as a fertilised egg. He is born as a man with the express purpose of showing us the Father. In Jesus' life on earth we learn of the Father's character. God uses Jesus to show us the Father's heart and how He reacts to us. For example, Jesus' handling of the woman caught in adultery was the way the Father wanted her to be treated. Jesus diverts attention away from her and on to Himself, exposing the hypocrisy and misogyny (hatred of women on the basis of gender) that she was experiencing. Jesus was doing the Father's will. The Father and Jesus are equally wise and kind and passionate. The Father is not remote and changeable, but as involved and understanding as Jesus. In His coming to earth as a man, we experience God as the second person in the Trinity who is able to help us see and hear God firsthand in the flesh, receiving His very nature (2 Peter 1:4).

In what ways do I know in my heart that the Father and Jesus are one?

Naming

Just as the Father named Jesus (Luke 1:31), He has a special name for each of us. God has given us a unique expression of His image in us. Our name should convey this, just as God's name expresses His fatherly love. Also, He is the Author of our life and His intention was that we would be named in an intentional way and be guided to become this person as an adult. We will see later in the course that this often did not happen well for us. Thankfully, God has hopes and plans for us that include our redemption and the restoration of our Father-son or Father-daughter relationship.

How much has anyone discerned who I really am and encouraged and blessed this unique person to become a reality?

A Father delights in His children

In the Bible we read that when the Father parted the heavens and spoke to Jesus, it was to reassure Him of His presence and to tell the world that He was well pleased and delighted with His Son. From this, we learn that we needed to be encouraged and also delighted in by our father. We notice, of course, that these words were spoken to Jesus before He began His active ministry after thirty years as a carpenter in mainstream life, not in Christian ministry! This is a wonderful example of the Father's unconditional love and true affirmation for who Jesus was, not what He had done, or would do.

Later on we will learn how important it was for us, as children, to identify with our father as a role model and as someone with whom we could intimately, easily and permanently connect. Jesus certainly identified with His Father in this way. Jesus knew who He was in relation to the Father, and He derived full security and identity from this knowledge. It was our earthly father's privilege to represent God's love to us through his affection; affirmation; attention; advocacy, acceptance and accompanying. We see Jesus publicly receiving all these from His father at His baptism. As we go to the Father as little children we can engage in this profound identification with Him and know our true identity.

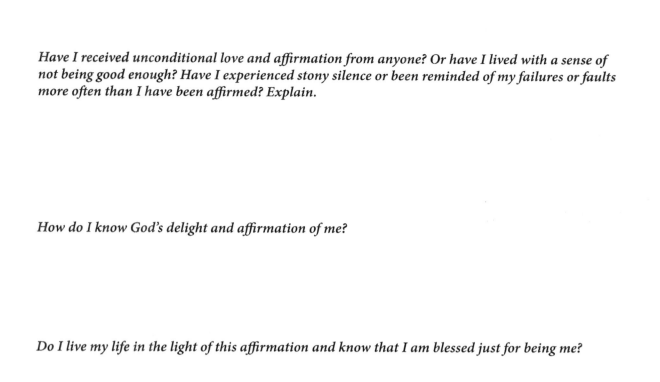

Have I received unconditional love and affirmation from anyone? Or have I lived with a sense of not being good enough? Have I experienced stony silence or been reminded of my failures or faults more often than I have been affirmed? Explain.

How do I know God's delight and affirmation of me?

Do I live my life in the light of this affirmation and know that I am blessed just for being me?

The Father also reminded Jesus that His gaze was fixed on Him. The Father knew where Jesus was and what was happening in His life all the time. We too needed to know our earthly father's affirming gaze on us: that he was fascinated by us, in awe and wonder at having fathered someone as fearfully and wonderfully made as us. We needed this level of engagement, not simply hearing his voice from behind the newspaper. In Matthew 5 Jesus reminds us again and again that the Father sees and knows all about us.

We need to know that we are seen by one who loves us, and who therefore understands us. In her worst moment God revealed Himself to Hagar out in the desert so she could say from her heart, "I have been seen by the God who sees me" (Genesis 16:13). We all crave this experience deep down in our hearts – to be really seen.

An awareness of the Father's gaze can act as a deterrent to sin. It encourages us to practise His presence and can be a resource in times of temptation. The lack of gaze from our earthly father, and the resulting lack of awareness of God's gaze, can be so acute that we search, almost frantically, for eye contact and gaze from others. We can need it so badly that we can assume people are looking at us when they are not, or we can be predatory and flirtatious in our desperation to be seen.

Have I known my father's real and appropriate attention and gaze on me?

How do I feel this has been lacking or unhelpful? Has it affected my desire for and knowledge of God's presence?

The Father accompanied Jesus

The Father promises never to leave us or forsake us. He accompanied Jesus through every step of His life on earth until the darkness of sin obscured Him from Jesus at the crucifixion. Jesus spent hours and hours talking with the Father and only did His will. He enjoyed the companionship, wisdom, and revelation of the Father with Him all the time. It was a blessing not a duty.

Yet, so often, we can live life on the run, squeezing in focused times with God as if they were a duty. Our times with God are often not the precious, life-giving father-son or father-daughter moments that they should be. We can treat our time with God as an added extra, or as if we are doing God a favour – rather than experiencing time with Him as the awesome privilege of being accompanied by the Living God – the one who is our life, our joy and our peace.

Is this so in your life? If so, why do you think this is?

Are you aware of God's desire to be with you as the Good Father?

It may be that our own father wasn't particularly present in our life as we grew up. As a result we can hardly imagine God being interested in us, or, that He would want to accompany us through life. Thinking back, we may have had very few deep and meaningful times with our earthly father, if any. He may have always told us to, "Go and ask your mother". Or he may have silenced us by asking what we wanted in an unwelcoming tone. He may have lived in his shed or behind his newspaper or spent long hours outside the home. He may not have known quite what to do with us, or, being unfathered himself, he may have found fatherhood too much.

So, if we detached or gave up on our father, or feel he did that with us, we may also feel detached from God. We will be unable to enjoy His presence or include time with Him in our life on an ongoing basis. Whatever happened in our story, **we need to separate God the Father from our earthly father**, and press through into a real and open loving relationship with God the perfect Father.

The good Father is REVEALED in Scripture

The Old Testament

In Genesis 1:25 God reveals Himself not simply as one person, but as a Trinity. He says, "Let us make man in our own image". Humanity is not alien, but can join the relationships of God. The whole of creation meets with God's approval and is tailor-made for us to enjoy. He sets up the family unit and the roles of father and mother – biologically, spiritually and sociologically. He has asked for our worship to be expressed as love towards Him, towards ourselves and towards our neighbour. In doing so, He invites us to take our place in an earthly community and in the community of the Trinity. These relationships invite us into something personal, intimate and ongoing that is revelatory on all sides. Our worship and obedience are to be expressed through relationship, not as abstract concepts.

In Deuteronomy 32:6 Israel is asked, "Is not he your father who acquired you for his own?" God proclaims Himself as Father to the fatherless in Psalm 68:5 and promises to have compassion on us (Psalm 103:13). He promises that when our earthly father or mother forsake us He will take us up (Psalm 27:10). He covers the effects of the Fall on our family life and on the ability/failure of our parents to provide what He knows we need.

In Psalm 89:26 the psalmist calls out to God, "You are my Father, my God and the Rock of my salvation". God continues to speak of His fatherly care and understanding in the Psalms and in the book of Isaiah, reminding us that His sons and daughters, who will come back from afar, have been created for His glory (Isaiah 43:6-7). He asks Jeremiah to say to the people, "But I thought you would call me father?" (Jeremiah 3:19).

He is passionate that we should grasp this truth – He is our good, eternal Father. He wants us to relate to Him first and foremost as beloved sons and daughters. He is the one who carries us close to His heart. He taught us to walk!

How do you feel about this? What is your response?

Does this help you separate out your earthly father from God the Father?

How do you feel about God's desire to be your eternal Father?

The New Testament

Jesus refers to God as His Father straight away in the Sermon on the Mount. The Pharisees are indignant in response – they cannot believe that Jesus equates Himself with God. Jesus commands us to address God as Our Father.

Jesus' mission was to bring us back to the Father so that God could enjoy having us as His children again and that we could receive our rightful inheritance as heirs of the eternal kingdom.

In Hebrews 2:13 and Jude 24 we read of Jesus presenting us to the Father as His children with great joy. Although Jesus is the one who makes us holy, He is not ashamed to call us His brothers. Jesus enables our relationship with God to move from hostility – being slaves – to servants, to friends and then to brothers and sisters and sons and daughters sharing the same Father. At the last supper Jesus calls us His friends, but after His resurrection He tells Mary that He is ascending to, "My Father and your Father, to My God and your God". He has achieved the restoration of the family that God originally intended.

As we look at the accounts of Jesus' life, He is constantly addressing and referring to God as Father. Jesus even says that He has revealed to us everything that He has learned from the Father. He teaches us about God the Father in His parables when He refers to God as an intimate and personal Father, not as some remote or disinterested deity. Throughout His last teachings in John's gospel we hear the Father and Jesus and the Spirit drawing us into the glory of eternal life and to the very heart of their relationship as the Trinity.

As we allow ourselves to share the passion and intimacy that is passing between them, we must realise that this is all for us and that it includes us. There is no other way to relate to God but as Father.

Paul begins each one of his letters by wishing us the grace and peace of "God our Father". In 1 Corinthians 8:6 Paul says that for believers there is, "Only one God, the Father, who is the source of all things and for whom we exist". Again, in 2 Corinthians 6:18 Paul quotes from Isaiah and Hosea reminding us that the Lord Almighty says, "I will be a father to you and you shall be my sons and daughters". Both these statements draw a clear contrast between the worship of impersonal idols and a living relationship with our Father God.

We are assured in Ephesians 1 that the Father has long planned for us to be adopted back into His family in love, so that we can become heirs of the Father's entire kingdom with Jesus. It is the Father who brings us revelation of these intimate secrets and plans of blessing. In Ephesians 3 we read the wonderful description of God being the Father who enables us to be rooted and grounded, not in insecurity or doubt, but in love. This is another Trinity moment – as the Spirit gives us the strength, deep in our inner beings, to comprehend the full scope and dimensions of Jesus' love for us, the Father fills us with the fullness of God's goodness and love.

He is passionate about being our Father and delighting in us as His children.

We may need to read the above sentence many times before it touches our heart and transforms our perception and attitude towards God. All through Scripture God reveals Himself as desiring relationship with us. Jesus' coming, is the means through which the Father, Son and Holy Spirit achieve this.

How do you feel about being God's precious son or daughter?

Can you live in the truth of this relationship?

How is God the Father described?

In Scripture every description of God's character repeatedly refers to God as a good Father or a just King. For our Eternal Father also to be the King of Kings and to reign in justice and holiness, means He is both trustworthy and the only advocate we need. There is no higher appeal. What He says about us is the final word. He is a Father who takes full responsibility. He is the living word and He has the last word. We need to allow His voice to override that of our earthly father and receive His goodness and blessing into our lives.

God is described as:

———————————————————————— ||| ————————————————————————

Faithful, just, holy, loving, patient, at peace, jealous, full of joy and light, everlasting, constant, wise, present, compassionate, understanding, strong, intimate, all-knowing, creative, tender, forgiving, kind, gracious, merciful, truthful, longsuffering, delighted, majestic, glorious.

———

We can complete the list from our own experience of God's nature.

As we look at these attributes, we realise that these are all the things we have longed to see, or indeed knew we needed, from our earthly father if we were going to flourish and be secure. The good news is that they are always there for us in God the Father.

How does this compare with your description of God at the beginning of this session? Has your heart warmed as a result of what you have read?

The most interesting of Jesus' teachings on the Father is His teaching about the 'waiting father'. The waiting father appears in the parable of the prodigal son, a story we are probably very familiar with. The description of the waiting father tells us so much about God's character and His attitude towards us, even in the midst of our waywardness. We need to be aware of the cultural context of the time if we are to fully appreciate the quality of the father's love, as Jesus moves his audience from the classic description of a Middle Eastern father, to revealing the totally radical nature of this father's love.

We could say that the main purpose of Jesus' coming and of the whole plan of salvation is to get us back into this father-son or father-daughter relationship: the Father first loving us with everything He has, including His own Son, and our increasingly being able to love Him with more and more of our heart, mind, soul and strength. We need to own before God and repent, of all the ways we have wasted the life and the gifts He has given us and ask Him to restore all that we feel has been robbed from us.

The parable of the waiting father, the prodigal son and the self-righteous son

In the story (Luke 15:11-32), the son had been brought up in what was probably the best home in the village. There were servants, livestock, ceremonial robes, sandals and a banqueting hall large enough to entertain the whole village. At the time, the village homes would have been built close together for safety, with balconies from which the father could view his lands or pass bread across to his neighbour on the Sabbath without contravening the law. Fields on every side typically surrounded the houses. The village may well have been at the end of a road, rather than on a route anywhere.

Before the son left, he had shamed his father in front of the whole village by asking for his inheritance while his father was still alive. It was normally assumed that sons would bless their father by being at their deathbed and it was taboo to mention the benefits of a will during a person's lifetime. In effect, the son publicly wished his father was dead. He walked out of the family home and the village with great bravado and pride. Some members of the village must have traded with him for him to exchange his assets (land, livestock) into cash. The village may well have heard later about the famine in the land and the son's high living and realised that the money had passed into the hands of Gentiles.

Despite his bedraggled appearance, and because desperate situations call for desperate measures, the son decided to return home. He came with a prepared speech and a plan to save himself – he had worked out that if he became a hired servant he would be able to work off his debt. He would also be able to live outside the family home and would not have to come back under his father and his brother's roof, keeping his independence and continuing to have no family obligations. He would have his freedom and enough to live off. It was a nice little win-win that only needed a few carefully chosen words and a bit of humble pie and it could all fall into place.

As he approached the outlying fields of the village the son knew that he would be spotted by the villagers and would have to run the gauntlet of their wrath. He assumed that his father would probably be so glad to know he was alive and back that he would agree to anything, including his plan.

The son could also have been subjected to the ceremony of 'The Kezazah', or cutting off, because he had lost the family money to the Gentiles and had dared to return home without it. This ceremony involved the public breaking of a clay pot on to the ground and the calling out of the name of the betrayer for all to hear. This action declared that the person was thereby cut off from the entire community.

But the son's father had other ideas for the son's reception. He watched for his son day after day. In his heart they were still father and son, no matter how the son had behaved. The father longed for the opportunity to restore him to his rightful place. The father needed to see him first before the villagers took matters into their own hands. So, every day he watched and was ready to run to him. The indignity of raising his robes and quickening his step enabled him to divert the shame and attention off his son and on to himself. We know the servants were hot on his heels and that there was already an audience present by the time the father and son spoke. The father held nothing back. His public display of pity and passion for his son took over and reduced the son's speech to empty words. For the father still wanted to have him as his son – to be in a real restored relationship with him – not just to know he was alive. He wanted to see him redeemed from his manipulative ways, from his hardness of heart and arrogant wheeler-dealer lifestyle.

Only the father could change the situation. Only he had the authority to forgive and redeem his son. Restoration and celebration were all that was on the father's mind. He had waited so long for this moment that nothing was going to quench his joy.

The son had not bargained for the radical nature of his father's love, nor for the father's desire to bless him as a son. The possibility of forgiveness and restoration was beyond his imagination, and at that point could even have seemed like a constraint.

But the son is touched to the heart and allows his father to reinstate him back into the family without any further conditions. He accepts the blessing of sonship, he receives the robe and the ring from his father and allows the servants to place sandals back on his feet. This was a clear demonstration to the whole village of whom the son still was and how he was to be treated by everyone. Once my son always my son – there was no servanthood here.

The killing of the fatted calf and the invitation to join the celebration are further expressions of the father's generosity and open heart and of his grace. He never minimises or excuses the son's abject behaviour, instead he covers it with his love and goodness. He takes the same stance with his elder son's self-righteousness – offering him grace and so much more. In fact, he reminds him that he has no cause to be resentful as everything the father has is his. By being bitter and detached he was no more desirous of being a son than his brother.

God loves us when we are unrighteous and when we are self-righteous. He understands the damage of both. It is the same mercy, the same restoration and celebration. He knows better than us the full extent of our sin, but He is determined that nothing will rob Him of His father-child relationship with us. He reiterates the terms of His covenant back to us, "All that I am and have is yours. Behold My Son". Following the son's example, we refuse to stay proud or rude. We look into the Father's welcoming face and say, "All that I have and am is yours. I am home".

Where are you in this story? (Please expand on the 'Notes' page if desired.)

Do you believe that God is equally compassionate to you when you are unrighteous and when you are self-righteous?

NOTES

CHAPTER 5 – JESUS, GOD THE SON

Jesus is the answer to our cry for God to open the heavens and come down to save us. In Jesus, God becomes Man. He is the person of the Trinity whom we have seen face-to-face and survived. He IS God and we are made in His image. Jesus came because the Fall took such a toll on our humanity that we needed to see and experience God, in Jesus, to see who we really are and what we have lost. Few of us are as full of grace and truth as we should be. As well as showing us the Father, Jesus also demonstrates how to be a beloved son/daughter and how to know God as our Father.

The Incarnation

Jesus has shared every aspect of our human journey, from conception to death. He experienced every human emotion from highest joy to extreme pain. Therefore, He expects us to share every part of our lives with Him – not just the "good" bits or our successes or panics. Nothing can shock Him or be outside His experience of life on earth. He has seen it all and borne it all, Himself, on the Cross.

We know from Scripture that Jesus experienced much on earth:

- He was branded illegitimate
- He was a refugee
- He was homeless as a toddler
- He lived in a small town
- He was misunderstood
- He was free and not institutionalised
- He was slandered
- He was betrayed
- He was swindled
- He exercised His free will in grace and truth
- He was physically beaten
- He was mocked and despised
- He experienced excruciating pain
- He was abandoned by His closest friends.

Jesus' family tree contained murderers, prostitutes, abusers, cheats, adulterers, widows and wanderers; we have no cause for shame before God. If we doubt His commitment or His understanding and compassion, His response is to invite us to examine the wounds on His hands and at His side. His death was for us. Nothing need separate us from the love of God in Christ Jesus. Jesus is the go-between. He intercedes for us to the Father asking Him not to hold our fallen nature against us.

Jesus is the Great Physician. When we go to Him He asks us, quite rightly, "What's wrong? What do you want me to do for you?" (Mark 10:51). He expects us to come clean and share our difficulties, including: doubt, pain, sadness or confusion, openly with Him, so that He can do something about them!

Am I trying to hide any aspect of my circumstances from God?

In Jesus, we do not have to deny any part of ourselves, or split off from the aspects of our lives that are unacceptable to us, as if they were also unacceptable to God. He invites us to love Him with ALL that we are – all our heart and mind and soul and strength. Even if that does not amount to very much in our eyes, it is precious to God.

We also have no excuse for doubting God's love and becoming cynical when we see that He did not even spare His own Son, but freely gave Him to us all. We would have been amazed at the Queen giving up Buckingham Palace in favour of a bed-sit in Moss Side or Willesden in order to understand her people. But Jesus did something infinitely more epic for His whole lifetime, not just for an interesting interlude. He had no respite at all and lived every minute in a perfect rhythm, and to the full. He has fully modelled our humanity for us.

There is therefore no shame in being human – in fact we are fearfully and wonderfully made with the capacity to be like Jesus Himself. Our humanity is made holy in Jesus.

The vision of each one of us being transformed from one degree of glory to another (2 Corinthians 3:18), until we attain our full identity in Christ, was the joy that enabled Jesus to endure the Cross for us. He believes in our redemption. Therefore, we too can believe for ourselves and for others.

Can I live in the truth that Christ is in me and is my hope of glory? (Colossians 1:27)

Jesus our brother

Jesus is not ashamed to call us His brothers and sisters. The word used for "brother" in Hebrews Chapter 2 means "sharers of the same womb". Jesus clearly identifies with us with ease and pride; we have no need to be ashamed. We are owned and welcomed by the highest authority.

The Cross

We will explore the Cross more, later in the course, when we will see that Jesus expects us to make ongoing exchanges with Him. At the Cross we can exchange death for life, shame for honour, lies for truth etc. In doing so, it is crucial that we identify with Him, allowing ourselves to die with Him and be raised in Him to new life.

Jesus says, "Whoever has seen me has seen the Father!" (John 14:9). We are not reaching into a void to get to know God. He has come to earth to show us Himself face-to-face. He is full of grace and truth and is a compassionate Father to us, the fatherless.

Our inheritance

God isn't called "Father" for nothing. Through the Cross, Jesus has won back, for the Father, an eternal family of children. Each member of the Trinity has His own role to play to achieve this. The Incarnation, the Cross, the Resurrection and the coming of the Holy Spirit are all means to this end: that God (Father, Son, Spirit) should have His family back. As a family we then inherit all that is due to us in Christ.

What is our inheritance? We inherit Christ's nature and likeness, and all the riches of His grace.

For where a will is involved, the death of the one
who made it must be established

(HEBREWS 9:15)

We are children of God and if children then heirs –
heirs of God and fellow heirs with Christ, provided we suffer with Him
in order that we may also be glorified with Him

(ROMANS 8:17)

Suffer can mean going the way of the Cross and humbling ourselves to the point of confessing our need of a saviour and facing the fact that we cannot save ourselves.

A will made on earth expresses the wishes of the person making it. This is the one time in our lives when what we request to happen is legally binding (apart from variations!) and the executor must carry out our wishes to the final detail – whatever his or her personal opinion.

In a will:

- No one has the right to expect anything
- You do not know the contents until the person is dead
- You only inherit if you are alive at the time of the person's death
- If someone wants to leave you a mansion or a few million pounds, they can. First you must accept. Only after that, can you decide what to do with it – once it is yours
- It is rarely performance based

- There has to be a death for the will to come into force
- The executors must carry out the wishes to the letter.

The Father has the property. The Son dies the death. The Holy Spirit is the executor/the guarantee of what we are going to inherit. We are the beneficiaries, whatever we think about it!

The benefits of our inheritance include:

- Life – we must be alive, or we can't inherit
- Our transfer from the Kingdom of darkness to the Kingdom of God, which is eternal (Colossians 1:13)
- Part of it now and part of it later (Ephesians 1:14)
- Our inheritance is a sign of our son-ship/daughter-ship (Galatians 4:7)
- Hope, riches and immeasurably great power (Ephesians 1:18)
- Immeasurable riches of His grace in kindness (Ephesians 2:7)
- Fellow heirs – we all share in the promise.

An extremely wealthy man died. His will instructed that his vast art collection of paintings and sculptures be sold at an auction at the property. The collection contained many important paintings by the Great Masters, and as a result the auction attracted a great deal of attention. On the day of the auction hundreds of art collectors and museum representatives arrived early, hoping to buy the works for display in National and private collections. The man who had died had left specific instructions for the auction – the first painting to be offered for sale was to be a portrait of the man's son. His son had been killed in action during the war and the painting was by an unknown artist. It was of poor quality and no one was interested in it. The painting was held up; the crowd fidgeted and chatted among themselves – they were impatient to move on to the important works.

The estate's gardener, who had been devoted to the family and worked for them for years was at the auction. He knew he couldn't afford to buy anything, but he wanted a memento to remember the family by. When he saw the painting of the son he offered £20. No other bids were made. The hammer went down and the gardener became the owner of the painting, which was entitled, "My Beloved Son". The auctioneer put down his hammer and read from the Will: "Whoever has My Beloved Son gets everything. The auction is over."

Whoever has the Son inherits everything.

What is my inheritance from God?

Jesus the Bridegroom

As well as Jesus giving the Father back His children, the Father also wants to give the Son a bride. We are also the Father's gift to Jesus. The Father prepares us as a worthy bride for His Son and He will make us pure and spotless. This can be a real source of hope for us. It means that God's ability to redeem is infinite and will include us, however we feel about ourselves today.

Is this preparation of the Bride a source of hope for me?

Jesus – filled with the Holy Spirit

As we study the Holy Spirit we see that He is indeed the Spirit of God and the Spirit of Jesus and that each person of the Trinity is consistent. The fruit of the Holy Spirit expresses exactly how Jesus was with us, even as sinners who misunderstood Him and betrayed Him. His character was steadfast, even on the Cross, and ordinary people loved Him for His integrity, delightfulness, gentleness and frankness. He was fully human, fully alive and thoroughly enjoyed Himself. Therefore, we are right to allow the Holy Spirit into our lives and to want to be like Jesus, because this is who we really are. This is eternal living (John 17:3). There is much to explore in our relationship with Jesus and so much room to grow and flourish.

NOTES

CHAPTER 6 – GOD THE HOLY SPIRIT

Our Comforter and Advocate

Isaiah 61 is a wonderful description of the Holy Spirit's work in our lives, reminding us that He knows us better than we know ourselves. He knows the places of mourning and regret; the places where we are trapped or sad; the places where we are in ruins and are devastated or filled with shame, and those places where we have been robbed and feel bereft. The Holy Spirit is able to move us from grief to comfort and into joy.

The Holy Spirit brings us the "double portion" reserved for the eldest son in the Parable of the Prodigal Son and the joy and delight of a garden springing into life. The Holy Spirit is the one who prays for us with sighs too deep for words and is the guarantee of our eternal life.

In a fallen world we suffer pain in so many different ways. We need a Comforter.

Some of us have never had anyone to fight our corner – someone who believed in us. Therefore, we need an "advocate". In Roman law, an advocate was someone who listened to you, interceded for you. He or she was often a best friend who would speak on your behalf, bring food to you if you were in custody and sit and hold you when you cried. This applied to grown men and women!

We can know God the Holy Spirit holding us close to Himself when we cry, even as adults. When we consider our lives before God we may cry the tears of ourselves as a baby, as a toddler, as a child, as a teenager, or as a young person. We can cry the tears of every stage of life up to today. Each time, we will release more of our wounded self to the Cross and allow more of our true self to emerge.

Where and how do I need comfort?

Our guide into truth

In this life, we have been lied to and deceived. We need to lay aside any false wisdom and naivety about this. We can open our hearts to the Spirit to show us, again and again, where this has happened and held back our true becoming. We have agreed with the lies when it has suited us, and even used them as fuel to maintain a defensive detachment from God. The Spirit lives in us to right these wrongs.

Isaiah 44:20 says, "Is there not a lie in my right hand?" This verse reminds us that, often, we cannot see where we are being duped and when we believe a lie. The right hand is usually a person's dominant hand – we may believe lies and allow them to influence and determine our lives more than we acknowledge to ourselves. Conversely, there are truths that we find hard to accept. So we must invite the Spirit to help us to accept God's truth, even when we cannot see how it could apply to us.

What lies do I still believe about myself, or God, or others? Am I ready to receive truth?

Our Counsellor

Life is complex and we need a Counsellor to enable us to understand what is happening. The Holy Spirit can bring order to our lives as we keep in step with Him (Galatians 5:25). We need to identify areas of chaos and compromise and invite the Holy Spirit to bring His counsel and wisdom into these places.

Am I able to ask the Holy Spirit to be my Counsellor?

Coming to repentance

The Holy Spirit leads us into repentance. This is not to make us feel bad or to prove who's boss, but rather because He knows the damage caused to us and others by our sin. The Holy Spirit works the work of the Cross into our lives physically and spiritually, and restores the intimacy we need with the Father.

The Holy Spirit also interprets God's word to us so that it resonates as truth in our hearts and becomes a living word rather than a law. We then engage with the spirit of the law in freedom. There will be a time for repentance later on in the course.

The gifts of the Spirit

We need to be in community to test out the gifts of the Spirit together. We need the gifts of healing, knowledge and discernment, as well as administration and preaching of the word, among others. For some, this will include the gift of speaking or singing in tongues. We may need to ask for this gift in prayer, or begin to use it again if we have neglected it. Paul used the gift of tongues regularly as a means of building up his relationship with God.

In order to experience God through His Spirit, to hear His voice and to be free in our worship we need a restored and holy imagination. If we have been overly involved in fantasy, for example pornography, we will need to ask the Holy Spirit to cleanse our imaginations for us so that we can use them to see the good things of God's kingdom.

Have I asked the Holy Spirit for more gifts recently? Which gifts would I like to receive? Which would I like to have in greater measure?

The fruit of the Spirit

Galatians Chapter 5 shows us the progression from walking in the flesh and under the law, to walking in the Spirit and in the freedom of God.

The Holy Spirit enables us to make the transition to walking in freedom. We notice that the word "but" is used three times in verses 16–20. This assures us that we are not stuck living under the law in our flesh. Instead, there is a way to move into our true inheritance that is life in freedom and all its fullness.

> ***But*** *the fruit of the Spirit is love, joy, peace, patience, kindness,*
> *goodness, faithfulness, gentleness and self-control*
>
> (GALATIANS 5:22-23)

Galatians Chapter 5 also tells us about the nine manifestations of the fruit of the Spirit. These are probably just a sample – there are many more. They are listed here in three groups of three. In Hebrew tradition the number three indicates the divine. This use of three threes emphatically states that this is God's divine character, and therefore it is to be ours. We need to hold on to the truth about who we are, especially when we have made our issues our identity e.g. victim, addict. These are lies. We are all fearfully and wonderfully made in the image of God and our issues need not define us. They are not the sum total of who we are.

The word "fruit" is singular; it does not say "fruits of the Spirit". This means that we must expect to grow in *every* aspect of the fruit of the Spirit. We cannot pick and choose which ones we want! God expects us to grow in maturity as well-rounded individuals. As we grow in one aspect of the fruit of the Spirit, the others will follow.

The wonderful truth is that when the fruit of the Spirit is in action in our lives, or we are on the receiving end of them, life feels right and good; we flourish in them. As people, we are made for the fruit of the Spirit and they sit well in us. They make life work properly and build trust and openness. They bring God to earth. They are also each essential to the growth of the body of Christ, and if we focused on practising them together we would know deep healing. The fruit of the Spirit are also essential building blocks for healthy relating. For example, when we have God's transcending joy in our hearts and want to be faithful to Him, each other and ourselves, we can find a new level of patience about singleness.

The fruit of the Spirit is to be cultivated and enjoyed at an individual level, inwardly, but it must be worked out at a corporate level. That's when we find out if it is ripening into sweetness, or if it is still immature and sour!

There are many books written on the fruit of the Spirit, but let's look at each one briefly in turn.

a. Love

We could say that love is finding a way to bless someone and feeling free to do so, without any expectation of a return. Here, the word for love, "agape" has been expanded to include the inexpressible quality of God's love. This agape love is wanting the best for someone now and in the future and putting this above our own needs. Anything that has gratification as its core or uses people is not love.

If we gave ourselves space, and were able to risk giving and receiving this blessing of love to and from each other, we would find many of our wounds being healed. The Holy Spirit can help us in this.

b. Joy

Joy is knowing an inner gladness beyond our outward circumstances. Joy does not come from instant gratification. Rather, it comes when we draw deeply from the wells of salvation and know in our hearts that we are secure in God's kingdom. Joy comes from knowing that who we are, at the moment, is enough to know God's pleasure. Our culture of instant gratification and pleasure-seeking does not do joy well – the good news is that we can hold fast to joy and allow it to anchor us in life.

c. Peace

The peace that comes from the Spirit is not simply an absence of conflict or worry, but the presence of Christ. Peace is not defined by what is not there (such as a lack of anxiety or trouble), but instead by the positives it brings to life. This peace is beyond our human understanding; it is counter-cultural and can often be opposite to our circumstances. It is about well-being, satisfaction, fulfilment and order. When we know God's peace we can live from a place of confidence, knowing we are centred in Christ. Living from this place enables us to face conflict righteously and seek higher justice, rather than taking matters into our own hands. Peace enables us to live in the reality of Psalm 112:7: "They will have no fear of bad news; their hearts are steadfast, trusting in the Lord." We are in Christ and He is in us.

d. Patience

Patience is the result of love and peace coming together. Patience is not resignation or passivity. We are truly patient when we freely give someone our time or energy, because they need it to cover their chaos, thoughtlessness or self- absorption. They may have genuinely wronged us, but we choose not to count it against them. Instead we give them the space they need but don't deserve. It is amazing to be on the receiving end of real patience – it is not patronising and makes you feel blessed not guilty. It always makes me want to have more of it naturally in my life. We need to recall how patient God is with us! Again, patience is another counter to instant gratification.

e. Kindness

Kindness is about choosing to respond from the kingdom of God, not from this world.

The wonder of kindness is that it recognises our fragility. It has a naivety and generosity about it that can be disarming, but is a welcome contrast to the harshness and competitiveness of our world. It is giving an unexpected gift of understanding and comfort and connection, because we have seen a real need or vulnerability in someone and want to meet the person there. It is a huge relief to experience kindness – it's as if our humanity is still valid. It leaves us wondering how the person showing kindness knew we needed it, but being really grateful that they did!

Scripture is full of instances of God's kindness. We know it is dear to His heart and is something we all need. A flow of understanding, comfort and kindness in our friendships and churches could go a long way to counter the loneliness that can lead to unfulfilling addictive behaviour.

f. Goodness

Goodness has the courage to be different – to hold on to integrity and to stay in the place of blessing, rather than in the place of compromise. It is an appreciation of the supremacy of the kingdom of God that recognises morality is purposeful and the ultimate source of blessing, rather than constraint.

Goodness wants the best whatever the cost, because anything less is a betrayal of our humanity and of God's love.

g. Faithfulness

Faithfulness is about building trust and offering opportunities to be trusted.

We really need each other's help to remain faithful. For that to happen, we need to be known by our communities and those around us. When faithfulness is tested it partners with patience, peace and goodness.

We first experience it from God, as the Trinity remain faithful to their plan of salvation. We dare to prove God's faithfulness every time we confess our sins and ask Him for forgiveness and absolution. Bit by bit, we discover He is not arbitrary, that "He is not a man that He should lie" (Numbers 23:19). He comes back with more and more. God's love is not performance-related. He believes in us and He invites us to believe in each other to keep faith, to trust in someone's potential and not be deterred by current events.

Even though it may cost, faithfulness enables us to keep our word.

h. Gentleness

Compared to kindness, gentleness is more of a disposition than an action. Gentleness has a humility and speaks of soul rest. It has nothing to prove, no axe to grind. It is about not quenching a dimly burning flame! Gentleness suggests depth and character. We are sometimes afraid of being gentle in case someone takes advantage of us, but God reminds us that we are in the business of healing and blessing, not self-preservation. It is the opposite of hardness of heart. Gentleness is a part of manifesting the goodness of God's strength.

i. Self-control

As we see in Galatians 5:16–21, the flesh, in and of itself, sees no need for control. The flesh sees indulgence as a rightful expression of the self, regardless of the consequences for others or ourselves.

In contrast to the indulgence of these behaviours there is an external restraint – the law. Our society also acknowledges how harmful these behaviours are. In addition to the external restraint, the Spirit creates an inner restraint, partly, through an understanding of the true destructive nature of what we are doing. When we cooperate with the Spirit we find we are able to control our flesh. Self-control is the opposite of instant gratification; it is choosing what is important long-term over what is urgent in the short-term.

The Holy Spirit is also the presence of God living in us. Because of His presence self-control then develops into the other manifestations of the Spirit: we put others first and realise our capacity to bless; we become patient; we know the joy of being right before God; we are not raging and we can be at peace and bring kindness and gentleness into our relationships.

Self-control enables us to treasure our own purity and honour that of others. We can be safe and open friends who are trustworthy and intimate. As we experience the benefits of self-control, we find that we are able to counter the demands of our childhood deprivations and unmet needs, and allow God to meet them in legitimate, adult ways.

The presence of the fruit of the Spirit means the world is no longer about the survival of the fittest. Instead it is a place where we can live out the vision and glory of the kingdom of God. It is worth noticing that against the fruit of the Spirit there is no law, i.e. I can be as lavish as I like with my kindness and patience; I can be overflowing with joy and goodness; I can be strong in peace and faithfulness. There are no limits!

Life is incredibly different when someone is really patient or gentle with us, especially when we expected a harsh response. Many of us never experienced the real thing in our early family lives. The only patience we knew was the gritted teeth or violent variety.

In showing kindness we have a choice. We can put on an act and behave as if we are at peace or being kind when we are really only tolerating the other person's behaviour. If we pretend like this the person will know, and they will feel shame. This kind of pretence could be called the 'plastic fruit'. It looks like the real thing at first glance, but it quickly becomes apparent that there is no goodness within.

In contrast, we can allow the Spirit to bring authentic patience and kindness into our lives, into those times when we are stretched and frustrated. If we allow the Spirit to do this we can genuinely bless the person on the other end, because our patience was given freely from an open heart. In this way, patience comes as a gift beyond our human capability and the recipient's expectation.

In Galatians 5:14 we read that love is in fact the fulfilling of the law! All the manifestations of the Spirit are ways of loving and of bringing God's blessing into our world in a variety of ways.

As we cultivate love, joy, peace, patience and kindness they naturally become a part of who we really are: a true Christ-like self. This is then expressed in every area of our lives. We facilitate new possibilities for meaningful fellowship in church; richer relationships at work, intimacy and relaxation in our peer group and new openness and freedom in marriage.

Which variety of the fruit of the Spirit is growing well in my life? Which do I need to cultivate more? Why?

Other work of the Spirit

In Romans 8:23 the Holy Spirit is called, "the Spirit of adoption". He secures our status with the Father as that of Christ – the firstborn son. Many of the struggles we have are the groaning of the orphan places in our hearts. We need the Holy Spirit to bring us to that place of adoption with the Father. The Spirit also prepares us as the Bride for Christ our Bridegroom. We can invite Him to work deeply in our lives.

So, we need to welcome every aspect of the Holy Spirit into our lives!

NOTES

CHAPTER 7 – THE CROSS – ISAIAH CHAPTER 53

Introduction

But God shows His Love for us in that while we were still sinners,
Christ died for us

(ROMANS 5:8)

At the start of this chapter on the Cross, please begin by reading Isaiah chapters 53 and 61 several times. You may wish to read it out loud to yourself. As you do so, acknowledge that Isaiah is describing us. The chapter speaks of our fallen nature and, in doing so, gives us the words with which to name and bring to God all the emptiness and dis-ease in our hearts.

The Cross is the natural follow on to our chapters on the Trinity because it is all their work and it is the key to our restored relationship as a beloved son or daughter, and to our taking our rightful place in the heart of the Trinity. It is the dynamic whereby we receive their ongoing gift of salvation into the core of our being and are prepared to be the bride of Christ.

The Cross therefore answers every aspect of the cries of our heart spoken of in Isaiah 53 and 61. It is indeed the Passion where the Father, Son and Holy Spirit show us the full extent of their love for us. It is not just for conversion but also for us to receive the health and healing of which salvation speaks. We will see it is the place of exchange for us.

Sadly, many of us have forgotten that the Cross is for life. On our Journey of Grace we need to come back to the Cross, remind ourselves of what it is for in our lives and cultivate the practice of spending time at the Cross each week. Here, we realise our need for mercy and love and forgiveness. Here, all the dead places in our hearts, all those areas in which we have lost hope and even given up, can go through a resurrection.

The Cross is enough

The Cross is for all the times when we need grace and cannot save ourselves. The Cross is sufficient for: the worst of sin; the deepest wound; the strongest fear and the deepest primal pain. It is a level playing field where we all can be known without fear of reproach. It is where we can say whatever is on our heart without editing the facts, without pretence or fear, to God and each other.

So, every aspect of the Fall is reversed and we are able to re-enter the intended blessings of God. Freely accessible, the Cross addresses our fear, our shame, our neediness and our desire to hide as we bring our orphan places to Him.

It is here that the Father demonstrates His compassion and care for us, even in our fallen state, filling our empty hearts with all the affirmation, acceptance, advocacy, attention and accompaniment we crave. He also gives personal attention to our sins and our wounding and promises to accompany us through the healing and restoration, sending His Holy Spirit to minister to us step-by-step.

The Cross also addresses the corruption of God's mandate to, "Be fruitful and increase in number, fill the earth and subdue it. Rule over the fish of the sea and the birds of the air and over every living creature that moves on the ground" (Genesis 1).

Jesus endures the Cross for us

The Cross is important because of the One who died there. Jesus, in becoming incarnate for us suffered everything that a fallen world throws at us, so He can identify with all our pain and losses. Jesus was tempted in every way, just as we are, by all the same things that tempt us, but He is without sin. Jesus went to the Cross blameless, having lived a life of full acceptance and communication with the Father. He was so alive without any of our baggage and guilt and shame – just full of grace and truth and mercy. No accusation against Him could stand; no one took His life from Him – He laid it down by His own will and authority.

The Cross – the place of exchange

Isaiah 53 and 61 remind us that Jesus gave His all so that we could receive His full gift of salvation and share His inheritance from the Father. It is at the Cross that:

- Jesus became despised, hated and rejected so that we can be honoured, loved, esteemed and accepted
- He carries our griefs and sorrows and infirmities – both physical and emotional – to the Cross so that we may receive comfort, consolation, healing and joy
- Men hid their face from Him, even His friends abandoned and denied Him, so that we may be looked at, seen by God, received, cared for and affirmed
- He was pierced, wounded and crushed so that we may be healed and lifted up
- He received punishment so that we may receive acquittal and peace
- His image was marred so that the image of God could be restored
- He was oppressed and afflicted (grievously affected by great harm) so that we may be set free from all oppression and be treated lavishly with an abundance of freedom and grace
- He was judged, taken away and killed so that we may receive mercy, be brought near to God and each other, and receive life.

At the Cross we are invited to pour out all our distorted perceptions, brokenness, every shattered relationship, our deepest sources of shame, our most sinful acts and our most intense anger and hatred. It is sufficient for all our disappointments and regrets, relational anxiety, addictive behaviours, self-hatred and great rebellion. We bring God all our poverty: where we have been robbed and missed out, whether because of others or through ourselves. Our hearts know these places. It is where we receive the lavish riches of His eternal grace into the specific gaps in our being.

At the Cross we can exchange shame for honour; anxiety for security; anger and hurt for justice, understanding and comfort; striving for peace; the need to be in control for rest and freedom. We exchange bitterness for thankfulness; abandonment and rejection for welcome and belonging; our orphan state for son-ship/daughter-ship; death for life; despair for hope and desolation for abundance and restoration.

Do we believe this can extend – even to us? Are we afraid of owning up to our worst places of shame? Do we dare to prove His grace and stay at the Cross long enough with our specific sins and wounds to make the exchange?

What are the exchanges you need to make at the Cross, and how much confidence do you have in God to provide in the exchange?

The exchange requires our active, intentional participation. It also requires time: time to allow ourselves to be present to the pain and reality of the situation, and time to receive from God. We need time to own our displacement activities and learn how to stop them kicking in. With great relief we can be real and lay down our self-hatred and narcissism, our shame and blame-shifting, and let our hearts be real and hurting. As we face this pain, rather than numbing it and retreating into detachment or fantasy or our cave, we encounter God's mercy and grace. God wants us to develop the rhythm of this in our daily walk with Him. He wants us to live as an honoured son/daughter in relationship and dialogue with our Father.

Throughout this process we:

- Fully face the consequence and reality of sin, both ours and that of others
- Fully acknowledge the holiness, goodness and compassion of God
- Fully express and feel the depth of our sorrow, wounding and pain
- Fully renounce the shame and guilt we feel and come out of hiding to live open, honest and known lives
- Fully recognise the depth of our orphan state and receive the robes and ring as the garments of salvation
- Fully walk out of despair and into healthy, life-giving relationship and community
- Fully receive His grace and forgiveness
- Fully take our place as people made in His image and likeness – the pinnacle of God's creation
- Humbly accept the truth, therefore, not only of our current condition and need, but also of the amazing restorative purpose of God for us, our value to Him and our true place in creation.

What are the griefs, sorrows, despising, oppression etc that you carry in your heart that you need to bring to the Cross?

Who inflicted these upon you, and how? They may have been a parent, family member, peer or, in the case of self-hatred, even yourself.

What have we inflicted on others that we would like Jesus to take for us?

Scriptures for worship and prayer

EPHESIANS 2:1-6

> *As for you (us), you (we) were dead in your (our) transgressions and sins, in which you (we) used to live when you (we) followed the ways of this world and the ruler of the kingdom of the air, the spirit who is now at work in those who are disobedient. All of us also lived among them at one time, gratifying the cravings of our sinful nature and following its desires and thoughts. Like the rest, we were by nature objects of wrath. But because of his great love for us, God, who is rich in mercy, made us alive with Christ even when we were dead in transgressions - it is by grace you have been saved.*

ROMANS 8:32

> *God did not spare His own son but gave Him up for us all.*

PHILIPPIANS 2:8

> *He humbled Himself by becoming obedient to the point of death, even death on a Cross.*

COLOSSIANS 2:14

> *God cancelled the record of debt that stood against us with all its legal demands, setting it aside by nailing it to the Cross.*

HEBREWS 12:2

> *Jesus, who for the joy that was set before Him endured the Cross, despising the shame, and is seated at the right hand of the throne of God.*

Applying the power of the Cross

We will look at many of these things in more detail later in the course.

The Cross was a place of torture and pain for Jesus. It is also the place to find restoration and healing. As we give time to process things at the Cross we can expect to feel pain. This pain can be from finally recognising the depth and consequences of our sin, the shame and hiding, the fear of being found out or moving on, the sadness over loss and our brokenness, the anger about what should have been. We may still be feeling the pain of ongoing addictions, confusion, unforgiveness, bitterness and powerlessness. We feel this and carry it in our hearts, minds and souls. But because of Jesus, the Cross is the place for restoration and healing, the place to which we can bring our pain and leave it there. Therefore, by facing and processing our pain we end up with salvation and life, rather than in death. This process can involve a number of things:

Confession of sin

Confession is done both in private and in public. James urges us to confess our sins with one another so we may be healed. As John 1:7 says, "If we walk in the light, as He is in the light, we have fellowship with one another, and the blood of Jesus, His Son, purifies us from all sin."

So we need to take responsibility for what we have done wrong, by commission or omission and specifically own this as sin before God – a sin which took Jesus to the Cross. We ask His forgiveness and ask that this sin will be laid on Him now not us, that His blood will cover it and the guilt will be taken away. We wait to receive this so that we can know we are truly cleansed and free and that sin is now as far from us as the east is from the west.

We also need to be known, so it is good to share our confession with fellow Christians and let them assure us of our forgiveness from God and their ongoing acceptance of us in Christ. Receiving mercy and grace from another person, especially when we least expect it can be very healing of itself. It also brings us out of shame.

Mourning of sorrows and loss

At the Cross we need to be real about the losses in our heart, allowing them to surface because our heavenly Father acknowledges them with us and will meet us in them. He moves us from grief to consolation to joy because Jesus became the Man of Sorrows for us. This takes time, with many sessions, and we should neither give up, nor become introspective and stuck in these sorrows. We may have spent years numbing the pain, so feeling again can feel overwhelming. Allowing ourselves to feel again can be a bit frightening but He promises to be with us in this valley place and to never leave us or forsake us there. The Father is with us through His Spirit and we can allow others to be there too. Some of our losses will include things we missed out of within our primal relationships and parenting that have impacted our lives from that time on.

Renouncing shame

Shame drives us to hide and to blame shift. We all have an inner place of shame and we are loathe to have this exposed. We may be ashamed of our own actions or of what others have done to us.

We may feel full of shame and have elaborate ways to hide this. Whatever our position, Jesus wants to lift all this off us and out of us as part of our healing.

We may feel we are despicable and, at some level, be ashamed of who we are. As we bring this shame to the Cross, we exchange it for God's acceptance, honour, value and place in community. Allowing others to know these shameful places also plays a powerful part in our healing.

Repenting of attitudes and actions

At the Cross we repent, both turning *away from* and *towards*. We turn away from sinful attitudes of the heart, from which all sinful actions spring, such as comparison, envy, despair, and from the actions themselves (James 1:14–15). We specifically name these before God and we repent of them. This list may include living out of an orphan mindset, harbouring resentment and hatred and being filled with sinful fantasies. We must be specific. The exchange here is for God to create in us a clean heart and for Him to renew a right spirit within us (Psalm 51:10). Then, as we turn towards the Cross the right actions will follow.

Lay down striving

It is time to stop trying to save ourselves from both the deprivations we feel and the wrongs we have committed. Jesus has done it all at the Cross, and this is more than sufficient. It is appropriate as a fallen creature to a Saviour, and the good news is that we have one. Our Father says that it is His delight to give us the Kingdom, not His demand that we earn it.

So, this chapter is profound and specific, even pivotal. During The Journey of Grace course, the Cross is available for us to use, both as a place of exchange and also a place of meditation. In everyday life, when we put out our rubbish each week, it is removed and carried away, but it is only ever moved from one place to another until perhaps it reaches a landfill site. It is still around somewhere as rubbish. In contrast, when we confess our sins and they are laid on Jesus, He bears them for us, is buried with them and rises *without* them. They have truly left us and are no longer traceable. This means that anything that Christ bears for us is open to transformation and resurrection.

The necessary process of sorting out what is in our hearts takes time. Revelation comes to us in all sorts of ways. We confess sin, we mourn our sorrows and losses, we renounce our shame, we repent of our bitterness and we lay down our striving. We need to put the right verb with the right noun! We can ask the Holy Spirit to deepen and develop our understanding of the Cross so that it becomes an ongoing dynamic in our lives. Use the exercise on the following page to start this process!

ISSUE	WHAT DOES IT LOOK LIKE FOR ME?
ANXIETY	
WOUNDS	
LOSSES & SORROWS	
GRIEFS	
SHAME	
REJECTION	
SINS	
BITTERNESS	
STRIVINGS	

NOTES

SECTION 2 - OUR FAMILY AND PEERS

For you, O Lord, are my hope, my trust, O Lord, from my youth.
Upon you I have leaned from before my birth;
you are He who took me from my mother's womb.
My praise is continually of you.

(PSALM 71:5–6)

OUR FAMILIES

With God by our side and in our hearts, we are now going to move onto our families. Each of us is like a new build house – we are a unique creation: with our mothers laying a firm foundation and our fathers providing the scaffolding, and being the clerk of works!

We are each like a new build house

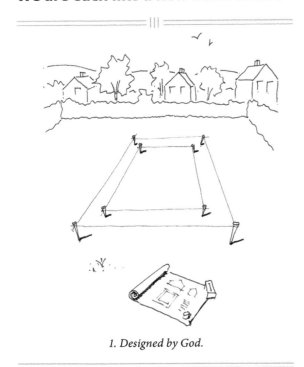

1. Designed by God.

2. Given firm foundations by our mothers.

3. Overseen and given scaffolding by our fathers.

4. A new home for us to live in with God.

CHAPTER 8 – OUR MOTHERS

NB: The purpose of reviewing our relationships with our earthly mothers and fathers is to have a clearer understanding of the roots of some of our issues. We can then reach out to God to receive healing, rather than apportioning blame. We may then be in a better place to honour our parents in our adult relationship with them. As we think about our grandparents' circumstances we can identify some of the difficulties our parents may have had to deal with.

A word of encouragement for those of us who are parents: we may see these wounds in our own children – God is as able to reach them with His healing, as He is us. We only need to be a good enough caregiver, not the perfect parent.

In an ideal world

It seems that God's original plan was that two individuals should have been parented in such a way that when they reached adulthood they could leave their father and mother and enter into a covenant relationship with each other. Within the security of this relationship, they were then invited to share in God's creation by becoming parents themselves.

We were to be conceived in a covenant union that was peaceful and ready to receive us. Our mother's womb was to welcome our presence and allow us to implant and grow in her. From a place of nurture, and covering by her husband, she could enjoy our growth within her and offer us a safe and secure home until our birth. Our job was to live in this place of peace and simply receive and be. Our delivery would have been straightforward and we would have been nourished at our mother's breast and been nurtured by her.

It is wonderful that a newborn baby can focus at the distance to its mother's eyes, when at the breast or in her arms. As far as we are concerned, we have life through her, and our sense of 'being' grows as we drink in her love and attention. Gradually, there is enough of a person in us for us to begin to draw away and we can start to explore our immediate world, but with our home base always there to go back to. The next step is that we realise this difference between our mother and ourselves, and that when she is not visible she still exists and will return. Another experience of this is when a child feels invisible when they have their eyes closed and the delight they experience when they are still there on opening them. Our moves away from our mothers were to be gradual and at a pace that was right for us, until we were filled up with enough life and being of our own to venture out and take on the world.

But it wasn't an ideal world

Sadly, things have happened to rob us of our birthright of order and blessing, even before day one of our existence on earth. Our parents may not have been mature or committed enough to embark on the journey of parenthood. The generations before them may have left a legacy of chaos or hurt.

Our mothers were given the amazing privilege of carrying a 'work in progress' as we were 'intricately put together' by God in her womb (Psalm 139:13-15).

But our coming into this world may have been far from ideal:

- **Our conception** may not have been planned, or may not have taken place in a context of love and commitment; our womb may not have been welcoming or ready for us

- As a result we may have been wary of implanting or embedding, and even now we may feel unwelcome and uneasy about having a valid place in life

- Realisation of pregnancy may not have been good news for our parents for any number of reasons, some very valid, others selfish or due to sin. We will have sensed this and we may have been left with a deep anxiety, ambivalence about our very existence, or an inability to settle, make a home or belong anywhere

- **The Pregnancy itself:** If we were not good news, we can be left with a deep unease about the way we were growing and could not stop it. It can leave us afraid of the future, or ashamed and needing to apologise for our very existence

- **The Delivery:** Birth is a dangerous process and despite everyone's best intentions it can go wrong. Some of us have been left with profound anxiety and terror as a result of our births

- **The Bonding:** This is a crucial moment and then stage for us all. It should have been a continuation of the bonding we knew in the womb. At birth, we needed to be welcomed and to keep that attachment to our mothers so strongly. For some of us, there are very valid reasons why this could not be, such as mother or baby health problems, but for others, it was that our mothers had nothing to give us, or that they saw us as a burden. Either way, this vital stage may not have happened. It may even have felt that our mother was trying to draw life *out* of us

- **The Relationship:** Our total dependence on our mothers was to be the preparation for us being able to just 'be' and to 'rest'. It would enable us, in adult life, to receive from others without shame and be intimate without fear. If we perceived that we were too demanding or there was no rest for us, then we will feel ashamed of having any needs, even as adults, and we will not be able to receive easily. We also may be unable to stop and be quiet or allow anyone close enough to know us without being afraid. This also links into our feeling that there may be no one inside us worth getting to know. We may well find it hard to sustain our adult relationships or move into commitment. We will not know how to trust

- **Growing Up:** As we became a toddler and on from there, our mothers needed to give us appropriate freedom to engage in life, and yet still be there for us when needed. This disengagement process should have been by mutual consent. If for any reason this happens prematurely, or it feels like a sudden rupture to the child, this will leave us seriously anxious and fearful of it continuing through life. We will also be wounded if the separating never happens at all! Those of us raised in an atmosphere of doom or anxiety about the world, will 'believe' this from our mothers, and never have the freedom or courage to launch out and grow up. If we were not allowed to explore or make mistakes, we will have been denied the chance to develop into an individual with a unique or clear sense of who we are.

The need to attach to our mothers cannot be overemphasised. If we did not attach to her, or we abruptly lost this attachment, we will have a desperate need to attach for the rest of our lives. We may not be able to trust and attach to anyone else, including God.

Attachment

It was vital that we attached to our mother/primary caregiver in an open non verbal way. A lack of attachment as a baby leads to profound difficulties as an adult:

A straight-forward attachment: allowing and managing feelings well, able to play, have empathy, recover from discomfort, be open and forgiving, tune into and read the body language of others, connect well.

Detached caregiver: unavailable to us > adult distancing, being rigid, critical, afraid of connection.

Ambivalent caregiver: confusing, inconsistent, invasive for us > anxious, insecure, controlling, blaming, confused, giving mixed messages in relationships.

Disorganised caregiver: not child-focussed, neglectful, traumatising > chaotic, fearful, desperate yet terrified of connection, commitment, trust, relationships, angry, abusive, cannot sustain connection.

Toxic caregiver: unable to give consistent care or reversed the flow of care > cannot rest or trust, numb, angry, unable to connect or see a place in life, aversion to care, intimacy, perceived demands in a relationship or to women in general.

We may have felt there was a strong attachment to mother, yet still feel empty. This may be because very little healthy bonding was actually present and it was more about her than us. We may find it hard to cut ourselves free from her and release ourselves and her into God's hands. We may be overwhelmed by terror or guilt, but we will need to do this if we are to emerge as the true adult.

We will need to identify any unhealthy experiences of attachment and seek to process the wounds and empty places within us.

We all needed to attach to someone or something and if we could not attach easily to our caregiver we will have attached to something else, for example: fantasy, anger, emptiness or death. It also means that our natural stages of independence will not be able to happen because we do not have a sure enough foundation from which to explore the world – is anything ever constant enough to be trusted to remain? We will live with a deep sense of having missed out and may experience anxiety.

So what is the damage?

No sense of self or well-being

If there was no welcome or life freely passing into us along our umbilical cord, or from our mother's arms then we will not have a clear sense of being. This sense of self was meant to grow out of our symbiotic union with our mother – starting in the womb and continuing after birth – until we were filled up enough to become ourselves. Our mother's acceptance and nurture becomes our self-acceptance and sense of well-being later.

If this did not happen to a sufficient degree, we are empty and we will know it. We will feel vacuous and empty and live in survival mode, maybe expecting to be snuffed out or found out at any point.

Everyone else looks as if they know how to 'do life' better than us, as if we missed the briefing. We will keep people at a distance, because we are afraid to let them see how empty we are.

If we had *some* life passed into us, but there was no nurture, safety or rest then we will lack a sense of well-being. 'Everything is right with the world' becomes: 'nothing will ever be right with my world'. We cannot settle or belong. Without a sense of self, it can be hard to make a home and live in it. It is easier to be on the move. We can avoid testing situations or taking risks. We have had enough. It is often stressful to be still or quiet even in God's presence as the vacuousness/emptiness can close in. Going to sleep can bring the same feeling.

Making decisions can be impossible, even choosing a meal: we don't know what we want or prefer, we can become a chameleon in the vain hope of fitting in, and we have nowhere inside to store our experiences or achievements or love. Life never seems to touch the spot or impact us. We can become narcissistic in the hope that the attention will sustain us, but this has a short shelf life so we are left always needing more.

How is my sense of self? Do I have a sense of well-being?

How do I view the world – with fear, with joy, with resignation?

Fear of abandonment

We may have actually been left, or we may have perceived this. Either way, this is the original rejection wound and leaves us feeling seriously unwanted and anxious. We may have protested our abandonment and got stuck in always being angry. We may think we are a very "feeling" person, but actually only feel different kinds of anger. We need God to come and soothe us into the comfort we so badly need.

We may have given up on anger and resigned ourselves to aloneness. This can leave us in despair and passivity or control and independence – both because deep down we are really afraid of everything. Wary of further rejection we may: get in first with our rejection; avoid commitment; hate goodbyes; test out people's care; find it hard to be a team player or fit in; hide behind taking care of everyone so they'll need us; be paranoid; expect betrayal; be a victim; find holidays and the unfamiliar or unknown stressful; be unable to relax or tend to be on our guard.

If the fear becomes too much to bear, we can cut off from our mothers or those who seemed to betray us and detach from life itself. We shut down and become frozen or numb, maybe vowing never to trust or love anyone again. This leaves us tense and we find it hard to just 'be'.

Do I have a sense of place in the world? Can I trust?

Separation anxiety

This is the deep and almost crippling anxiety that we are left with if we have been abandoned, or felt we were abandoned, either as a baby or a small child. The absence makes our hearts grow frantic. It can be free floating, in that our sense of abandonment seems to be there all the time and not be associated with anything in particular. We may feel silly and different, with ongoing feelings of self-hatred and shame, or we become driven and controlling in an attempt to keep the anxiety down. We will have been looking after ourselves since we were babies, so receiving or having needs or being out of control is a terrifying prospect for us. When this anxiety becomes sexualised it can lead to addictions or acting out in other ways, despite our faith. We will have needed to bond to something to survive: it may be being angry at everything, it may be despair, it may be to an object or fantasy or death.

Do read Psalm 23 out loud and check how your heart responds to the truth it contains. For some of us, what we read is no more than wishful thinking as we have never felt any care or shepherding, our souls feel empty or uneasy, we cannot be quiet, we are not sure if goodness or mercy really exist and our cup has always been half-empty. Maybe no one has ever prepared anything for us, let alone something lavish, and we have never felt welcome or at home, often camping in the valley of the shadow of death. Let your heart speak – God longs to hear its cry.

A broken heart

As these wounds are so early and preverbal they will have broken our hearts. To have a broken heart is biblical. We know that, "a broken and a contrite heart, God does not despise" (Psalm 51:17) and He "heals the broken hearted and binds up their wounds" (Psalm 147:3).

If we are living with a broken heart, it is hard for us to 'do joy' and to watch others live life. Our heart may be full of sorrow and we may be living with an over-riding sense of disappointment and guilt that we are not happy or grateful enough for our lot.

God promises to be our safe place, our rest and our comfort. He is the One with whom we can share our hearts because He is the One who knows how to bind them up. Try to share what is in your heart with God. For some of us, despite years of being a Christian, these areas of our lives have gone unaddressed. This may be partly because we may not have had the opportunity to tell anyone about it, or we have lacked the words to describe it and bring it all out into the open, or perhaps there did not seem to be any solution.

Self-hatred

If we did not feel welcome – or were given a message of rejection for who we were – and did not elicit a response of care or attention from our mothers (for whatever reason) then we will have taken this on board and assumed there is something intrinsically wrong with who we are. This may be subconscious but will be present, and like Job we may even "despise the day and fact of our birth" (Job 3:11). This is self-hatred, and we will need to repent of it and ask God to replace it with our true worth and love for whom He has made us to be.

Gender insecurity

If we do not have a clear sense of personhood and being, then our sense of gender will also be impacted, as it is such a key part of who we are. Our gender becomes consolidated within our sense of personhood. We will look at this in more depth later in the course.

Inability to receive

If we perceived our mother's attentions and 'milk' as a mixed blessing or unsafe or harmful, even as a newborn, we may have cut off from her and the desirability of being on the receiving end. We may then become wary and sceptical of receiving at all and cut off from all life-givers from then on. (Just check this out as a possibility in your heart.) Any receiving we do will be strictly censored and we will make sure we are in control. We will then live on in a place of "famine" and "emptiness" (Psalm 33:19) and may be unable to receive "life-giving" things from anyone, including God.

Coming to God

As these wounds are inflicted so early on, and can be so painful, they can eclipse the presence of God for us. If we are living in a vacuum, then it can feel as if we live in a silent and dark world that not even the voice of God or the light of His presence can penetrate. We may need to agree with God that this can't go on any longer and ask Him, even now, to break through the emptiness and speak to us in a way that we can hear (see Job 3:1–7). We may also be numb and feel the presence of God is futile or unnecessary.

Scripture is full of invitations from God to come, to pour out our hearts, to be found by Him and to be comforted. We can admit how hungry we are for good things, for the essentials of life. We can bring Him the places that are still not satisfied, where we feel different and deprived. We may feel we only exist and live in a place of detached survival – in a bubble out of touch with the 'normal' and with God. In fact, He speaks of His longing to comfort us very often. He will never leave us or forsake us (Joshua 1:5) – that promise is for eternity. He also talks specifically about anxiety (Philippians 4:6-7, 1 Peter 5:7), letting us know that He understands all about it and wants to bring us peace and security in a way we have never known before.

A prayer

Thank you, Lord, that You understand all the circumstances of my family, including my birth and early life. I ask that You will come and reveal Your goodness and comfort to me now, so that I can allow You to bind up my broken heart and rebuild trust within me. May I come to know more of Your healing presence in all the ways that You see I need it and please can You give me peace.

Amen

NOTES

NOTES

CHAPTER 9a – BEING MY MOTHER'S DAUGHTER

The effects of a mother wound in women will be specific and will link back to:

- Who God made women to be
- Being under the curse which brings enmity with the serpent, and broken relationships between men and women
- Dealing with a broken relationship with the same-sex parent
- Any attachment issues with our mother.

Who are women?

Women and men are both essential in conveying the image of God on earth. Each is unique. While we share our basic humanity with men, our ways of knowing and being are different and provide a very necessary complement to them. It is not a question of men being somehow superior and women adding a few niceties!

Jesus honoured women in many ways during his time on earth. He assures us that we are blessed and are vital to God's glory being seen on earth. In fact, when Adam saw Eve he proclaimed, "This at last is bone of my bones and flesh of my flesh" (Genesis 2:23). This is a statement of awe, but it also speaks of equality. "Bone" was a symbol of strength and "flesh" was a symbol of weakness. Both strengths and weaknesses are shared between men and women – men and women have the opportunity to bless and complement each other.

There is a specific feminine quality, which is in us all as human beings, but is seen more evidently in women. It is about valuing 'being' as much as 'doing'.

It is about seeing *beyond* reason; to be intuitive and to bring together the many aspects of a situation and allow them to distil into a new truth. It is about making room for more, weighing up, receiving, and not settling for the obvious, but including feelings and consequences. It is about valuing intimacy and relationship. It is about providing balance to a functional world.

Without this quality, we merely exist and society loses its heart, becoming driven and competitive. When reason prevails, we can lose the desire to hear God or to receive from Him and each other. In our restlessness we can reject the prophetic, the weak or the imaginative. We become cynical about life itself and our decisions become driven by economics or pragmatism. This is the devaluing of women and all they represent; this is present to some degree in all cultures. Women can internalise this, expecting rejection and feeling marginalised.

In the Fall, the feminine presence is challenged and made an ongoing target of antagonism by Satan. As a result, the gift and contribution of women becomes a continuing source of contention and is undervalued.

The Fall also leaves women with a tendency to need men to tell us who we are or to make us feel significant. We can give away our dignity and place to them. Men under the curse will act this out, so while we can be aware of this and try not to fall into these traps, they can still be there. We can also find we tolerate pain as our lot.

So, women have an appreciation of:

- The need to 'be' as well as 'do'
- Intuitive ways of knowing as well as just plain reason
- The need for relationships and connection and loyalty
- Their feelings, and those of others
- The need to take in all aspects of a situation and consider and build: in decisions and in life
- The desire to care and protect and nurture.

But there will also be the tendency:

- To internalise and take the blame or responsibility for more than our own part
- To be on the back foot
- To live out of our feelings
- To feel shame or to expect to be treated as less of a person than a man
- To need other people to tell us who we are and to reassure us.

Why it hurts and how it surfaces

Because of this inbuilt capacity to 'be' rather than 'do', it is harder for women to hide the effects of a mother wound in action. Instead, a woman's awareness of feelings, and of the importance of connection and relationships, heightens the sense of emptiness. The knowledge that something vitally important is missing and cannot just be reasoned away, can add to the aloneness and the emptiness. Without a sense of being, life can get very frustrating.

Relationships

As women, we often cannot find a good outlet for our need for relationships, connection and loyalty. The lack of a solid sense of self, our attachment issues, the fear of being abandoned and the anxiety that will come if it all goes wrong, is too much to risk. We may also define ourselves by our relationships – daughter, mother, friend, wife – so a lack of relationship affects our sense of identity.

As a result there can be:

- A downward spiral of impossible relationships, either with men or women, that cannot take the weight of our needs. We may settle for any relationship rather than have no one, or go into overdrive and throw ourselves into caring for others

- A sense of always being on the outside

- A need to fit in and become the person we feel will be rejected least

- Attention seeking behaviour that keeps affirmation flowing

- Manipulation and deceit as we try to keep relationships going

- A need to sabotage good relationships. We may find it impossible to believe anyone cares for us and spurn the love we crave. Tenderness can be terrifying

- Anger and rage and self-pity and the need to control

- No boundaries as we dare not say 'no', or do not realise what is appropriate

- A withdrawal into fantasy and seclusion.

How are my relationships with men and with women?

Are there any patterns in my way of relating that I would like to change?

There are two classic patterns of unhealthy relating that we can all tend to fall into, either from time to time or as a lifestyle. Each tends to have a poor sense of self as the root:

Co-dependency

This is when we live our lives through others, anticipating and responding to their needs rather than our own. It is care taking as a defence and enables us to stave off rejection by making ourselves indispensable. Co-dependency avoids real intimacy or being known and means we leave no time to feel our own pain or loneliness. It is as if we have got stuck in the infant stage of detachment and stay cut off and hurt – longing for love but afraid to risk having it. We need to be in control, even at enormous personal cost, because inside we are terrified of change, rejection or being alone.

Emotional dependency

Here, we appear to be a chaotic and needy person attaching to others out of fear of aloneness. We usually do not believe we have anything to offer in relationships and see ourselves as only being able to take. It is as if we have stayed stuck in the infant stage of crying out to be held and loved. Boundaries are difficult for us; we are often living out of our feelings or our fantasies.

We will often oscillate between co-dependency and emotional dependency in response to what buttons are pressed in our relationships. Of course, the codependent needs someone to be emotionally dependent on them, and vice versa. These dynamics can play out in our family relationships, through hanging on to old patterns, at work and church, or in our marriages or parenting. The start of the way out is to recognise what is happening and to bring the underlying aloneness, fear and lack of confidence to God. He will bring His comfort, ongoing intimacy and consolation.

Feelings

As women, we will tend to let our feelings dictate how we are and our view of ourselves.

We can also internalise other people's feelings and make them our own. As a result, we may believe that we are 'useless' or 'helpless' or 'unimportant'.

Without a sense of self, we are more likely to:

- Suffer with low self-esteem, self-doubt, self-hatred, self-harming
- Feel invisible and overlooked or ignored
- Be unable to be assertive, take a rightful place or achieve our potential
- Try to find an identity but not take the risk of commitment or success or completing something
- Find that life becomes a self fulfilling prophecy of rejection and being marginalised
- Develop, or stay in, a victim identity
- Experience deep shame, both at being a woman and in being in such chaos or anxiety
- Be pole-axed by our inability to make decisions and be open to control by others
- Use care taking as a means of appeasing people and fending off further rejection
- Experience a life that is restricted: being too insecure to take holidays, make a home, buy clothes or make choices
- Tolerate too much pain and aloneness as our lot and then become angry and bitter.

Do I live out of my feelings too much? Are they a range of feelings or just anger, and am I numb underneath?

How satisfying are my relationships at the moment?

Gender

Being let down by our mothers can leave us confused about our gender. If we got angry and cut off from our mother then we will have cut off from our same-sex parent, our most important female relationship. This can leave us without any good role model or feminine presence in our lives.

We can find we are:

- Reacting badly to other women of our mother's type, eg needy women or cold, controlling women
- Insecure as a woman, as well as a person, making us uneasy with our peers or with other women
- Wanting to repeat that symbiotic connection with our mother through someone else. This can sometimes become overwhelming and lead to further rejection as people avoid us and our neediness
- Left with a trail of broken sexual relationships (if this need is eroticised)
- Needing men to tell us who we are
- Despising ourselves as we saw how our mother despised herself
- Hating men, feeling jealous of them or vowing never to give them any room in our life.

How do I feel about being a woman?

What was my mother's version? This is my main role model.

How do I take my place with other women?

As women we are made to convey the glory of God's image, uniquely and in our own way. Trying to live to a stereotype of who a woman should be is a key cause of not enjoying our gender. Another cause of dissatisfaction is when we live in reaction to our role model. Some of us have made vows never to be like our mother, and we then wonder why our womanhood is a source of angst for us. We need to renounce such vows in order to be free to embrace our own true self. When we do this, we allow God to bless us with new ways of becoming and of being a woman in our own right.

What are some of the ways that we, as women, convey the glory of God? By our mystery, by showing the importance of receiving, intimacy and intuition, by being relational, understanding the need for wisdom, healing and comfort.

Women display the radiance and beauty of God, whereas men tend to convey His majesty and different strengths. Women show, by their God-given nature, that God is to be sought after, that He takes risks and works collaboratively, that He sees the big picture and is radical. We live out the truth that there are many ways of knowing and seeing life, not just in concrete terms or only with the mind. Women show that things take time to be revealed and that beauty and creativity and the works of our hands and hearts are vital for a true balance and quality in life. A culture needs all these qualities, including ways to explore using the imagination and valuing what is unseen.

We can ask God to give us the imagination to see who we really are as a unique woman, fearfully and wonderfully made in His image – realising that this will express all the fullness of who we are as a person. We will also need to welcome the masculine *and* feminine parts within ourselves as equally valid and as part of our unique creation.

A prayer

Lord, I thank you that You know me better than I know myself. Thank You that You invite me to come to You as the healer and restorer of my soul. Thank You that You want to offer me comfort in all the places where You see I need it. May I trust You to be my Comforter now and let Your comfort reach down into my heart and soul.

Lord, I ask, too, that You will reveal any ways in which I am at odds with being a woman, where I am lost or living out of an untrue understanding of who I am, or who men are. While I bring you my wounds, I also pray that I may be ready to take responsibility for my behaviour and find forgiveness and healing in You.

I ask this in Jesus' name.

Amen

A useful exercise!

Write a letter to your mother, telling her what it was like for you growing up as her daughter. (The letter is not to be posted; it's just between you and God.) Also, if she wrote you a letter, what would you hope it would say?

Scriptures for worship and prayer

PSALM 62

PSALM 71:1-8

ISAIAH 44:1-5

ISAIAH 43:1-4

MATTHEW 6:28-34

JUDE 1:20-21

Questions for women

What does being a woman mean for me?

What is my stereotype? Why?

What do I find comfortable about being a woman?

What is a challenge?

What is being/receiving like for me? What was my mother like?

What was her message to me about women?

How have I received from her?

How have I cut off from her?

Please read Appendix A: Co-dependency vs emotional dependency.

NOTES

CHAPTER 9b – BEING MY MOTHER'S SON

The effects of a mother wound in men will be specific, and will link back to:

- Who God made men to be
- Being under the curse which brings enmity with the serpent, and broken relationships between men and women
- Dealing with a broken relationship with the opposite-sex parent
- Any attachment issues we have with our mother.

Who are men?

Men and women are both essential in conveying the image of God on earth. Each is unique. While we share our basic humanity with women, our ways of seeing and doing are different, and complementary to, those of women. Both are necessary for God's glory to be seen on earth.

There is a masculine quality that is in every human being, but is more evident in men. It is about valuing 'doing' rather than 'being'. This difference will be partly due to the different physicality and strength that men possess, as well as the biological difference of providing the covering and security for pregnancy, but not carrying the young themselves.

This masculine quality involves the capacity, under God, to define and initiate truth, and then to stand in it and persevere until it is achieved. This can be at an individual, family, church, corporate, national or global level. It is to understand God's order and bring the 'world' in line with it, and to do this under God's authority (a delegated benevolent authority), that can give form and order, find a way through, cover and bless. It wants to enable and release others (whereas woman have a need to care and protect). It is ready to take responsibility and understand the principle of reaping and sowing. It is expressed in Psalm 62:11–12 as strength, love and reward.

This means that, as men, we make things happen. We can pare a situation or task back to the bare essentials and keep an objectivity that is often necessary, both for the work to be done and for it to be completed. We act using reason, function, structure and decision; this is not a path of rugged independence, rather collaboration and interdependence. Properly balanced by the feminine and operating under God, the masculine presence gives us a functioning world that is creative, dynamic and structured, but with a heart.

When this is lost and the Fall is allowed to reign, then we are open to cynicism, competitiveness, finding our identity solely through work and the survival of the fittest. Decisions are then made out of independence and pride, on economic or pragmatic grounds, or as an exertion of power. We become heartless or aloof.

The fallen position from which we live as men is through toil. Because of the cursed ground, men will "toil the earth". Our work takes up most of our energy, and gives us our value and reason for living. It can become an idol. If this is the means by which we have significance, then it follows that it is devastating to be out of work or in the wrong job. We can feel worthless and ashamed or angry. If we do have a job, we are vulnerable to drivenness, workaholism and being manipulated into working long hours . We may become 'devoted' to our work and we may feel too insecure to stop or even to take our annual leave. We may not know what to do with our free time or how to relax and just 'be' at home. We may also have a tendency to blame-shift, especially on to women.

The effect of the curse on men and women, and the serpent's enmity with them, will mean that the feminine ways of knowing and being, of having feelings or the desire to have relationship are seen as a threat because they challenge this way of being. We can become ashamed of having needs and receiving. We can be afraid of having feelings and being intimate. We prefer to be defined by our work than our relationships and do not want demands made on us that we cannot understand or meet.

How do I find this description?

What do I find an encouragement and what do I find irritating or a threat?

Men have a capacity to:

- 'Do' as well as 'be'
- Use reason and objectivity to make decisions
- Bring structure and order into life
- Enjoy taking responsibility and initiative
- Provide covering and stand alongside women, blessing who they are
- Invest in and release others.

But there will also be the tendency:

- To find identity in work and hide there
- To drivenness, keeping busy, 'survival of the fittest'
- To be heartless or independent or to see relationships as too demanding
- To feel shame in needing anything or anyone, and be afraid of intimacy
- To be passive and avoid responsibility
- To participate in misogyny and misuse strength
- To blame shift, especially on to women
- To feel bewildered about the world of men and that there is not enough of me to belong.

Why it hurts and how it surfaces

The male inbuilt need to 'do' requires a sense of self to make anything happen, let alone take risks, persevere and take a stand. If we are empty inside, or are full of chaos, we will not bring any order into life. We will be fearful of real responsibility and of being a covering for anyone, including a wife and children. We will want to hide our insecurity by being on the go or by cutting off, rather than stopping and being known. We will do this as a strategy to keep the painful feelings at bay and as an attempt to survive life on our own.

Boarding school/fostering

If our boyhood relationship with our mothers was cut short for any reason, especially by being sent away to school and being expected to handle it bravely, our relationship with our mothers will have ended abruptly and will never have been quite the same again. We will not know how and to whom we can express any needs or pain. We will not have been able to break away from our mother properly as a teenager with the mixture of anger and ambivalence that we should have felt. We were supposed to have done the separating out then, rather than being banished at an early age. This often leaves us in a state of limbo or guilt around our mothers, and we can stay overly attached or feel bereft long into adult life, even transferring this ambivalence onto women in general.

Relationships

Our need for relationships, connection and a partner is there inside us, but often it cannot get met. Perhaps this is because we keep on the move or because we expect devotion without relationship. The lack of sense of self, our unresolved attachment issues and the fear of being left will often be subconscious, but may well be dictating how we live as we try to stave off future rejection by avoidance, escape, or control and manipulation.

There are two classic patterns of unhealthy relating that each of us can fall into from time to time or as a lifestyle. Each tends to come out of a poor sense of self:

Co-dependency

This is when we live our lives through others, anticipating and responding to their needs rather than our own. It is care taking as a defence and enables us to stave off rejection by making ourselves indispensable. Co-dependency avoids real intimacy or being known and means we leave no time to feel our own pain or loneliness. It is as if we have got stuck in the infant stage of detachment and stay cut off and hurt – longing for love but afraid to risk having it. We need to be in control, even at enormous personal cost, because inside we are terrified of change, rejection or being alone.

Emotional dependency

Here, we appear to be a chaotic and needy person attaching to others out of fear of aloneness. We usually do not believe we have anything to offer in relationships and see ourselves as only being able to take. It is as if we have stayed stuck in the infant stage of crying out to be held and loved. Boundaries are difficult for us; we are often living out of our feelings or low self image. We may use fantasy to compensate for our relational deficits.

We will often oscillate between co-dependency and emotional dependency in response to what buttons are pressed in our relationships. Of course, the codependent needs someone to be emotionally dependent on them, and vice versa. These dynamics can play out in our family relationships, through hanging on to old patterns, at work and church, or in our marriages or parenting. The start of the way out is to recognise what is happening and to bring the underlying aloneness and lack of confidence to God. He will bring His comfort, ongoing intimacy and consolation.

This can lead to:

- Depression and a feeling of defeat, that we will never make the grade as a man
- Feeling adrift and unable to connect to other men
- Fear of our peer group: becoming competitive, aloof, overly cool, supercilious
- Inability to trust and be a team player
- Promiscuity, seeking to prove our masculine prowess, but afraid to be known
- Fear of commitment and a chain of broken relationships
- Fierce control of girlfriends or wives to avoid being abandoned again
- Withdrawal and aloneness, perhaps into self-pity and an addiction
- Our infantile rage feeling dangerous for us in a strong adult body
- Being abusive or violent or showing passive aggression towards women
- Workaholism and an inability to relax or be quiet in case there is no one there inside
- Fear of our own feelings and of having a heart.

Sexual fantasy

Another fear in relationships is of rejection or emasculation. This may reach such a level that we are unable to relate to anyone in the flesh, only in fantasy. We will then be prey to pornography or distant relationships such as on internet chat rooms, floorshows and clubs, chat lines or prostitution. This can happen even when we are Christians because we have split off from our real need for people and only feel safe at a distance. We may feel too empty and uninteresting to dare to engage with anyone in reality.

How do I feel about myself as a man, as well as a person?

In the light of this, how are my relationships with men? Easy, a peer, enjoyable, satisfying, fearful, care-taking, aloof?

How are my relationships with women?

Separation anxiety

This anxiety is often much deeper than we realise and can reach the point of terror. As little boys this may well have been felt as genital pain, hence the need to reassure ourselves by clutching our genitals. This may have paved the way for masturbation to become compulsive. We may then fall into addictive ways of managing this fear or of maintaining the stimulus for masturbation, as mentioned above. Until this anxiety is brought to God and replaced by His peace, constancy and love, we will not make any headway with our addictions. Similarly, we may have a fixation for a certain part of a woman's body that feels like a connection back to our mothers. This leads to particular kinds of pornography or fetishes.

How is my heart?

Do I live with any deep-seated anxiety or secret places?

How have I sought to fill up my empty places or ease my anxiety?

Gender

Being let down or wounded by our mothers, or being left in a detached and anxious place by our attachment issues can make us unsure about who we are as men. In our anger, we can cut off from our mothers and just go through the motions of being her son. This can leave us without any good role model or feminine presence in our lives and unsure of how to relate appropriately to women.

If our lack of sense of being was combined with a controlling, emasculating mother then we may never have emerged and still remain attached to her in an unhealthy way. Or, we may have cut off and have been punishing every other woman in our path ever since, perceiving them as another version of mother! Conversely, we may have been overly attached to our mothers and experienced a powerful meeting of minds and understanding with her that we look for in other women. If we then marry we can transfer this on to our wives and then have difficulty separating the two out – tending to be a 'good boy' or 'troublesome teenager' in the relationship – and at times resenting the commitment of a marriage. This can even lead to a new kind of acting out.

This can leave us:

- Reacting adversely to women of our mother's type, eg needy women or cold controlling women
- Fixating on, for example, women's breasts, especially if they are large as this is our primal memory of our mother's engorged breasts
- With an insufficient sense of personhood, let alone manhood, with which to take our place as a man
- Only able to be macho or misogynistic as a man
- Needing a woman as an accessory to bolster our masculinity or feeling we are God's gift to women!
- Treating women as objects, for example through pornography
- Vulnerable to a wounding by our fathers which undermines our sense of masculinity
- With a fetish for women's clothing: one aspect of what is happening here is the need to stay attached to mother becoming eroticised on to objects of women's clothing. There is usually a history of some early lack of bonding with mother and a deep separation anxiety.

What was my mother's attitude to men? (She is my main role model for learning how women relate to men.)

A prayer

Lord, I thank You that You know me better than I know myself. Thank You that You invite me to come to You as the healer and restorer of my soul. Thank You that You want to offer me comfort in all the places where You see I need it; and strength and direction where I feel at sea. May I trust You to be my Comforter and my enabler, my advocate and my brother and let Your comfort reach down into my heart and soul. I put my mother into Your hands as I work through my relationship with her.

I ask this in Jesus' name.

Amen

A useful exercise!

Write a letter to your mother, telling her what it was like for you growing up as her son. (The letter is not to be posted; it's just between you and God.) Also, if she wrote you a letter, what would you hope it would say?

Scriptures for worship and prayer

PSALM 62   *PSALM 71:1–8*   *JUDE 1: 20–21*

ISAIAH 43:1–4   *ISAIAH 44:1–5*   *MATTHEW 6:28–34*

Questions for men

What does 'woman' mean for me?

What is my stereotype? Why?

What do I find comfortable about being a man?

What is a challenge?

What is being/receiving like for me?

What was my mother like?

What was her message to me about women?

Please read Appendix A: Co-dependency vs emotional dependency.

NOTES

CHAPTER 10 – RECEIVING MOTHERLY LOVE

The healing presence

We need to check out our hearts before God and tell Him about anything that prevents us drawing near to Him. He knows what these things are already, and He is longing to clear our path to Him. We need to press through any of these ill feelings or distrust and simply wait in His presence. This may feel like emptiness and we might be afraid that we will disappear. Or, we may feel unattached in a sense of space. This can be quite distressing, but if we can call out to God from this place and find Him with us, it can be the start of a new reality in our relationship with Him.

The wait

As we become more able to wait, His presence becomes the healing presence. As we quieten our hearts we will feel the full security of Him being God for us. We can become rested and comforted by this deep inside. We may well not be able to put what is happening into words, until we feel Him knowing us and being there for us. When we are ready, or when it seems to be the right next step, we can start to 'pour out our hearts to Him'.

(We may find it helpful to carve out some time to tell God about our lives, from our perspective, from the beginning until the present day. If we then wait in His presence He will speak back to us about how He sees our lives. This process can be very freeing. If we feel we have no voice then it is good to find some private space and cry out to God our Father as loud as you can asking Him to come and find you. As the healing presence comes He will fill us with life.)

As we enter the healing presence our unmet needs will start to sort themselves out from the wounds, the disappointments, the griefs, the sorrows, the rejection, the questions and the powerlessness. As we give them to God on the Cross, He takes them and gives us back life in exchange.

For some of us, the wait is impossible because we do not have a sense of being – a deep knowledge of our own existence that was set in to us from the life of another. We may not have a sense of well-being – an inner sense of being secure and having known some goodness.

Or our primal discomforts can start rising up inside us:

- Anxiety for our mother's presence
- Panic that she isn't there strongly enough for us
- The feeling that we are alone
- Real distress
- Anger and protest at her apparent absence
- A craving need for her attention or any attention
- A desperate need for touch, or to attach
- A sense of hopelessness that I am alone
- A numbness and deadness
- A deep sense of detachment from our mothers and a fear of losing the protection of this independence
- Terror
- The inability to relax, let go or even to get to sleep each night.

What is being healed?

When we have not received the best that God intended for us, for whatever reason, we are wounded and will have lost out. What wounds may there be?

- A very particular rejection wound – towards our very existence, as a person, or towards our gender
- An insecurity wound from expecting security and welcome and being disappointed
- An anxiety wound at not being able to bond and rest – a feeling of being at sea, unanchored
- An emptiness wound at not having a sense of self
- A distress wound at not having a sense of well-being or getting the basic care we needed
- A nakedness wound where we feel exposed in life, unsheltered or uncovered
- A raw wound of anger, frustration or self-hatred
- A guilt wound at being here at all or being a nuisance
- A death wound of feeling more present to death than to life, a sense of living in a non life-giving place or in a vacuum, a sense of death being a friend and a way out or means of relief
- A fear wound of giving in to death or being overtaken by non being
- A fear wound of being found out and rejected again
- A wound of unreality as we detach from life itself and go on as an 'observer'
- A deprivation wound of still never having enough to live off in life
- The wound of a broken heart.

What ten words would describe how I feel inside and how life seems to me?

What is missing?

We have already seen that a basic sense of self, of well-being, of security, of care and nurture, of personhood, of boundary and of confidence may well seem to be missing. There may also be other gaps in our lives. We may not have developed a capacity:

- To trust anyone except ourselves, and even then this can be dodgy!
- To choose – this is difficult without a sense of self
- To have needs
- To receive or give, or both, depending on the circumstances
- To connect or be known or share
- To be thankful or enjoy ourselves or do fun
- To be still or rest or to relax
- To join in
- To take risks or cope with the unknown
- To make a home, feel safe or welcome others.

What else might be present?

Our hearts may be full of hurt and survival and sin:

- Self-doubt, self-hatred
- Jealousy, envy, despising of others
- Anger
- Self-pity, despair
- Lust and sexualised needs
- Hatred or murder
- Pain and a sinful means of managing it, for example an addiction
- Numbness and isolation
- Bitterness and blame shifting
- Care taking
- Appeasement
- Grief, and a sense of being inconsolable.

We will need to offer these responses and survival mechanisms to God. He knows they are there and through the Cross He is ready to relieve us of them. He will be our Comforter and shield and our source of life, consolation and care.

What are my wounds?

What is missing in my life?

What am I carrying in my heart?

Forgiveness

Earlier in the course when we looked at the Cross we discovered God's grace to us as He forgives us our sins. Now, we have a chance to use that grace towards our mothers.

Relating to our mothers as adults

We have all survived into adulthood, or we would not be reading this today. Our mothers may still be alive and we may have resolved many of our issues with them. Or, our current relationship may be an outworking of our childhood days. For others, our mothers are no longer alive, or we are so estranged that there is no meaningful contact.

God wants to enable us to do all we can, from our side, to find at least a rest position in our relationship with our mother that does not sap our energy or keep us as a child. We need to be objective and realistic about who our mothers are and what changes are feasible for them. We might need to lay down the expectation that our unmet needs will be met by her, and turn to God instead.

Starting with the positive, we thank God for all that has been good: our mother did bring us into the world! (It may be a challenge to our self-hatred to agree that this was a good thing to have happened!)

In thanking God for the good things we can go right back to our infancy and early childhood. We may begin to see some of the issues that our mothers were up against. There may have been a difficult mother-in-law, a lack of covering from a husband or partner, poverty, a lack of emotional support, fear, conflict, etc.

Then, in God's healing and holy presence, we can gradually go back over all that seemed to be missing. We will need to name this as sin against us. We then seek to realise the full effect of this in our lives and seek God's grace to move on into forgiveness. The move into God's grace will allow us to move beyond our detachment and hurt into a place of objectivity and forgiveness. We must take our level of hurt and woundedness fully into account before we embark on forgiveness. We find a new sense of adult empowerment to face the issues and process them. As we release our mothers to God, the Righteous Judge, we are letting go of our right to be judge and jury and from the ongoing burden of revenge or pity.

As we assess our current relationship with our mother we can see where we are in it. We can seek to change our behaviour to that of a Christ-like adult. This may involve setting good boundaries, trying not to keep score of wrongs, not taking the bait, holding our ground, allowing our mother space – whatever would be corrective for us. As we do so, we are "beating our swords into ploughshares" (Isaiah 2:4)!

Very often our mothers do not know what they have done wrong, and they may well respond to a change of approach from us. God may even take us to a new position of peace where His love enables us to relinquish our resentment and anger and approach our mothers as a free adult.

Come before the Lord. Let Him remind you that you have been fearfully and wonderfully made. Tell him that you want to know that deep inside. Explain to Him what you are carrying in your heart and what you try to run away from. He has provided the Cross as the place of healing, comfort and restoration for us – let Him find you and take you there.

A prayer for a renewed sense of being

Lord, I come before You now and ask that You will find me where I am. I need Your comfort and life-giving presence in my life. I bring those parts of me that were wounded before I had any words to describe what was happening. But the wounds and memories are still within me.

Please find my heart and begin to take my woundedness into Yourself. Give me a safe place within my heart to store the goodness and life that You want to give me. I ask that You will exchange my lack of being with Your life; the presence of death for Your resurrection, and set Your ongoing healing into the very core of my being.

I ask this in Jesus' all-powerful name.

Amen

We may need to pray in a true 'sense of being' every day. We can do this by putting our hands on our heart or stomach and asking God to create a place within us where we can store good things. We can then receive His life and comfort and well-being until it builds into a solid self!

Scriptures for worship and prayer

PSALM 139

PSALM 138:3

> *On the day I called, you answered me; my strength of soul you increased.* [1]

PSALM 13:3

> *Consider and answer me, O Lord my God; light up my eyes, lest I sleep the sleep of death.*

PSALM 16:6, 9

> *The lines have fallen for me in pleasant places; indeed, I have a beautiful inheritance. Therefore my heart is glad, and my whole being* [2] *rejoices; my flesh also dwells secure.*

PSALM 18:4

> *The cords of death encompassed me; the torrents of destruction assailed me* [3].

ISAIAH 28:15-16, 18

> *Because you have said, "We made a covenant with death. Behold I am the one who has laid a foundation in Zion, a stone, a tested stone, a precious cornerstone, of a sure foundation. Then your covenant with death shall be annulled and your agreement with Sheol will not stand."*

ISAIAH 33:6

> *He will be the stability of your times, an abundance of salvation.*

JOB 3:11

> *Why did I not die at birth, come out from the womb and expire?*

PSALM 22:9-1

> *Yet You are He who took me from the womb; You made me trust You at my mother's breasts. On You was I cast from my birth, and from my mother's womb you have been my God. Be not far from me, for trouble is near, and there is none to help.*

PSALM 27:10

> *For my father and my mother have forsaken me, but the Lord will take me in.*

PSALM 31:21-22, 24

> *Blessed be the Lord, for he has wondrously shown his steadfast love to me when I was in a besieged city.*
> *I had said in my alarm, [4] "I am cut off from your sight." But You heard the voice of my pleas for mercy when I cried to You for help.*
> *"Be strong, and let your heart take courage, all you who wait for the Lord!"*

PSALM 33:19

> *...that He may deliver their soul from death and keep them alive in famine.*

PSALM 71:5-6

> *For you, O Lord, are my hope, my trust, O Lord, from my youth. Upon you I have leaned from before my birth; You are He who took me from my mother's womb. My praise is continually of You.*

PSALM 94:17

> *If the LORD had not been my help, my soul would soon have lived in the land of silence.*

PSALM 95:6-7

> *Oh come, let us worship and bow down; let us kneel before the Lord, our Maker! For He is our God, and we are the people of His pasture, and the sheep of His hand.*

PSALM 116-3

> *The snares of death encompassed me, the pangs of Sheol laid hold of me, I suffered distress and anguish. Then I called on the name of the Lord: "O Lord, I pray, deliver me."*

PSALM 131:2

> *But I have calmed and quieted my soul, like a weaned child with its mother; Like a weaned child is my soul within me.*

PSALM 147:3

> *He gathers the broken-hearted and binds up their wounds.*

ISAIAH 66:11-13

> *That you may nurse and be satisfied from her consoling breast: that you may drink deeply with delight from her glorious abundance. For thus says the Lord, "Behold I will extend peace to her like a river, and the glory of the nations like an overflowing stream; and you shall nurse, you shall be carried upon her hip, and bounced upon her knees. As one whom his mother comforts so I will comfort you; you shall be comforted in Jerusalem."*

ISAIAH 50:10

> *Who is there among you who reverently fears the Lord yet has no shining splendour in his heart?*

Come all you who are thirsty, come to the waters; and you who have no money come and buy and eat. Come buy wine and milk without money and without cost. Why spend money on what is not bread, and your labour on what does not satisfy? Listen, listen to me, and eat what is good, and your soul will delight on the richest of fare. Give ear and come to me; hear me that your soul may live.

End-notes for scriptures:

1. Hebrew: you made me bold in my soul with strength

2. Hebrew: my glory

3. Or terrified me

4. Or in my haste

Many of us do not realise how dead we feel inside, or how deep our sense of deprivation and hunger really is. We can feel extremely frustrated that none of our own efforts really change this, and we do not know what it feels like to rest and be satisfied. God wants to meet us in this dead place and bring us life, full healing and comfort.

NOTES

— III —

CHAPTER 11 – OUR FATHERS

In an ideal world

Let us remind ourselves that God's original plan was that two individuals should have been parented in such a way that, when they reached adulthood, they could leave their father and mother and enter into a covenant relationship with each other. Within the security of this relationship, they were then invited to share in God's creation by becoming parents themselves.

So, we were to be conceived into a relationship that was peaceful and ready to receive us. Our fathers would be committed, both to our mothers and to this adventure. They were to welcome our presence in their relationship and not see us as an intrusion or an inconvenience. We would sense the covering of our father for our mother, feel safe and grow. We would know that provision was being made for us and at our arrival and we would have been welcomed by someone who felt strong and present for us. That strength was to provide the safety for our mothers to nurse us and for us to take in all she had for us. We could then just 'be' and receive rather than fret.

Gradually there is sufficient presence in us, as children, to begin to draw away to explore our immediate world – but with our home base always there to go back to. Our movement away from our mothers was to evolve at a pace that was appropriate for us, until we were sure enough of life to venture out and take on the world.

During this time, our fathers should have been present as a benevolent strength for us. They would be our advocate and help us to become objective about the world and our place in it. They were to be a source of reality and self-belief for us, providing the scaffolding within which a new person could begin to take form and grow. We needed our fathers in different ways as our lives evolved.

The bridge

Our fathers needed to come and find us on our mother's side of the bridge into life and lead us – both away from our mother and over onto the other side. We needed to get to the other side to start our unique life. For some of us, there was no father to come, so we remain stuck with our mother or she is unable to let us go. An understanding mother may have tried to take us over herself, but we will feel the lack of father and know she needs to remain on her own side. Sometimes we may have tried to go by ourselves – maybe we make it but we are left horribly alone. Or, our father may be abhorrent to us and we have declined the invitation to go with him, or he may have got us over the bridge only to abandon us there to make our own way off into life.

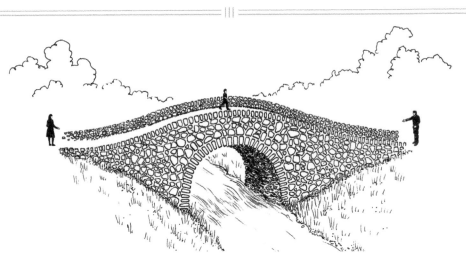

The ideal – our father needs to help us across from our mother's side of the bridge into life

Our mother may try to help us over herself, but there is no father to come

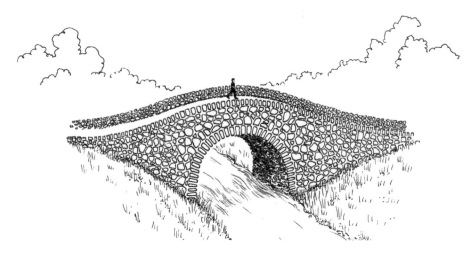

We are left alone to make the transition into life ourselves

The role of our father

Model of good humanity

Our father had the privilege of modelling good humanity for us. He would do this so that we would want to belong to the human race too and find our way into it via him. His desire to connect to us through his benevolent strength was to be a powerful source of identification. We needed to latch on to him as soon as we were mobile, feel a deep connection to him and know that we belonged and were covered. This is vital for all of us, but particularly for boys. If this early identification stage is not completed then we feel adrift from life itself and cannot see where or how we can ever fit in. We will attempt to find identification and connection with others but know in our hearts that this is not sufficient. If this need becomes eroticised through puberty, we may seek to meet it in sexual ways.

Priest to the family

Our fathers were to have a living relationship with God, representing God the Father to us in a positive way. They were to live before God themselves, working out with Him who we were becoming so that they could father us appropriately. They were also to pray for us.

Husband to our mother

Our father was to love our mother and provide for his family so that our mother felt secure and able to nurture and care for us. Our parents were to be in a relationship that was an equal partnership, well-coordinated and with good communication. We should not have been a diversion for their difficulties, a surrogate parent to whoever needed one, or a threat to their relationship. They were the adults – we were children.

To be delighted with us

It is a huge privilege to be a father and our father was supposed to be awed and chuffed by this. He should have been able to communicate this sense of delight and privilege to us, just as the Father did to Jesus.

Source of discipline and advocacy

While our mothers cared for us, our fathers were to provide the scaffolding of discipline, advocacy and relationship that would prepare us for life in the big wide world. He was to help us develop the objectivity, the inner strength, the will, the conscience, the sense and knowledge of self and the back-up that we needed to gradually take our place in the world. This would happen first at school, then with our peers, then as a teenager and as a young adult.

His external discipline was to be administered in such a way that we could make it our own – developing our own sense of what was right and wrong, with enough conviction and strength to live with our own integrity and take our place in life. We could make mistakes and actually learn from them; we would not be afraid to risk or try. We learnt to face the consequences of our actions.

This need for advocacy and blessing is vital. It cannot be underestimated. Many of us are still listening, long into adult life, for that word of ownership, favour and pride in us as his child: 'That's my son/that's my daughter'. If Jesus needed to be blessed publicly at the start of His ministry as a son, rather than for His achievements, how much more do we need it? He was also reassured of this in the transfiguration, just before He embarked on the journey to the Cross. Here we see that the Father's words of ownership were vital for His strength and courage for the task.

Some of us have never had a word of encouragement, ownership or pride spoken to us. Our hearts know it and are empty. We are deeply disappointed and this can lead us to feel that we are a disappointment as a person. We crave a word of affirmation so desperately that we seek it from anyone and everyone. We then live a life of raised expectations and flattering others in the hope they will return the favour. The sense that we 'had hoped' for this encouragement can become the overriding narrative in our hearts. We can feel like an orphan, adrift and unimportant.

How have I been affirmed and by whom?

Am I still seeking affirmation now as an adult? If so, how?

Being named and being known

Our fathers were to name us (in partnership with our mothers, obviously!) In the Bible the act of naming often had a prophetic quality. Names were to express something of who the person was to become. This was to be the start of our father's commitment to knowing us and owning us (Isaiah 49:1).

Our fathers were to be the person who discovered who we were becoming, who dialogued with us so that he could discern the unique stages of our development. A useful analogy is to think of each of us as a new build house. Our mothers were to lay firm foundations, and our fathers were to form the scaffolding and make sure we continued to be a work in progress and did not get stuck or lost.

Our fathers heard our dreams, noticed our preferences, saw our skills developing and created the space and opportunities for these to be tried or tested. Within this process we were not meant to feel beholden, nor locked in, made to feel like a threat or a waste of space. So, if we showed artistic tendencies, he would realise that these may need room to grow. We would then see together whether they would become our career, or simply a hobby. Either way our 'house' would need a studio. Others of us would need a 'kitchen' or a 'garden', a 'study' or a 'consulting room', ' a great hall' or a 'pulpit' etc. Of course, the house that we were becoming was unique and would be different from that of each of our siblings!

Our fathers would give us the chance to be an apprentice to them with their skills and hobbies. We should be free both to overtake our fathers and also not to be as interested as them. We would learn to try things and also to persevere. It would be a journey of discovery, not the creation of a clone, or the life he never had.

We needed our fathers to engage directly with us eyeball to eyeball not hiding behind a paper or telling us to go and ask our mother. That kind of detachment or passivity was not good masculine presence.

We will also experience deep confusion and wounding if our father committed sexual unfaithfulness or deserted our mother. We will feel angry or ambivalent about what he modelled for us. But in our desperation to identify and connect with him we may deny the hurt to our mother and we will need to find him through the divided loyalty.

Have I been aware of real interest and investment being made in who I was becoming?

Was this welcomed? Who am I as myself, and not just the child of my parents?

Am I still a work in progress? Is God interested in me and who I am?

Good masculine presence

In these ways, our fathers were modelling sound masculinity for us, which brings a benevolent strength and has the ability to act and accomplish. For men this is as the same-sex parent. For women this is the example of man as a safe companion and the one who represents the opposite sex to us.

Ideally, this interest needed to be **genuine, consistent and continuous**. But some of us will remember our fathers finding certain stages of our lives harder for them than others. But there may also have been some better times, so we need not dismiss our whole relationship as a non-starter.

But it wasn't an ideal world

The Fall can step in and rob us of our birthright of order and blessing, even before day one of our existence. Our fathers may have not have been mature or committed enough to embark on the journey of parenthood. They may have been so busy providing for us, or been away for some reason, that they missed being present for us. They may well have been fatherless themselves, with the generations before them leaving a legacy of chaos, hurt, passivity, fear or violence. The demands of a wife and then a family might have been too much. We may realise that the whole household had to revolve around our father's mood or behaviour and we were never free to have a relaxed time as a child. It was all about him.

The fatherless

Throughout Scripture people are called after their father as "son of" back through the generations. For some of us this connection is fine and a source of pride. For others of us it is a big unknown. We may not even know our father's name or have met him, let alone his ancestry. Our father's behaviour may have left us ashamed to be part of his family.

Whatever our circumstances, our adoption into God's family has been secured. We can receive it with joy and gratitude. We now share the same Father as Jesus and He will never leave us or forsake us. He will always treat us with dignity and grace.

Throughout the Old Testament, God asks His people to defend the cause of the fatherless and provide for them. He describes himself as, "Father to the fatherless" (Psalm 68:5). The Old Testament ends with an appeal for fathers and children to be reconciled in Malachi 4:6. The reconciliation is to happen whether it is the fathers who are estranged or the children who have been rebellious. (The loss can come from either side.) The New Testament opens in Luke 1:17 with this reconciliation and fathers turning back their hearts to their children. This is to be one of the purposes of Jesus' coming – to bring about this reconciliation through His Cross. We are all, therefore, fatherless to some degree.

Orphans and first-born

It is interesting to make a list of the characteristics of orphans and of first-born and see the difference. Where am I still living out of an orphan place?

Jesus shows us the Father

But Jesus also came: to show us the Father, to do only the will of the Father, and to demonstrate that the Trinity is relational. Jesus and the Father lived out a Father/Son relationship in every sense with obedience, delight and freedom. The way Jesus was with people was exactly how the Father would have been with them if He had been incarnate. For example, every moment of Jesus' encounter with the woman caught in adultery was Jesus doing the will of the Father.

Jesus shows us how to move from being slaves towards God, to being servants, to being His friends, and finally to being His sons and daughters. However good our earthly fathering has been, we all need to know God as Father. If we have had the advantage of a loving and appropriate earthly father then the idea of God being Father will sit well for us. In contrast, if our experiences were unhelpful, destructive, or if our father was indulgent or totally absent, then these experiences can eclipse a true knowledge of God in our hearts.

Types of father

Our earthly father, or our lack of him, will seriously colour our perception of God, our heavenly Father. The more difficult the relationship, the more likely we are to tar God with the same brush and find it hard to separate them out.

For example:

An arbitrary father – may leave us thinking: Will God be there when I need Him? And, how will I find Him today?

A perfectionist father – may leave us believing that God is equally demanding. We have no experience of grace.

Absent father (physically or emotionally)

We can perceive an absent father as rejection. This can lead to a sense of unworthiness, self-doubt or self-hatred. There can be a sense of betrayal and broken trust. We will not have had any scaffolding so can feel adrift and without a proven or established sense of who we are. Our mothers may have tried to compensate for our lack of fathering and have left us either too tied to her, or feeling guilty for breaking away. The reason for the absence will also, of course, leave its own scars. Is God equally 'absent' for me?

Critical father

Often, a critical father will not know how to nurture. He will see us as an extension of himself and his own insecurities. We can respond to his demands to perform in a variety of ways. We may rebel, suppress our anger into later addictions, anxiety, depression, or feel like a constant failure and be seriously lacking in confidence or ambition. We may detach so that our relationship becomes perfunctory, though we are seething inside, or we can try to appease him with performance, knowing it will never be good enough. We can be so worn down that we no longer take responsibility for anything. We may be left with the questions: Can I ever please God? Will I have ever done enough?

Insecure father

An insecure father will leave us with very little sense of well-being or confidence, no real relationship and a fear of both letting him down and adding to his worries, or surpassing him and being a threat. Again, there is no good scaffolding. We are left wondering if God can cope with the weight and details of our life.

Controlling father

With a controlling father we do have scaffolding, but usually only in the shape of the house that he wants to build, or the one he thinks we are evolving into. He may keep us financially dependant or unable to make decisions without his input. Everything is external and about him, rather than about us developing our own inner conscience, will or character. We can feel like a mere shell.

We may never feel we have reached adulthood. A controlling father can crush our spirit, or we can come out fighting and either rebel or 'take everyone on'. We will not have experienced grace or have an idea of what free will is.

Indulgent father

If we have an indulgent father we can either become a spoiled brat, or the 'baddy' in the family – spurning our father's generosity. It will be hard for us to stand in life and discover or trust our own resources. There will be some insecurities in him that need to appease us in this way, to keep us indebted to him. We may well view God as the provider of magical solutions and not understand the joy of collaboration or taking responsibility.

Violent father

A father who was violent will leave us insecure and ashamed with no scaffolding and very little building. We may just feel like a pile of rubble and we will be deeply wounded. If we can make the transition to God as our comfort and shelter then we will be able to begin to feel safe enough to embark on life again.

Passive father

A passive father is deeply frustrating. Often, he would be present but he would feel of no use to us. Perhaps there was no active interest or support, no engagement or presence when we needed him. If he was also dominated by our mother, this will significantly affect our view of marriage. We will be left asking: Is God up to the task too?

Your father

What ten words could I use to describe my father (to God)?

So what is the damage?

An empty space

We will have an empty space in our hearts and almost physically in our whole bodies. This empty space is where we should have had blessing, advocacy, covering, strength, belief, ownership, personhood and a sense of belonging. (Note this is different from a lack of sense of being.)
We can be more aware of this loss. We feel orphaned, unnoticed, needing to prove our existence or just a disappointment.

Unaccompanied

We wonder if there is anyone travelling the road with us, a good ear, a sounding board. We need someone to help us be objective and to get clarity about our lives.

Self-doubt

Without good constructive input and the chance to learn from our mistakes we might be lacking in real confidence – doubting our own ability and resources.

Anxiety

Anxiety can lead to compulsive masturbation, addictions or a cycle of failure.

Shame

An inadequate attachment to our mother and a disconnection or antipathy towards our father will leave us with deep shame inside, whether we feel it or not. We prefer to blame ourselves, rather than our parents, and will assume we are deeply flawed and not special enough for them to parent us well.

Drivenness

Our lack of an adequate father may lead us to become driven: either out of a craving for words of affirmation at last, or to prove that we can manage without our father. There may be a sense of showing him who we really are and what he has missed by not getting to know us. Or it can just be a promise to ourselves that we are going to succeed despite him.

Lack of masculine strength

This can manifest in difficulty persevering, making decisions, taking risks, taking responsibility or facing consequences. Or it may lead to blame shifting, despair and bitterness, even self-pity. We can be narcissistic or cynical as we seek to cover up our weakness.

Gender insecurity

If we have cut off from our fathers then we have rejected his version of the masculine and this actual part of ourselves. Without much in its place we may seek to fill the gap through immoral sexual behaviours such as promiscuity and pornography. For women, we may then despise or wish to punish men, or ask to be fathered.

Fathering ourselves

Fatherless men can sometimes relate in a fathering way, and not as a peer. This feels safer and at least brings some fatherly presence into their lives, albeit self-generated. In the long-term this is exhausting and only increases the loneliness because there is no receiving, or mutuality in our relationships, only giving and defensiveness.

Heartless

If we are in survival mode then we can cut off from the hurt or from any emotion and become heartless and even bitter and angry. We are not able to relax, enjoy ourselves or let others do so.

What ten words would I use to describe myself?

What male role models do I have?

Where does my covering and advocacy come from?

Coming to God as Father

We must clearly separate out our earthly father from God the Father. Otherwise we will be wary of engaging with Him in a meaningful way. We will just expect or dread more of the same, but on a grander scale! We may feel too unworthy to be called a son or daughter of God, but it is the Father who determines this, not us, as we see in the story of the prodigal son. Some of us have managed for so long on our own that we are afraid to give up our independence, like the elder son. There is no shame or blame in owning before God our need of more, or better, fathering.

The Father is expecting us to come to Him. He invites us to take down our defences, or gather ourselves together, and pour out our hearts to Him. Like the father in Luke 15, God is waiting for us to come and express our need for Him to be our eternal good Father. He longs for us to let Him embrace us and welcome us into the eternal blessing and covering of the Father's house.

At the last supper Jesus called us His friends, which is lovely, but at His resurrection appearance to Mary in the garden (after His death for us) He said, "I am ascending to My Father and your Father, to My God and Your God" (John 20:17). Jesus has achieved our full adoption by the Father. He has paid all the debts that needed to be settled and is not ashamed to call us His brothers and His sisters. We are now co-heirs with Him of all the Father's blessing, advocacy and the eternal inheritance of life and goodness and mercy and love. We have a Father in heaven and, through His Spirit, we can know and be known by the Father whilst we are on earth.

A prayer

Thank you, Lord, that You understand all the circumstances of my family, including my father – who he is/was and who I am. You know what I needed and where the gaps in my fathering are.

I ask that You will come and reveal Your goodness and comfort to me now, that You will be my advocate and that You will bless me as Your son/daughter, as Your own.

Please forgive me where I have allowed my family experiences to affect my relationship with You. Please rebuild trust within me and may I come to know more of Your healing presence in all the ways that You see I need it.

Amen

Scriptures for worship and prayer

PSALM 62   *EPHESIANS 1*   *LUKE 15:11–32*

HEBREWS 2:9–18   *PSALM 103*

NOTES

CHAPTER 12a – BEING MY FATHER'S DAUGHTER

In the last chapter, we looked at our own father and God as Father. The incarnate Jesus was masculine, but God obviously also includes all the attributes of the feminine in His being as we are described as made in His image "male and female". In this chapter we will look at what we needed to receive from our fathers when we were children, and at how we may relate to men now as adult women.

The effects of fathering in women will be particular and will link back to:

- Who God made us to be
- How we were fathered in our family
- Dealing with a broken relationship with the opposite-sex parent
- Whether we could identify with the good of our humanity in our father.

Women as daughters

As women, we needed the presence of a safe father. This would enable us to grow up beyond our mother's care. A safe father would help us to emerge from the family with a clear sense of who we were becoming under God and help us find our unique path as a woman in life. As our culture loses sight of God, we create a vacuum for everyone to do what is right in his or her own eyes. As we lose our way for men and women to live together with a complementarity that blesses each other, we all become less clear about who we are and how to be. This can disable and anger us, leaving us confused, cynical and hurting.

Wounded women

As women we have a tendency:

- To need men to tell us who we are or make us feel significant. So, it is very important for our fathers to have expressed a genuine interest in us, by getting to know us, investing in us and opening up a place and a future for us – in the same way as they might have done for any boys in the family
- To tolerate pain as our lot. So, we may well have suffered in silence about any unfairness or rejection or lack of interest, and found it hard to express this clearly

- Come to expect rejection and feeling marginalised: so we may have detached, making it hard for our fathers to get close to us
- To find our identity in relationships. That's how we work so the lack of relationship, the absence of our father or a destructive relationship will affect us deeply
- To expect people to 'second guess' us. Our fathers may not have been able to do this and we perceived this as rejection
- To internalise or take as 'ours', feelings or messages that weren't specifically for us. This can lead to a build-up of disappointment and feeling misunderstood or neglected by our fathers. We may have taken in his 'messages' to us as the truth, because they came from him and that is what we were listening for
- Any of these can lead us to feeling deep shame or insignificance or lacking in confidence.

The role of our father

A representative of God our heavenly Father

The way we experienced our father will have given us a blue print for how we see men in general. As both the Father and Jesus are male, our fathers may have seriously affected our perception of God and our relationship with Him. It is worth checking out how much we have been able to separate out our earthly father from our heavenly one, and ask God's help to do so.

Which ten words would I use to describe God (my heart response, not the 'right' answers)? How many of these ten words apply to my earthly father too? (Can I separate out God from my father?)

Husband to our mother

An absent or ineffective father can have resulted in independence, control and insecurity in us. An abusive, arbitrary or controlling father can have led to blame or hatred. Again, we may need to process this as an adult and bring our father to God, seeking His objectivity so we can release him to God, the Righteous Judge, and move into a place of forgiveness. Seeing how our fathers treated our mothers, or how our mothers allowed themselves to be treated, can affect our view of marriage, men and ourselves. Again, we will need God's perspective on this.

What is my view of being a wife? What are my expectations of a man as a husband?

Delight

We needed to be a source of delight to our fathers. If there was any devaluing of women on the basis of their gender in our upbringing, then this will be engrained in us and will need to be renounced. If our father saw us as too mysterious, as being demanding or expensive, or if he viewed us as a sexual object, as just another girl – not a boy – or labelled us as being 'like your mother', then we will feel shame.

What was my experience? Did I feel valued as a girl and young woman?

Discipline and advocacy

As a child, we will have needed an advocate. We needed to be offered the same degree of care, blessing, opportunity and interest as a boy. There may be a generational line of discrimination against girls on our mother's side (or our father's side), and we may have internalised this. This will need to be renounced before God so we can now receive from Him, from our father and from other men.

We may embark on, or stay in, unsuitable relationships with men, as we seek to be affirmed by them and plug this gap inside. We can be perceived simply as being needy, and not as who we really are. We may even live out of this place of neediness just to keep the relationship going. We may have been the favourite in the family and this leaves us feeling only a conditional acceptance.

On the discipline front, we may have felt unfairly treated, been seen as trouble, or been able to manipulate. Any of these will not have given us a good start for our self-esteem or internal discipline as adults. Without good scaffolding we will feel adrift, misunderstood and like an orphan. This may run deep within us and will need to be touched by God.

Did I have an advocate?

How was I disciplined?

Have I heard a word of blessing – just for me – and received it right into my heart? Do I believe it?

Being named and known

Isaiah 49:1 talks about God naming us. We need to feel named in an honourable way by our fathers and be ready to recall and bring to God any labels and wrong names that were used against us. These will stick and we may have allowed them to define us, even subconsciously. The names that have been used to describe us may have left us believing wrong things about ourselves. For example, labels may have left us feeling that we are only there to be decorative; that we will never come to anything; that we will never be like our brother; that we are hysterical; thick; a nuisance; daddy's little girl, a princess etc. We need to take these names/labels to Jesus on the Cross.

Was I labelled in any way? Am I living out of any of these labels?

Good masculine presence

Our fathers needed to model a healthy masculinity to us – we needed to see a model of God's benevolent strength and advocacy so that we could be open to Him later. We also needed to experience a good representation of the opposite sex. As we grew up, we needed to be at peace with the masculine – the strength and the ability to act and persevere – that we welcomed it as part of who we were. If we were at odds with our fathers this good masculine presence will not sit easily in us. It will either be in overdrive as we show we can manage without men, or we will be defeated and passive, or swing between the two!

As adults, it is helpful to ask God to show us our father in a new light, so that we can be more objective about our relationship with him. With God's help we can sort out the suitable and good from the unsuitable or destructive or absent. We may then be able to benefit more from what was helpful and be in a better place to process and forgive what was missing.

Fatherlessness

It can be a real shock to see ourselves as fatherless, but if we were lacking a good, steady fatherly presence, it is the word that God would use to describe us. Whilst our father probably did his best for us, we realise that compared with what God intended for us it may not have been enough, nor what we uniquely needed from him.

We will need to come to terms with our fatherlessness and realise that our fathers will probably never be able to make up the lost ground with us as adults. We need to move on from being a needy child inside to being an adult who must leave home and begin to transfer these needs to God. Then, as we receive the love and advocacy that we need, we are able to see our families objectively and release them to God. We can then begin to relate to them from a new place.

In life, we all needed our fathers to draw us away from our mothers, especially if we had a difficult relationship with her and she was critical of us or saw us as competition. We needed him to give us the backing to take on life and help us stay in the game when we might have been tempted to retreat back to home. We needed help to cope with mistakes, to take risks and to try out different opportunities. If these things were not present for us, then this is a sin of omission needing our forgiveness.

Just today, a little boy got on the bus with his parents and pointed to the man opposite him and said, "That's my Dad". He was so proud of him. How many of us could say that? In different ways, we are all fatherless. We need to be adopted as daughters into the Father's family and find a covering and blessing that we never dreamt we could know.

Relationships

If we did not receive good fathering then our need for relationships, connection and being understood by men often cannot find a healthy outlet. We can be left with a real ambivalence about men: on the one hand needing them, but on the other hand despising, hating or being afraid of them. For women, a lack of relationship with men can affect our sense of identity and echo back to our teenage years and the all important question, "Who are you going out with?"

As adults, our unresolved issues with our father can also drive us *away* from men into:

- Independence and a living in a walled-off place
- Being frigid: fuelled by despising, passive aggression and fear
- Feeling ambivalence towards men - preferring their company yet fearing and avoiding real intimacy and connection
- Emotional dependence on other women
- Militant feminism.

Or, our unresolved father issues can have the opposite affect and drive us *towards* men and:

- Punishing men by toying with them or being unable to commit
- Needing them too much for our identity or a sense of well-being
- Being in romantic fantasy about them
- Sexualising our relationships
- Trying to play happy families and right the wrongs of our family script
- Allowing ourselves to remain in unhealthy relationships where we are treated badly because we feel it is all we are worth, or all we know (and at least it is familiar)
- Wanting a man to fill the father gap inside us and take care of us – leading us to regress
- Pornography.

We can find ourselves avoiding men like our fathers, and extending this to all men, or we can find ourselves drawn to them like a magnet, for the reasons above.

Very often we will swing between love and hate, as often the thing we need the most we fear the most! This may lead us to operate out of a place of real ambivalence. This can be confusing for everyone and can make us feel hopeless and misunderstood.

Feelings

As women, we will tend to let our feelings dictate how we are and our view of ourselves. We can also internalise other people's feelings and make them our own. Therefore, we may believe that we are 'useless' or 'helpless' or 'unimportant'.

Without the good masculine inside us to balance this over reliance on feelings we can:

- Feel lost and pathetic or needy
- Find it hard to be assertive and stand our ground
- Find it hard to bring order and clarity to projects
- Find it hard to make decisions
- Be unable to be objective and sift out the truth from our feelings
- Buckle when the going gets tough or when we are challenged
- Not be as articulate as we want to be or be able to communicate our understanding of a situation well
- Remain a victim or live out of old identities or vows, or under a ceiling imposed by our father.

Lack of a real voice

If we were silenced or ignored too many times as a child, we may have given up on having our own voice or ever being heard. We may not believe we have anything useful to say, or that we are heard – even by God. Our hearts are desperate to be heard. We may never have cried out to Him in full voice and released ourselves from our "land of silence" (Psalm 94:17). We need to find our own voice and use it freely. We need to dialogue with God and start to believe in His desire to hear us and to know us.

Anger/passivity

Some of us are incredibly angry with 'someone' or simply with 'life'. We may be depressed, have issues with authority figures, be unable to commit or initiate or complete. We may not know the root cause of all this, but if we trace it back it may well be rooted in our relationship with our fathers. We may never have dared admit this to ourselves, let alone expressed it aloud. If this is the case, we can bring this to God and start to sort through how we have been sinned against. We will need to embark on a journey of forgiveness and freedom.

Intense frustration

Many of us know deep down that we have not reached our full potential on many fronts. We may be living on too small a canvas, or only in black and white, not technicolour. We may have felt too anxious or empty to press into new areas. Perhaps we have felt unable to break the family mould, or we are still under our mother's influence (mother wound), or without the necessary advocacy or guidance we need (father wound). We will need to spend time with God allowing our real heart's desires to begin to take shape, however unattainable they appear in the early stages. At first, we may not have words for our desires, but in time they will take form. The more we are true to who we really are in Christ, the more we will grow into the real selves that God intended us to become.

What ten words would I use to describe men?

What is the connection between this and how I am fathered?

How balanced am I inside between being and doing? Why is this my current position?

A prayer to the Father

Lord, I thank You that You know all about my family and the father I had or didn't have and that You know my needs and the gaps in who I am.

Please help me to see this vital relationship in a new way as an adult and sift through it – help me to find good things that I can hold on to and to release all the damaging or difficult parts to You.

May I come to a place of peace, that can lead to a deeper trust in You as the good and eternal Father, and in time enable me to forgive my father for the unhelpful things he did and the necessary things he failed to do.

I need Your kindness and benevolent strength and advocacy for me. I need to hear you calling my name and owning me as your daughter.

Lord, I ask too, that You will reveal any ways in which this has affected how I see myself as a woman, where I am lost or living out of an untrue understanding of who I am, or who men are.

While I bring you my wounds and ask You to be healing me, I also pray that I may be ready to take responsibility for my behaviour and find forgiveness and blessing in You. I ask this in Jesus' name.

Amen

Scriptures for worship and prayer

PSALM 62	*EZEKIEL 36:33–36*	*ISAIAH 49:1*
EPHESIANS 3:14–21	*ISAIAH 43*	*PSALM 71:1–5*

NOTES

NOTES

CHAPTER 12b – BEING MY FATHER'S SON

Masculinity needs to be conveyed to us, and the key person to do this is our father. He needed to have something substantial to give us, otherwise we will feel empty and ashamed. Instead of a vibrant masculinity, many fathers just gave us their brokenness: their passivity, fear, distraction or sin. We need the Father's blessing of true masculinity at every level of our being.

The effects of a father wound in men will be specific and will link back to:

- Who God made men to be
- How we were fathered in our family
- Dealing with a broken relationship with the same-sex parent
- How I identified with my father's masculinity: positively or negatively.

Men as sons

As boys we needed the presence of a safe father. This would enable us to grow up beyond our mother's care. A safe father would help us to emerge from the family with a clear sense of who we were becoming under God and how we should live as a man in a culture that is unsure about who we all are. As our culture loses sight of God, we create a vacuum for everyone to do what is right in his or her own eyes. As we lose our way for men and women to live together with a complementarity that blesses each other, we all become less clear about who we are and how to be. This can disable and anger us, leaving us confused, cynical and hurting.

The role of our father

A representative of God our heavenly Father

Our fathers may have seriously affected our perception of God and our relationship with Him, as we assume that God is like our father. If our father was critical, arbitrary, remote, awkward, indulgent or cold, we may wonder why we only have a perfunctory and head relationship with God rather than one that is open or from our hearts. If we see God as critical and impossible to please, we may well feel angry with Him. Our faith can then seem pointless, but we carry on anyway because we know it is the truth. This can lead us to be cynical, passive aggressive or angry towards God. We can become rebellious, disillusioned or find an outlet in addictive behaviours. It is worth checking out how much we have been able to separate out our earthly father from our heavenly one, and ask God's help to do so.

How do I view God the Father and Jesus?

What ten words would I use to describe God (my heart response, not the 'right' answers)?

How many of these ten words apply to my earthly father too? (Can I separate out God from my father?)

Husband to our mother

An absent or ineffective father can have resulted in independence, control and insecurity in us. An abusive, arbitrary or controlling father can have led to blame or hatred. Again, we may need to process this as an adult and bring our father to God, seeking His objectivity so we can release him to God, the Righteous Judge, and move into a place of forgiveness. Seeing how our fathers treated our mothers, or how our mothers allowed themselves to be treated, can affect our view of marriage

What is my view of women?

What are my expectations of a man as a husband?

Delight

We needed to be a source of delight to our fathers and for there to have been some warmth or depth of feeling modelled for us.

What is true for me? How have I been shown affection?

Discipline and advocacy

As children, we needed to hear a word of favour and blessing from our fathers that was specifically for us – not for our achievements, but because we were our father's son. We may have had negative sentiments for us: that we were a nuisance, that we wouldn't come to anything, that we needed to get a haircut etc. Or we may have been the favourite. This negativity will mean that we only feel accepted conditionally.

On the discipline front, we may have felt unfairly treated, been seen as trouble or been allowed to manipulate. As adults, these things will have had a negative affect on our internal discipline and on our self-esteem.

Without good scaffolding we will feel adrift, misunderstood and like an orphan. This may run quite deep within us and needs to be touched by God.

Did I have an advocate?

How was I disciplined?

Have I heard a word of blessing – just for me – and received it right into my heart? Do I believe it?

Being named and known

Isaiah 49:1 talks about God naming us. We need to feel named in an honourable way by our fathers and be ready to recall and bring to God any labels and wrong names that were used against us. These will stick and we may have allowed them to define us, even subconsciously. The names that have been used to describe us may have left us believing wrong things about ourselves. We may have been grouped with 'the boys' instead of being allowed to be a new person in our own right. Or, our father may have felt he understood us completely because we were another male and therefore made a club together. We need to take all this to Jesus on the Cross.

Was I labelled in any way?

Am I living out of any of these labels?

Good masculine presence

Our fathers needed to model a healthy masculinity to us – we needed to see a model of God's benevolent strength and advocacy so that we could be open to Him later. We also needed to be at peace with masculinity – the strength and ability to act and persevere – in order to welcome it as an essential part of who we were, our masculine part. If we were at odds with our fathers this will not sit easily in us. It will either be on overdrive as we show we can manage without him, or we will be defeated and passive or swing between the two!

We may feel that the version of masculinity offered by our fathers wouldn't work for us, or that we hated him and had cut off from all he was. If so, we will be empty and will not have any real masculine presence in us. As a result, we may feel insecure about relating to other men. Or, we may have a sense of being a man, but be left wondering how to fit in. We may feel our dad hasn't blessed our unique version of being a man, as he needed to. Perhaps we weren't technically minded and that was all he understood, perhaps we were musical and that wasn't a career he considered safe, or perhaps we wanted to pursue an academic path and he didn't value this. We needed recognition and blessing.

As adults, it is helpful to ask God to show us our father in a new light, so that we can be more objective about our relationship with him. With God's help we can sort out the suitable and good from the unsuitable or destructive or absent. We may then be able to benefit more from what was helpful and be in a better place to process and forgive what was missing.

Fatherlessness

It can be a real shock to see ourselves as fatherless, but if we were lacking a good, steady fatherly presence, it is the word that God would use to describe us. It does not ignore that our father did his best, rather it simply admits that our fathering wasn't enough or wasn't right for the person we were becoming.

We will need to come to terms with our fatherlessness and realise that our fathers will probably never be able to make up the lost ground with us as adults. We need to move on from being a needy child inside to being an adult who must leave home and begin to transfer these needs to God. Then, as we receive the love and advocacy that we need, we are able to see our families objectively and release them to God. We can then begin to relate to them from a new place.

In life, we all needed our fathers to draw us away from our mothers, especially if we had a difficult relationship with her, if she was critical of us, overbearing, indulgent or didn't 'do' boys. We needed him to give us the backing to take on life and help us stay in the game when we might have been tempted to retreat back to the safety of home. We needed help to cope with mistakes, to take risks and to try out different opportunities. If these things were not present for us, then this is a sin of omission needing our forgiveness.

If our fathers were passive our mother may even have made us her little husband. If so, we needed to be drawn away from her even more and this will have sorely tested our loyalty to our mothers. But the truth is that we need to leave our mother and release her to her chosen life. We will not be able to cleave to God or to a wife unless we have left both our father and our mother. If we have cut off from one and are ambivalent about the other we may need to go back over our leaving and tidy it up. In this way we will have left properly while keeping as much of the relationship as we can.

If we were placed in boarding school at an early age then we will have been a little boy in an adult world and may well have felt lost. If we had to be brave, we may have lost an open relationship with both our parents and moved into a required role. We may find it hard to admit needs, handle affection or intimacy, pick up nuances or be intuitive . We may live life through gritted teeth and only be able to be purposeful.

Just today, a little boy got on the bus with his parents and pointing to the man on the opposite seat said to me, "That's my Dad". He was so proud of him. How many of us could say that? We are all fatherless. We need to be adopted as sons into the Father's family and find a covering and blessing we maybe never dreamt we could know. Hebrews 2:11–12 tells us that Jesus is not ashamed to call us His brothers, even though we are still in process of being made holy. We need to take this on board completely and find the advocacy and belonging we are longing for. It will transform our confidence, our authenticity and give us a resting place to live out of, rather than having to prove our worth.

Relationships

In a culture where sometimes the jury is out on society's need for men, let alone for our value and contribution, we need a deep-seated confidence about our masculinity. If we are fatherless in any way this deep-seated confidence will be missing and there will be chinks in our armour.

Our lack of sense of self, or self-hatred, can mean we feel inferior to other men who seem to have it all.

Detaching from our father may hinder us from connecting with other men and we may even look at them as foreign and threatening. Our own gender can become a challenge for us. Conversely we are at ease with women because there is no demand to belong or identify with them. Any sense of inadequacy as we compare ourselves with other men, is agonising and alienates us into acute loneliness.

This lack can drive us *away* from other men into:

- Independence and living in walled-off place
- Being driven and competitive – needing to outstrip others or becoming a workaholic
- Avoiding men's company, except when absolutely necessary, fearing intimacy or competition
- Never joining the herd, then justifying or complaining bitterly about our position of isolation
- Being cynical, intellectual or heartless
- Needing attractive, decorative women as a trophy
- Feeling safer with women and settling for their affirmation
- Not knowing what to do with the numbness or rage inside – being cut off from our feelings.

Or it can drive us *into* other men through:

- Comparing ourselves to see how we measure up, e.g. personality, looks or achievements
- Being drawn to men who engender strong or confident masculinity
- Longing for their validation, approval, acceptance and affirmation
- Emotional dependency and codependency
- Yearning for father figures and role models (finding these can be positive and helpful on our journey, unless it becomes a fixation. We need to look to God first as these father figures will not be able to carry the weight of our needs).

These can leave us vulnerable to being abused and manipulated.

Only God can meet our deepest needs and quieten our anxiety and hunger. It will be a process but He can give us the blessing and fathering we need and restore the deficits we feel inside. He can accompany us back into our peer group on equal terms so that we can relate appropriately and easily to our fellow men again.

Pornography

As mentioned above, we may find that masturbation, fueled as an adult by pornography, goes back to an infantile anxiety. We will need to allow God into the deepest place of our isolation and shame. He longs to meet us with His love and cleansing at that deep place.

With women we may:

- Try to play happy families and right the wrongs of our family script
- Hope women will ease our anxiety
- Hope their adulation and flattery will boost our sense of being a man
- Use them in the hope that we can create a smoke screen over our sexual attractions to other men
- Ask them to affirm us and bolster us as men.

Why fatherlessness hurts and how it surfaces

Cut off from our feelings

Because we are human beings we have been made to be blessed and loved by our fathers. Any lack of this will hurt. If we had no help in how to manage any of our feelings, as a man, least of all the uncomfortable ones, we may well have pushed them all down and cut off from them. We will have broken hearts just as deeply as any woman, but we won't know that Jesus is talking about us when He says He has come to heal the broken hearted. We won't know that anything can be done about our broken hearts. As we are so unused to allowing ourselves to feel pain (compared with women who feel pain is their lot), we may not even register that anything is wrong. Often, we live solely out of our heads – when we are asked what we feel we have no idea how to answer, or even what the question means!

We need to own that we have hearts and feelings and that they may be broken or suppressed. God can lead us through this in such a way that who we are will survive. He will give us back our hearts – not at the expense of our minds, but as an essential component for life!

Heartless

Fatherlessness can mean that we appear as if we don't care. Women especially can pick up on this. Often we simply lack awareness of dealing with emotion and having empathy. We may have no practice in this area, or we may have a sense that if we become more connected to our emotions the fragile masculinity we have may be diminished. It's interesting to note that usually anything that increases our humanity also increases our whole sense of well-being, rather than diminishing another part of us. We do not need to be afraid that we will lose our masculinity.

Restless

We may feel restless and this will link back to our mother wound – we cannot find a resting place, even in God alone (Psalm 62). But this may also tie into our lack of connectedness and belonging. We can keep busy to avoid feeling anything, or we are always 'on the go' to ensure we feel we exist, or to justify our place in life. We need to dare to stop. Christian philosophy professor and author, Dallas Willard, talks of the discipline of solitude[1] being very helpful in this area. Once we have broken the fear barrier of stopping and realised we are still alive, we can find a new rest position in life. We will then start to enjoy the benefits of it more regularly until it becomes a part of us.

Stuck

We can also feel stuck as a lost or hurt little boy and we may well need to own this before God. Under His care this part of us may then be able to grow up and become a valued part of our adult self. We may also be aware of a pattern of regressing when we are under stress, or the need for alcohol to relax, and this equals a childishness as we do not know how to relax or have fun in an adult way. Jesus spent most of His time eating and socialising with people. This may terrify us. A Bible study on 'joy' or 'life' might help here.

Lack of a real voice

If we were silenced or ignored too many times as a child, we may have given up on having our own voice or ever being heard. We may not believe we have anything useful to say anymore, or that we are heard, even by God. Yet we know deep down that our hearts are desperate to be heard. We may have never cried out to Him in full voice and released ourselves from our "land of silence" (Psalm 94:17). We need to find our own voice and the freedom to use it. To deal with this we need to dialogue with God and start to believe in His desire to know us.

Anger/passivity

Some of us are incredibly angry with 'someone' or simply with 'life'. We may be depressed, have issues with authority figures, be unable to commit or initiate or complete. We may not know the root cause of all this, but if we trace it back it may well be rooted in our fathers. We may never have dared admit this to ourselves, let alone expressed it aloud. If this is the case, we can bring this to God and start to sort through how we have been sinned against. We will need to embark on a journey of forgiveness and freedom.

Intense frustration

Many of us know that our full potential has not been realised on many fronts and we are living on too small a canvas or only in monochrome not colour. We may have felt too anxious or empty to press into new areas, unable to break the family mould, still under our mother's influence (mother wound) or without the necessary advocacy or guidance (father wound). We will need to spend time with God allowing our real heart's desires to begin to take shape – however unattainable they appear in the early stages. We may not have words for them but in time they will get form. The more we are true to who we really are in Christ, the more we will grow into the real selves that God intended us to become.

---

1. Dallas Willard, *The Spirit of the Disciplines* (HarperCollins, 1991), 100-101.

Fear of emasculation/misogyny

If we suffered any emasculation from our mothers, and our fathers did not help to rebuild us or stop it, then we may be living in reaction to women. We may not want to open ourselves up to emasculation again and as a result we may have difficulty with women bosses and live life out of a place of misogyny. Again, once we know His protection and blessing of us as men, we will need to bring this misogyny to God and renounce it.

How do I feel about myself as a man, as well as a person?

What is the connection between who I am now and how I was fathered?

In the light of this, how do I conduct my relationships?

How do I take my place with other men?

A prayer to the Father

Lord, I thank You that You know all about my family and the father I had or didn't have and that You know my needs and the gaps in who I am.

Please help me to see this vital relationship in a new way as an adult and sift through it – help me to find good things that I can hold on to and to release all the damaging or difficult parts to You. May I come to a place of peace, that can lead to a deeper trust in You as the good and eternal Father, and in time enable me to forgive my father for the unhelpful things he did, and the necessary things he failed to do.

Lord, please help me to know that I need a heart and I can start to feel without losing my sense of being a man. Please help me where I have escaped into fantasy, sexual sin, work, busyness or cynicism. Help me to own those parts of me that are afraid, or isolated or walled off so I can emerge out of them into life and into Your good protection and Fatherly presence. I need Your kindness, Your benevolent strength and advocacy for me. I need to hear You calling my name and owning me as Your son.

Lord, I ask too that You will reveal any ways in which this has affected how I see myself as a man, where I am lost or living out of an untrue understanding of who I am, or who women are. While I bring you my wounds and ask You to be healing me, I also pray that I may be ready to take responsibility for my behaviour and find forgiveness and blessing in You.

I ask this in Jesus' name.

Amen

It can be very healing to go somewhere where you can be completely alone and to call out to God as Father as loudly as you can. As you call out to Him, ask Him to find You in Your isolation and tell Him that You want to know Him and love Him.

Scriptures for worship and prayer

EZEKIEL 36:33-36   *ISAIAH 49:1*   *EPHESIANS 3:14-21 (AMP)*

PSALM 62   *ISAIAH 43*   *PSALM 71:1-5*

Questions for Men

What does being a man mean for me?

What is my stereotype? Why?

What is comfortable?

What is a challenge?

What is doing/persevering like for me?

What was my father like?

What was his message to me about men?

How have I received from him?

How have I cut off from him?

NOTES

CHAPTER 13 – RECEIVING FATHERLY LOVE

Our father's blessing is a vital part of our parenting. We are desperate to be seen and valued and blessed by him. Many of us did not receive this – there may have been silence, or we may have received too little to take us into life. At a very profound level, we need to separate out our earthly father from God the Father. As we receive healing from the Lord, we will be able to welcome Him into our lives as the good father and understand that this is an ongoing process.

A father should be for life, not just for Christmas, or when we tow the line, get into trouble, do well or make him proud.

> *And not only the creation, but we ourselves, who have the first fruits*
> *of the Spirit, groan inwardly as we wait eagerly for adoption as sons,*
> *the redemption of our bodies. For in this hope we were saved*
>
> (ROMANS 8:23-24A)

Our orphan nature – our fatherlessness – is not a theological concept, but a physical and emotional reality. These verses profoundly express our need for holistic redemption: body, mind and spirit. All of us are orphans and are feeling the pain of this, whether we can express it or not. As the verse describes, inwardly we are both groaning and eager, frustrated and trying to keep hope. We need to accept our adoption by God, not just in our heads, but through welcoming Him into our whole being as the Father and the family we have always longed for. Our unmet emotional and physical needs are like groanings in our bodies and will be evident in our posture, relationships, perceptions, addictions, self image and shame. As we release these to God and choose to exchange this pain and emptiness for His provision we will notice a difference in our whole demeanour.

This is as primal, radical and profound as you can get. It is the redemption of our whole self, of all the pain in our broken hearts, of all the ways we feel imprisoned, of all the shame and sin and false comforts. We welcome the Father's healing presence into our whole being.

The healing Presence

We need to check our hearts before God and tell Him about anything that prevents us drawing near to Him. He knows these things already and longs to clear our path to Him. We also need to press through these ill feelings or any distrust to waiting in His presence. God acts on behalf of those who wait for Him (Isaiah 64:4).

The wait

As we wait for the healing presence, the ideal is to stop and stop again until it is just the Lord and us together. This can be frightening and may even be painful, but it is the place we need to reach. His presence is the healing presence. His ear is the one that is bent towards us to hear our heart's cry, and His voice is the one we need to hear. If we can quieten our hearts we will feel the full security of Him being God and us just being a creature.

As we welcome His presence, we may not need to put anything into words yet. We begin to feel Him knowing us and being there for us. Then, when we are ready, or when it seems to be the right next step, we can start to 'pour out our hearts to Him'. As we do this, the unmet needs will start to sort themselves out from the wounds, the disappointments, the griefs, the sorrows, the rejection, the questions, our guilt, their guilt, the detachments, the might-have-beens, the powerlessness and the chance for change.

Underneath all this sadness we may well reach:

A profound sense of aloneness

This is a longing to be accompanied and affirmed and to hear a sincere word of blessing and favour; to be gathered up into a loving secure relationship and to belong unconditionally.

A deep sadness or resignation

We may feel a deep sadness or sense of resignation, and, if we are honest with ourselves, we even feel this towards God. It's as if we turn away from Him with the deepest part of our sadness, resigned to the fact that even God is not sufficient for it. This is called 'acedia', or sloth, and it includes passivity and hopelessness. As the waiting father He longs to console us and comfort us to the very depths of our being and replace this sense of death and despair with His real life and fatherly care.

What is being healed?

When we have not received the best that God intended for us, for whatever reason, we are wounded and will have lost out. Our wounds may include:

- A wounded view of God
- An inability to trust God or see Him as different from our father
- An over-riding sense of insecurity because of his failure to provide for us
- Anxiety

- Feeling fatherless, unaffirmed or adrift
- Aloneness and a difficulty for men to reach out to other men and build good friendships
- Feeling pain when we see children being fathered eg when they are carried on their father's shoulders or have their hands held by a man
- Hearing a crushing silence where there should have been affirmation and encouragement
- Living with raised expectations that we will get affirmation at last, or from somewhere, and usually being disappointed
- Feeling less than, or a disappointment
- Lacking in confidence because there was no external belief or confidence set in us
- Needing a Dad – our hearts know what this means
- A sense of having to prove our worth
- A sense of 'What does all this matter anyway, as I don't matter', including depression, frustration or rebellion
- No sense of personal pride or dignity
- Cycles of failure or non-perseverance
- Difficulty taking responsibility or understanding the concept of 'sowing and reaping' in life
- Relational issues
- Still being attached to our mother
- The wound of a broken heart.

You may well have your own way of describing what is happening inside.

What is missing?

We may not have developed the capacity:

- To trust – especially if we cut off and have been independent from early on in life
- To stand or persevere, instead flipping in and out of control or strength
- To draw near to God merely on the basis of being His son or daughter
- To relax and lead a balanced life
- To take responsibility or make mistakes or take risks
- To understand grace
- To become a new, separate and valid person
- To concentrate and focus, especially if we are stuck in a restless busyness
- To be known.

We can ask God to restore these things to us and for Him to be there for us as we practise having them in our lives.

What else might be present?

Our hearts may be full of hurt and survival and sin including:

- Self-doubt/self-hatred
- Anger towards my father/other authority or caring figures/all men
- Anger towards my mother for not intervening or overcompensating
- Self-pity
- Lust and sexualised needs (in practice or as fantasy)
- Hatred or murder
- Pain and a sinful means of managing it, eg an addiction
- Numbness or passivity
- Bitterness and blame shifting
- Care taking and appeasement
- Drivenness and a need to succeed.

We will need to be offering these responses and survival mechanisms to God. The good news is that He knows they are there already. Through the Cross He is ready to relieve us of them and be our advocate and good father.

What are my wounds?

What is missing in my life? What am I carrying in my heart?

Am I prepared to leave my earthly father with God – as the Righteous Judge of all that happened or failed to happen – and transfer my allegiance to God, my Eternal Father?

How do I make the move into the Father's house and tune myself in to His voice and provision and care?

Psalm 112 explains this very well. Take time to read the Psalm through a couple of times. We will learn that:

- If our father has rightly conveyed the goodness of God to us then we will be able to delight in God as He delights in us (v 1)
- We will have received a valuable inheritance from our father (v 3)
- He will have dispelled our darkness and we will have experienced someone who is gracious, merciful and righteous (v 4)
- We will have a heart that is firm, trusting in God; a heart that is steady and not afraid of bad news that will look on its adversaries with triumph (v 7).

As we have seen, Psalm 112 describes wonderfully the solid start and enabling that we all needed. It also expresses the strength to persevere and that we are resourced and accompanied for life by God.

We need:

- Affirmation, for who I am, not for what I have achieved or how I look
- Affection, so that I know I am loved and can share my feelings
- Attention, so that I know I am being seen and understood just for who I am
- Advocacy, so that I know I am owned and worth defending
- Accompanying through life.

After Jesus' baptism, the Father blessed Him with attention, affection, affirmation and advocacy, and we know He also accompanied Jesus throughout his earthly life:

- "You are my Son" – the Father gave Jesus attention and identified Him
- "Whom I love" – showing affection
- "With you I am well pleased" – showing affirmation.

The Father's advocacy is also shown by the Father's voice being audible – He was fully associated with Jesus. In recognising Jesus' need for the above, we also see our need for someone to bless us in the same way.

Every aspect of the Father's blessing contributes to the deep sense of acceptance that we all need to be able to live, to be part of the community and, more importantly, to join our peer group as an equal member. It is never too late to try to salvage and develop a relationship with our fathers or, if that is not possible, to unpack the details so that we can reach a place of peace.

Forgiveness and relating to our fathers as adults

We now need to extend God's grace to our fathers for their sins of commission and of omission, especially if they were passive or absent in their fathering of us.

As we compare what God wanted for us from our fathers, with what we actually received, we can start to list what needs to be forgiven. We are not being disloyal in doing this, because we are clearing out the debris from the relationship. The other side of this is that we will need fully to repent of all our sinful reactions, such as our detachment, hatred, despising and fear. We will then need to offer the wounds beneath each of these reactions to God, for example, the loneliness and the shame that we have carried.

We can start by thanking God for all that was positive. For some of us this will be a pleasant surprise because we thought there was very little. In listing the positives, nothing is too simple – God will use these as a symbol of goodness in our hearts. It can help to think back to our father's story and remember his circumstances. This gives us a better context in which to hold our fathers responsible for their actions (or lack of them) and then to forgive – fully weighing up the consequences of each of the sins. We release him to God the Righteous Judge. This whole objective process is very empowering and it is important to let God breathe new power and being into us, without us being afraid of it.

Some of the key actions our fathers should have taken included: to create a stable home; to support our mothers; to really notice and affirm us; to see who we really were; to draw us away from our mothers; to allow us to identify with our fathers and to see our humanity and path into life through them (especially for men). In our teenage years, they needed to bring us the order and grace of God – not modelling Him as disinterested or a hard taskmaster.

The more specific we are in bringing our fathering to God, the more release we will know and the more we can then draw near to God as a totally different Father. We move from orphan to beloved.

It is vital that we clear our hearts of all that blocks us from receiving the ongoing love and grace of God. He wants to flood us with welcome, favour, son-ship/daughter-ship, belonging, glory, warmth and blessing.

A prayer

> *Lord, I come before You now and ask that You will find me where I am.*
>
> *I need to hear Your voice and allow Your life-giving presence into my heart.*
>
> *I wait before You, for You to reveal my needs and bring order and meaning to the void I feel inside. May I allow You to be the true Father I need and as I put my hand in Yours may You lead me into all the fullness of life and blessing that You have for me.*
>
> *I ask this in Jesus' all powerful name.*
>
> *Amen.*

It is good for us to live our days in communication with the Father, as Jesus did, getting to know Him more and letting Him 'get to know us more'!

We have also found it useful to review what our 'house' looks like. One way of doing this is similar to an architect's plans, which would have a drawing of the 'existing' house and of the 'proposed' house. We suggest you prayerfully draw your 'house' in its 'existing' and 'proposed' states.

Scriptures for worship and prayer

ISAIAH 43:6

Bring my sons from afar and my daughters from the ends of the earth, everyone who is called by my name, whom I created for my glory, whom I formed and made.

PSALM 62:2, 7-8

He only is my rock & my salvation, my fortress. I shall not be greatly shaken. On God rests my salvation and my honour; my mighty rock and my fortress is God. Trust in Him at all times, O people, pour out your heart before Him. God is a refuge for us.

ISAIAH 33:6

He will be the stability of your times: an abundance of salvation, wisdom and knowledge – the fear of the Lord is Zion's treasure.

ISAIAH 49:1, 5, 8

The Lord called me from the womb, from the body of my mother he named my name. And now the Lord says: he who formed me from the womb to be his servant, to bring Jacob back to him and that Israel might be gathered to him – for I am honoured in the eyes of the Lord and my God has become my strength. Thus says the Lord: In the time of favour I have answered you in the day of salvation I have helped you.

PSALM 71:1-5

In you, O Lord, do I take refuge, let me never be put to shame. In your righteousness deliver me, incline your ear to me and save me. Be to me a rock of refuge to which I may continually come. You have given the command to save me for you are my rock and my fortress. Rescue me, my God, from the hand of the wicked and from the grasp of the unjust and cruel. For you O Lord are my hope, my trust, O Lord from my youth.

PSALM 5:3 (showing that He welcomes dialogue)

O Lord in the morning you hear my voice: in the morning I prepare a sacrifice for you and watch.

I PETER 3:12

For the eyes of the Lord are on the righteous and his ears are open to their prayer.

EZEKIEL 36:33-36

Thus says the Lord your God: On the day that I will cleanse you from all your iniquities, I will cause the cities to be inhabited and the waste places shall be rebuilt. And the land that was desolate shall be tilled, instead of being the desolation that it was in the sight of all who passed by. And they will say: This land that was desolate has become like the Garden of Eden and the waste and desolate and ruined cities are now fortified and inhabited. Then the nations that are left all around you shall know that I am the Lord: I have rebuilt the ruined places and replanted that which was desolate. I am the Lord. I have spoken. I will do it.

EPHESIANS 3:14-21

For this reason I bow my knees before the Father from whom every family in heaven and on earth is named, that according to the riches of his glory He may grant you to be strengthened with power through his spirit in your inner being. So that Christ may dwell in our hearts through faith – that you being rooted and grounded in love may have strength to comprehend with all the saints what is the breadth and length and height and depth and to know the love of Christ that surpasses knowledge, that you may be filled with all the fullness of God.

PSALM 68:5

Father of the fatherless and protector of widows is God in His holy habitation. God settles the solitary in a home.

PSALM 27:10

For my father and mother have forsaken me but the Lord will take me in.

PSALM 31:21-22

Blessed be the Lord for he has wondrously shown his steadfast love to me when I was in a besieged city. I had said in my alarm "I am cut off from your sight." But you heard the voice of my pleas for mercy, when I cried to you for help.

PSALM 34:18

The LORD is near to the broken-hearted and saves the crushed in spirit.

PSALM 103:13

As a father shows compassion to his children, so the Lord shows compassion to those who fear him. For He knows our frame.

PSALM 33:19

He has delivered my soul from death, and keeps me alive in famine.

PSALM 18:6

From His temple he heard my voice and my cry to him reached his ears.

PSALM 138:3

On the day I called you answered me; my strength of soul you increased.

ISAIAH 35:3–4

Strengthen the weak hands and make firm the feeble knees. Say to those who have an anxious heart, "Be strong fear not. Behold your God will come with vengeance and the recompense of God. He will come and save you."

ISAIAH 61:7–8

Instead of your shame there shall be a double portion, instead of dishonour they shall rejoice in their lot; therefore in their land they shall possess a double portion they shall have everlasting joy. For I the Lord love justice. I hate robbery and wrong. I will faithfully give them their recompense.

JEREMIAH 9:24

Let him who boasts boast in this: that he understands and knows me, that I am the Lord who practises steadfast love, justice and righteousness in the earth. For in these things I delight, says the Lord.

ISAIAH 9:6

Everlasting Father.

JOHN 20:17

I am ascending to my Father and your father and my God and your God.

EPHESIANS 1:5, 11

In love He predestined us for adoption through Jesus. In Him we have obtained an inheritance.

ROMANS 8:23

We wait eagerly for our adoption as sons.

ROMANS 8:15 (AMP)

But you have received the Spirit of adoption [the Spirit producing sonship].
It is in the bliss of this that we cry Abba, Father, Father.

ISAIAH 51:10 (AMP)

Who is among you who reverently fears the Lord, who obeys the voice of His Servant, yet who walks in deep trouble and has no shining splendour [in his heart]? Let him rely on, trust in and be confident in the name of the Lord and let him lean on and be supported by his God.

LUKE 24:15

Jesus himself drew near and accompanied them.

NOTES

CHAPTER 14 – SIBLINGS

We very rarely stop to review our relationships with our siblings.

We often hear church described as our family – that we are all brothers and sisters in Christ. This can strike fear and panic into those of us who come from dysfunctional families and for whom sibling relationships were at best complicated or non-existent and, at worst, abusive and terrifying.

A huge range of sibling relationships are described in Scripture:

Cain and Abel: ending in murder; Joseph and his brothers: riddled with sibling rivalry, pride and envy; Jacob and Esau: cheating his brother and fleeing the nest; Moses and Aaron: needing each other to fulfil God's call; Miriam: becoming bitter; David: relegated to the fields by his brothers; Amnon and Tamar: incest and rape; Mary and Martha: total opposites. The list goes on.

We can safely review our sibling relationships because God has seen it all! He is not shocked or perplexed by our experiences.

In fact, as Christians we are all brothers and sisters, that is siblings of each other and of Christ because we all share the same heavenly Father. Hebrews 2:10–13 reminds us that Jesus is the first born in the family and is not ashamed to call us His brothers and sisters. Even if we were ashamed of our siblings or they were ashamed of us, Jesus is not. This means that our key eternal status in heaven will be as beloved children of the Father. Therefore our relationships with each other will be as siblings. In God's eyes this is the most honoured and wonderful eternity He could give us, even if we don't feel like it would be! It follows that it is good to work out some of our sibling issues beforehand down here on earth!

If we are an orphan in God's eyes then our siblings are a collection of orphans all seeking to get their needs met from a limited pot of care and resources. No wonder we all resorted to our own survival mechanisms. In fact, the quality of our sibling relationships could be an indicator of how well our parents were doing. How much was appearances and how much went undiscovered because no one ever asked or we had no one to tell?

We also need to remember that each child has its own two-way relationship with each member of the family, not just with the parents. Our experiences may well be very different from our siblings, for a myriad of reasons. It also shows us why we may have felt left out, overlooked, unheard, or different and why we developed the coping mechanisms that may still be with us, such as, withdrawal, organising everyone, care-taking or raising our voice to be heard.

In order to take our rightful place within our peer group, we need a real sense of who we are. This includes being secure about ourselves and about our gender. Our sense of self will have been formed and tested within our family and among our siblings. We will usually visit our sibling issues on to our peers.

God set us to live in families here on earth to show us that life is about relationship and enjoying who we are in Him, together. He wanted us to be able to develop our capacity to love within our families and then transfer it on to Him. We needed our parents, as the adults, to take full responsibility for the family. We needed their commitment to each other to be firm; they shouldn't have needed us to be the glue in their relationship, or for them to stay together 'for the sake of the children'.

As we move on to look at our relationships as siblings and then as a peer we need to review our parents' issues and what sort of family they created.

What was the over-riding atmosphere in my family?

How was my parents' relationship?

Did it create security and happiness, or was it full of angst and concern for us? Could I just be a child?

What were some of the key factors? (Poverty, wealth, overbearing grandparents, disconnection from the extended family, pride, keeping up appearances, chaos, order, homeliness, fun, worry?)

What words would describe your family of origin when you and your siblings were children?

A sibling

We could say a sibling is someone with whom we share at least one parent. Some of us were one of the proverbial 2.4 children in the family, while others had a more complicated arrangement. Depending on each of our circumstances we may need to use the term 'sibling' loosely.

Special sibling relationships

- Being an only child or having too many siblings
- Non-relatives living with us or seeing us as a sibling, for example as the result of a complicated family history
- Siblings who are unknown to us, for example due to their/our adoption or other parental relationships
- Loss – through the death of a sibling in childhood or early adult life or divorce or separation
- A sibling who needed extra care or resources, for example because of health conditions or a disability
- Multiple births
- Intrauterine death of a twin
- A large, or very small, age gap.

Being an only child

Not all of us have siblings – some of us are only children. We may always have been the only one or we can become an only child through the death of a sibling, the break up of a marriage or a big age gap that means others leave home long before us. Each person's experience will be unique and will change over time.

Negative aspects or assumptions:

- You are the focus of attention
- You carry all the expectations
- You are lonely
- You lack competition and instruction from other siblings
- You have no one to buddy up with against the parents
- You have no one to play with at home
- You are spoilt
- You don't have practice at handling conflict
- You are the sole carer of your parents
- You are the sole (adult) child at Christmas or other family gatherings.

Positive aspects or assumptions:

- You are good at doing things on your own
- You have more resources
- You don't have to share
- You have more access to adults
- You have more space to be alone
- You value friends.

Siblings

It's worth noting that:

- Siblings are not chosen
- Being a sibling at all carries its own trauma, guilt, loss and injustices
- Being an only child carries its own guilt, weight and loneliness
- Each of us is different but we may have been treated en masse as 'the kids'
- Each of us will have had our own relationship with our parents and with each other
- We will have participated in some family secrets, and not in others. Our siblings may know secrets we do not
- We are siblings for life regardless of whether we have a living relationship with them or not
- Siblings are both a source of blessing and hurt: even leaving us under a fear of death.

In every family each child will have their own personality, gender, place in the birth order and their own relationship with each of the other members, including mum and dad. We will each have been at our own individual place during different family events, such as a death, a redundancy or a move. Our parents and our siblings will have perceived us in different ways, perhaps seeing us as quiet or reliable, an annoyance or someone not to be trusted, so we will have felt more ourselves with some people than with others. We will have accepted some labels or expectations that were put on us, but not others. We will have made different alliances with other family members at different times.

As adults, an interesting exercise is to get together with as many siblings as we can and compare our perceptions of the family and our recollection of key events. Each sibling could write their own account of life and allow each other to read them. This could easily be done by email to include those living far away. We can also talk about how each child was seen by the others – we may find some real surprises, such as having assumed another sibling was really happy or popular, when in fact that wasn't their experience.

As children we needed the opportunity to:

- Be an individual in the family – to have space to be ourselves, even if we were different from the rest of the family
- Make a contribution and be valued for who we were uniquely
- Be understood for who we were without our families assuming they knew already, or being endlessly compared with another
- Be connected into the whole
- Be a child
- Grow and change
- Have a childhood, not just experience the survival of the fittest.

What ten words would describe my family and my place in it?

Our family should have been a safe environment in which we could grow and develop at our own pace. We should have been able to build some solidarity as children in preparation for a peer group outside the family. We needed enough space:

- To find our voice and be heard, and also to listen
- To take turns and see others further ahead of us in life
- To learn that life isn't fair
- To try out our opinions without being shouted down
- To have a sense of property and ownership, but also to learn to share
- To admit our worries or ignorance without being mocked
- To learn boundaries
- To take appropriate levels of responsibility and be carefree
- To see conflicts resolved well and to understand that actions have consequences
- To pass on our skills to others, and also to learn from them
- To identify where we are similar, but also to celebrate our differences.

In the space overleaf please draw your family in whatever way you would like. Name each person and include any extra influential or absent people. We can arrange them as a family portrait, or as they functioned – some may be closer together than others. We can then draw in the lines of connection – some will be negative connections and others positive ones. They may include us or not!

What are your feelings as you look at this portrayal of your family? (Sadness, gratitude, shame, disappointment, anger, distance?) Are there any surprises? Any confirmations?

What is the most significant legacy of my family?

Was there anyone in whom I could confide? Did I?

What are my memories of meal times?

What word(s) would best describe my role or place? Eg the Joker, the Runt, the Professor, the Dumb Blond, the Reliable One, the Outcast etc. What would my siblings say about this?

In looking at our sibling relationships we see that:

- The blessings of community can also mean that members get left out and feel excluded, or dominate
- Making a contribution means that we will be better and worse at some things than others
- The age range means that others may have paved the way for us, eg tying shoe laces, showing us how to handle our parents, or taking risks. But we may also have had to pioneer everything if we were the eldest, or if we are younger we may feel injustices.

As we recall our family life we can review certain key areas:
(NB Nothing is too shocking or too trivial.)

Words we remember that blessed us and the words that hurt us (still!) This includes the words used against us or by us – words that we now regret. We can bring these to God.

Voices that we still hear: they may have blessed us and been a source of comfort, or they may have caused us trauma and even now feel louder or more authoritative than those of our heavenly Father.

Events or Actions that proved to be significant, for better or worse, such as a move, a change of school, a sibling lending us something or helping us at a critical moment. There may also be actions taken by us that were deeply damaging for someone, including ourselves, and we can bring these to God for His forgiveness, consolation and comfort.

Vows or Assumptions that we have taken or agreed with. We will need to revoke specifically any vows we have made, for example: 'I will never become like my brother', 'I will never cry again', 'I will always need help', 'I will never do as well as them' or 'I will never trust anyone again'.

Promises that we recall being made to us, or by us. They may have been kept or we may still feel disappointed if they are unfulfilled. It is good to clear these up with God and let them go.

Where did we live? Where was our safe place? We may have lived in books, up a tree, at someone else's house, out of the house, at school or under someone's thumb.

Where did we feel most unsafe? We may have unsafe places into which we need to invite Jesus to come to find us and rescue us. For example, school games, the playground, our bedroom, or someone's house.

Labels. It is good to release to the Lord any/all the labels we were given or names we were called and allow Him to take on to the Cross for us. Even if they were 'well meant' they will have limited our freedom to become who God made us to be. Labels may have come from family or peers or teachers.

As adults, it is likely that we are still playing out the labels that were put on us as children. We may do this at family reunions and in any institution or situation where we feel threatened. Or, we may be exhausted and have jettisoned whole parts of ourselves that are in fact valid and would thrive again in the right context. Also we may spend our adult lives attempting to replay our family relationships with a happier ending. We may be left wondering why this doesn't work or people don't change as we want them to.

Our families are a system under constant tension, like an elastic band wrapped around something, that mustn't be stretched to snapping point. We will have been careful never to stretch the system to this point – we may well have sacrificed part of ourselves for the sake of family stability, rather than cause extra tension.

When we forego our needs for the sake of stability, or to avoid shame, we may seek out another means of venting our energy. We may have appeared to be a totally different child at school from at home. We may have thrived in the order or opportunities at school or, we may have released our negative behaviour there and been in endless trouble/attention.

As we read the Bible we can take heart that everything we may have felt at the hands of our siblings is scriptural! God has seen it all before so He is well able to bring us redemption. In the parable of the Prodigal Son the elder brother disowned the prodigal calling him "your son" to their father. Joseph made his brothers jealous and then suffered betrayal. James and John had real sibling rivalry issues and an interfering mother! The Father can buy back the inheritance that we should have received from our families.

Uniqueness

God has made each of us a unique person, but we may never have been noticed as an individual, yet, by anyone.

- Our families may have assumed they knew who we were rather than appreciating that we were a 'new build' and did not yet know whether we were an extrovert or an introvert, musical or sporty

- We may have looked like the spitting image of great 'Aunt Esmerelda' or 'Uncle Dan' but we weren't them

- We may have tried to establish our uniqueness by taking up a role that no-one else had, such as, the clown, the caretaker, the rebel, the trailblazer but we then got stuck with this as our identity. As we are all adults we can safely leave these roles behind: our families don't need us in role anymore. We are no longer at that meal table; we have moved on. Perhaps we can now be the leader we always knew ourselves to be because we are no longer under the shadow of the family leader

- We may have felt that our contribution was undervalued compared to another's, for example, our sense of humour, our cooking, but in fact it was equal or better

- We may have genuinely not liked a group activity but we were press ganged into it, or criticised for not joining in
- Our attempts to be an individual may have met with derision and we feel like a freak rather than being special
- Maybe we remember past rivalries and we realise we need to forgive and release our siblings in order to be free ourselves
- Maybe we remember how we hurt others and want to ask God's forgiveness and have our consciences cleansed. Someone will have paid the price in the family. Perhaps we need a reconciliation
- Perhaps space and attention for me were not given within the family to develop my own personhood (e.g. being practical, intellectual, musical or creative) and I was left with a hole in my identity
- Maybe they overdid the 'special' bit and I have never been able to feel ordinary enough to fit in
- As an only child perhaps I felt unique but lonely and not confident about taking my place in a group.

What does unique mean for me? Am I an individual? Do I know that I am special?

We will also need to notice where we are trying to play happy families as adults or where we have recreated our family of origin with its dysfunction.

Spending time processing our sibling relationships with God is a vital step in our growth as people. It can also be rewarding for the whole family. We may well need to ask for forgiveness and give forgiveness at the profoundest level. We will need to release our expectations and turn to God for justice, comfort and advocacy. We may also need to change our stance or lay down our pride in our family relationships. We need to be prepared to see our siblings, and ourselves, in a new light as adults and move into reconciliation, or not, as the case may be.

What could be your most creative way of exploring these sibling issues?

NOTES

NOTES

CHAPTER 15 – PEERS

A peer is a fellow child or adult from our current generation who is not a family member.

What kind of preparation for joining our peer group did we receive in our families? For example, we may have joined our peer group too soon as an escape from home. We may have had very little parenting except from our peers as a result. An overbearing mother may have filled us with fear about our peer group and tried to keep us tied into her. Or, an abusive sibling may have undermined our confidence so much that we deeply feared venturing out.

Peers may be known to us or not. We may have a relationship with them based on any common factor, such as, work, church, neighbourhood or interest group. Whether we like it or not, if we are to function in life we need to belong to various peer groups. Belonging to our peer groups also enables us to live out the fact we are made for relationship.

Our peers:

- May be chosen, but some will be foisted on us
- May not be chosen by us for the reasons we think: family patterns may determine our friendships
- Our experiences within our family will play a key role in how and where we place ourselves in our peer group (inferior/confident/shown up)
- Our experiences in our family and in our peer group will determine how easily we take our place in our gender group, how we perceive ourselves and how we function
- Each relationship will have its own agenda, which may or may not be met righteously.

The importance of good peer relationships as we grew up cannot be overemphasised. We cannot take our place in our adult peer group any better than we did in our childhood sibling/peer group. We move from our families into the world via our peer group and we needed a clear place of belonging outside our family in order to take our place in the world. If we never had a secure, fulfilling place in our family, we may be able to make up for it by joining a good peer group. If not, this will compound our inability to belong and our sense of isolation. We remember too that, compared with what God intended for us, we are all orphans and so will display orphan behaviours towards each other, particularly at times of pressure.

Two key areas that compound our shame are stereotypes and comparison. Our culture creates fantasy stereotypes and in our teenage years we are vulnerable to believing these are the key to success and acceptance. We can then compare ourselves constantly with this unattainable standard to which we will always fall short. This compounds our shame and makes us even more vulnerable to rejection – or perceived rejection – from our peer group. It can seem as if everyone else belongs in the group except us.

For some of us, our rejection by our peers has been obvious, including serious abuse. For others, it is more subtle. Whatever the case our hearts will be saying that we never really made it into the group that mattered. We may feel like an outcast. We may have looked as if we were in the group to everybody else, but we didn't feel secure or relaxed.

We will then tend to carry this threat of rejection into adult life and be always weighing up situations and thinking about our place. We may continually feel, 'It must be about me', and we are not able to be objective and see others as being in a similar position of insecurity. This is actually rather narcissistic, but we stay there because it is familiar. There is also an aspect of self-fulfilling prophecy about remaining in this place. We can repent of being stuck and ask God to give us a new objectivity about others. We can ask for new courage to risk being known and open. We can seek specific help for trauma and abuse.

If we do not have much sense of being we can feel detached from both our own gender group and our opposite gender group. We feel at odds in every situation and feel that we do not belong anywhere. Our own gender peer group can even feel more alien than the opposite. We need to make peace with our place there and choose to rejoin.

It is as if our failure to identify properly with our same-sex parent carries over into our peer relationships. We are literally desperate to identify with them, but we feel such a lack of belonging to our gender that we cannot join in. For some of us, this yearning is so strong we would give anything to belong – even paying with our own bodies and life. We think that connecting as a victim is better than the pain of isolation.

Most of us have issues in this area: of not belonging well; feeling inferior or a bit paranoid, or being wary of taking risks and adding to our shame. However, being made in the image of God we need a full range of ordinary relationships. We must start somewhere to develop them.

We must embrace the 'ordinary stuff' of life and not despise it, realising that everyone else is in the same boat. We despise the ordinary because mundane life brings up so much shame for us. This will be hard if we have a history of eroticised behaviour, but it is essential and extremely rewarding if we persevere.

Our progression in life would ideally be:

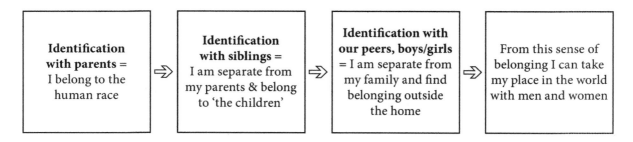

| **Identification with parents** = I belong to the human race | ⇨ | **Identification with siblings** = I am separate from my parents & belong to 'the children' | ⇨ | **Identification with our peers, boys/girls** = I am separate from my family and find belonging outside the home | ⇨ | From this sense of belonging I can take my place in the world with men and women |

For many of us this progression did not happen and we are left in a no man's land, not really belonging anywhere.

Belonging

We all need to belong or matter to somebody *and* to a group – not just on our own terms but with mutuality and the means to give and take, but this too can be a mixed blessing. This belonging empowers us to grow into an adult making our own full contribution.

- If we were brought up in a herd then we may score too highly on belonging and not at all on uniqueness. We long to have an existence outside the group, but we may feel too unsafe out there, or we may be so exhausted that we have vowed never to get caught up in 'belonging' again

- The cost of belonging may have been to surrender our individual identity. We may have been doing it ever since and do not know who is left as our individual person

- We may have joined a group that we did not want to belong to, such as, the rebels or the clever ones and we have never found a way out

- We may only feel safe in a group so we are like a chameleon and accommodate whatever is required in order to keep our place.

Where do I belong? Do I want to belong or am I trying to escape?

What is my core identity? Do I function out of this even now?

Can you visualise feeling special and belonging in a way that feels comfortable and is a good 'rest position' to live out of?

Our inner child

Some psychologists describe us as adults with parts of us inside still feeling or behaving like a child. We can get lost or stuck at particular key stages of our childhood through trauma, detachment, vows, fantasy or pain. We can then accommodate this part of us, or we can feel ashamed or angry with it, sensing that this needy childish part may let us down or become too demanding. It can be the reason we regress when under pressure or it can be our place of escape and our 'friend who understands'.

Isaiah 48:16 says, "At the time it happens I am there". God is the all-knowing Father who sees us from far off. He wants us to be so sure of His Fathering that we will come before Him with anything, even with our past. He wants us to come to Him with the moments, the relationships and the scenarios that we have been unable to fix or forget. Many of us are heavy-laden with significant events from our childhood; others have a catalogue of apparently trivial or domestic moments that have never left us. Some burdens can be relieved by us taking responsibility and confessing our part as sin and being forgiven. Others need to be resolved by allowing ourselves to be relieved of the responsibility and naming the sins against us or just accepting they are a set of circumstances we could do nothing about.

We can use this time to wait with God and pour out our hearts to Him. We may have been carrying our families with us all our lives, and as a result we may have never been free to live our own life, let alone enjoy ourselves! When we overreact to something or feel lost or anxious, it is worth asking ourselves how we feel inside and what this incident may be referring back to. It might well be felt as a replay of an earlier wounding and will set us on track for healing.

Our adult relationships

It is worth spending time on this review of our place in the family, as it will clear the ground for us to have more choice about our relationships now.

- We can give our childhood and any false identities to Jesus to bear on the Cross for us (for example, the clown, little miss helpful, big boy) and listen for His word of life back to us about who we really are
- We can recognise patterns – knowing where they come from can help us make new choices
- We can understand our frustrations as we give room to previously dormant gifts and talents within us
- We can allow for our families to have been a mixed bag and extend grace to those members whom we are at odds with – perhaps even finding some reconciliation or peace
- We can allow God to meet our needs in new ways rather than feeling deprived or looking to other mere mortals to plug the gaps
- As we leave all the members of our family and childhood peer group with God, the Righteous Judge, we can move on knowing that He can take better care of them than us and that He will be a better Judge and Jury than we can for all that was wrong or missing.

These difficulties and traumas will affect our ongoing relationships with God, ourselves and others in the following ways:

With God: Our hearts may still be wary of really trusting Him and we will assume that God is ashamed of us, displeased with us or merely tolerating us. We may feel accusatory towards Him and the fact He has allowed this to happen. We want to cry out to Him in anger asking, "Where were You?"

This ambivalence explains any reluctance we may have to come into the Father's house and allow Him to father us: we need to acknowledge this anger and grief. It explains why we might feel a need to appease God or hold out on Him, and why we may not be able to relax and enjoy His presence.

Jesus has carried all our betrayals and experiences of shame, assuring us of God's involvement and total commitment to our healing and salvation. Earlier in the course we saw how the Father, Son and Holy Spirit were all intimately involved at the Cross. It doesn't matter how many years have elapsed, He is ready to hear from us.

With Ourselves: We may be living with shame, self-hatred or rage at our core, or we may live with a victim identity or despise our own neediness. We may feel dirty and excluded or defined by others' words. If any of these are true for us then we will not be comfortable with who we are, and may not allow ourselves to thrive or become our true selves. We may not be able to look after ourselves well.

With Others: If we are stuck in independence, control, detachment, cynicism, rage or victimhood we will not have developed our social skills and place among our peers. We may manage for so long and then need to withdraw or leave in order to regroup or feel safe.

Without others weighing us down, we may even find that we can walk before the Lord in the land of the living, rather than waiting for heaven for everything to be made right. With our trust and our choice restored to us we can move out of the old family home into the Father's house and enjoy our inheritance in Christ. He has decided to share it with us – His brothers and sisters. May we receive the spirit of adoption that we all need and enjoy being special and at home forever.

Becoming a peer

No one has the right to define us except God. Only He has this authority, so we need to seek His face for our true dignity and healing. I must not even define myself! We will need to exchange lies for His truth and be prepared to release ourselves from any vows we have made and from being in control, or being the victim, the exception or a special case. There can be huge relief in accepting that, 'I am an ordinary person', but we may also experience an anticlimax as we realise that this is all there is. From this place, ongoing sexual addiction can bring us a sense of tension or excitement. We also need to reference back our attachment issues from our mothers. These may explain why we may feel so disconnected from everyone and why trust and staying present is so hard – causing us to resort to alcohol or sex to relate at all. We may also note that fun is difficult for us – a lot of easy connection comes when we are relaxed or through having fun.

With Him accompanying us, we will need to find some safe people with whom we can become friends and press into deeper relationships. If Jesus needed the three, then the twelve, plus the other people around Him, how much more do we need to belong and journey with others in life? It's worth noting that Jesus was criticised for having such a full and joyous social life; we need recreation and fun too.

There is no harm in using structures such as classes, interest groups, prayer triplets etc to get started. We may also need to re-evaluate our current friendships, perhaps taking care to deepen and value the ones we already have. Most people are as lonely inside as we are – we may have written them off unjustly.

The need to have people in our lives with whom we can be 'real' and share the ordinary stuff of life with cannot be overemphasised.

A Prayer

Father, thank you that I am fearfully and wonderfully made in Your image. Please may I go on to know that full well.

Thank you that Jesus has paid all my debts so that I can be adopted into Your family as Your beloved son/daughter.

May I continue to grow up, and keep growing, in every way into You, that I may enjoy becoming like Jesus while I enjoy becoming more and more myself in You.

Please help me to take new risks in building relationships and as You heal my rejection wounds can I realise that I bring life to others as well as their bringing it to me.

I thank You in Jesus' name.

Amen.

Please read Appendix B: Adult children from dysfunctional families.

NOTES

SECTION 3 - SIN AND THE FALL

"I will not leave you as orphans"

(JOHN 14:18)

CHAPTER 16 – ABUSE

Again I saw all the oppressions that are done under the sun.
And behold the tears of the oppressed, and they had no one to comfort them!

On the side of their oppressors there was power,
and there was no one to comfort them

(ECCLESIASTES 4:1)

This is a chilling reminder of how we are all suffering under the Fall, but seeking to manage or displace the pain in different ways, some of which appear much more damaging than others. As we think back to creation and the Fall, we see that abuse is not acting according to the glory of being made in the image of God. Abuse leaves everyone being cursed, rather than blessed, and is a misuse of authority and power.

We need to look at the area of abuse because some of what happened in our families and stories will need to be described in this way. There are many kinds of abuse, but there may have been an intensity that left us traumatised: for example, the extent of the neglect we experienced, or the vehemence of the control or brutality that we suffered. All abuse is damaging and we need to see it for what it is. Other abuse is much more subtle or violent and traumatic.

Kinds of abuse

Omission

As a child we needed basic levels of care. When these were not met, we may well have suffered abuse. As children, we all needed:

- Shelter, food, clothing, warmth and supervision
- Education and play
- A valid understanding of who we were
- The opportunity to express our feelings in a safe environment

- To be a child and not an adult
- To have a sexual innocence
- To have an emotional connection with those around us, and not to be frozen out or ignored
- Enough sleep
- Other.

The following can be described as abuse in childhood:

- Never to be spoken to in your own right as a child
- To be the carer of your parents, instead of them caring for you
- Not to know where the next meal is coming from
- To have to work all the time, rather than having enough time to play
- To be forced to live out family expectations without your true self being taken into account
- To be used as a surrogate spouse
- To witness marital infidelity
- To be violated.

An incident is classed as traumatic when we were unable, or denied the space, to process it. Therefore, the full weight of the incident remains locked inside us. There may have been an isolation that made us powerless and there may have been some kind of connection forged with us by our abuser that answered a deep cry in our hearts. Being on the receiving end of abuse in childhood can set us up for more later in life from a different source. Often, those who abuse us have suffered abuse at some point in their lives too.

What gaps are you aware of that have left you traumatised?

Commission

A definition:

Any act of power that is forced upon a child and leaves them traumatised. The level of destruction/abuse is not judged by the facts of the act itself, but must also include its effect on the recipient. It includes the child's perception of what happened, their view of it now as an adult and the objective view of a trusted third party. The damage can be gross or subtle.

Are you aware of any abuse in your life?

It can include:

- **Physical**: brutality, shouting, beatings, rage, passive aggression, silence, locking up
- **Sexual**: pornography, grooming, sexual acts, incest, rape, indecency, voyeurism
- **Emotional**: being idolised, being pushed to achieve, being emasculated, being controlled, being shamed, being manipulated, having the will beaten out of you, withholding of a relationship, incest
- **Spiritual**: overly religious, being a member of a cult, being controlled by fear, occult activity, satanic ritual abuse.

Vulnerability

A lack of sense of being and well-being, or a situation of isolation and detachment from a lack of fathering, can render us vulnerable to abuse. This obvious need for attention, care and connection is discerned by the perpetrator and used to win 'trust' leading to a 'special' relationship. This is the grooming stage.

Key factors in assessing the damage

- The nature of the abuse and how we were left afterwards
- The frequency of the abuse – the more often, the more deadening of our hearts there will be
- The age at which it occurred and therefore how much we could understand that it was not right and objectify it. The younger we were, the more significant the effect
- The identity of the perpetrator and their relationship to us. If they were in any kind of caring role or ongoing relationship this is significant. Also if they were in a position of trust or power, such as a teacher or babysitter
- The level of threat or terror used to swear us to secrecy
- The response of any adults we tried to tell: it is essential that we were validated and invited to disclose more without fear of repercussions. Disbelief or ridicule is devastating
- If we suspected that someone knew and was not doing anything to save us, for example, if we felt our mother knew about our father's sexual abuse of us or a sibling but did not own it. The web of helplessness feels bigger in this situation. We also may have wrongly believed that they knew and couldn't understand why they did nothing for us
- If family members are involved it is more difficult to break the silence. It is also very destructive and confusing to have to keep up normal appearances.

Are any of these factors true in the case of your abuse?

Disclosure, or rather non-disclosure

Non-disclosure is an ongoing mystery. Why do most victims of abuse find it so hard, or even impossible, to tell a key adult what is going on, even if they have not been threatened with secrecy? There is a dynamic whereby a victim will rather assume the blame for the incident than apportion it to another, especially if that person is a supposed caregiver. We can also feel that nowhere, or no one, is safe after the abuse has happened. We can also assume that our responsible adults or siblings must have known and we are waiting for them to reach out to us. After all, parents know everything else about life, so why wouldn't they know about this?

Why it is so hard to disclose abuse:

- Being threatened with dire consequences if anyone finds out our secret
- A sense that something is so wrong that it is too deep for words
- The abuse puts us into a bubble of detachment and silence
- We may have tried to tell someone and not been believed
- If there has been 'grooming' of a child there is an awareness that we are special at last and have a 'friend'
- There is confusion: shame, secrecy, terror, or even a warped enjoyment of the attention or the sexual stimulation – how can we articulate this to an adult?
- The terror is beyond words
- Protection of parents: 'this feels so awful I do not want to overwhelm or distress them'
- An assumption that we must be bad for this to be happening to us, and wanting to pretend that everything is OK
- Having no idea what would happen if it all came out: perhaps it would be worse and we would be accused of lying or causing trouble, or something too big to handle would be set in motion – thoughts that are too big for a child.
- The abuse may have felt normal to us if it came through a parent/caregiver. We trusted that they knew what was right and wrong. Even if something didn't feel right we don't question it, so it remains unspoken.

Effects of abuse

Any kind of abuse predisposes us to more and needs to be taken seriously and brought to God as it will be affecting our whole personhood. Nothing is too trivial to bring to Him.

Personal

- Living in victim mode: powerlessness, taking the blame, living with self-hatred, exhaustion, detachment, lack of emotion, anxiety, fear of rejection and shame
- A sense of being dirty, different or less than

- Anger: frustration and anger that it happened, that no one came to rescue us, but also the anger of the perpetrator dumped inside us
- Detaching to live in a place of numbness
- Bodily memories and night-terrors
- Secrecy and independence
- Feeling the weight and perversion of the perpetrator's sin
- Self-hatred and self-blame, because as a child you assume it must be your fault. 'I must have deserved it. Bad things happen to bad people.' Also, it is hard to bite the hand that feeds you, so if the abuser is a family member you have a warped sense of loyalty as well as despising and fear. You also despise yourself for your weakness in allowing it to happen
- Fear of future powerlessness and assault
- A sense of being imprisoned and defined by the abuse and this overriding any other identity. This can also cause a fear of success or attention
- Self-harming, both to release the pain and to feel the pain
- An inability to allow emotion to surface and be expressed because it wasn't safe to do so as a child – part of the heart has died
- A deep sense of grief and sadness, without necessarily understanding why
- Lack of initiative and perseverance – also indecision
- Addictions as a way of numbing the pain
- Gaining weight (particularly for women), as a form of self-protection from further abuse or unwanted sexual interest
- Bodybuilding for a sense of power
- Fear that we might become, or have become, abusive ourselves
- Eating disorders for a sense of control and comfort, or due to a poor body image.

Relational

- Can become abusive, or a bully, to those seen as weaker
- Staying in victim mode
- Intolerant of weakness in self and others
- Inability to form trusting relationships
- Precipitating rejection before it happens
- Issues of control so that no one will ever have power again
- Anger as a defence: no one can do right or no one understands
- Being a caretaker and assuming inappropriate responsibility for others
- Depression and despair that sound relationships will ever be possible.

Spiritual

- Deep relationship with God combined with a distrust of God, because He did not open the heavens and come down to rescue us
- Jesus can feel too masculine
- The Holy Spirit can feel too invasive
- Complex reactions can occur following spiritual abuse
- If our father was the abuser then there will obviously be issues seeing God as a good Father.

Sexual

- Eroticising of care or connection: promiscuity, fantasy and pornography
- Frigidity
- Hatred of feminine weakness or masculine strength
- Eroticising of pain leading to a tendency to sadomasochism
- Sexual addiction: compulsive masturbation to deal with sexual tension and anxiety; promiscuity after teenage sexual abuse/rape; pornography if early exposure to it
- Provocative dressing as if to precipitate further attraction
- Vengeful sexual behaviour, harming self or others.

The healing process

Abuse of any kind usually eclipses the presence and goodness of God for us. It can help to think back to a time of ministry or a moment when we *did* feel the presence of God. Maybe this was a time when we heard His voice, or when we just knew He was there for us and with us. We may not be able to do this if the abuse started early, continued for a long period or was very traumatic. Although we may be detached from God, it is good to be open to the possibility of bringing the abuse before Him, especially with someone else there to support and validate us. We may still feel confused and be desperate for Him to open the heavens to come down to help us.

We need to bring all that happened before God and allow Him to be the compassionate one, even if we are fighting to remain independent. Also, we need not feel ashamed of what happened to us, nor of our powerlessness in it and our inability to save ourselves – nor of the ongoing hurt and difference we feel. He longs to hear all about it from us in our words – or lack of words – and in our own time. So, we pour out our hearts to him, realising that He is infinite, but actually that the pain and shame are finite. Some of us may find it hard to 'mind' about what happened because we are still in victim mode and are blaming ourselves, to a greater or lesser degree. We can ask God to help us with this and get us in touch with the necessary anger.

As we tell Him what happened from our point of view we become aware of Him validating it. Tell him about the shock and trauma and also any 'good' feelings we got from it: attention, being noticed, orgasm, warmth, as well as the shocking and painful feelings of shame, being slimed, afraid, terror, the presence of death, threats and secrets, fear, blame, misplaced loyalty, panic, anxiety, bitterness, cynicism or aloofness. We notice where and from what we wanted to detach and did detach: from life, myself, family, lack of control, vows never to...

There is no part of it that we cannot share with God/Jesus and allow the Comforter to come into.

One of the most poignant things we need to face is our vulnerability and loneliness inside. This is part of the reason we were targeted. We can easily deny or despise this in ourselves, but it will be in the core of our heart and we will need to come to a place of tenderness and truth about it.

We will need to be very gentle and gracious with ourselves. We will need others with us, as we may be confronting our desperate need for connection or for others to notice us, and as we realise how exquisitely painful this is. We may sense the breaking down of walls and have an acute awareness of exposure and vulnerability – even though we know this must come. Or we may be aware of the weight of the devastation of generations before us. We will also be facing the truth that we have survived and will need to adjust to the possibilities and demands of our ongoing life and adulthood.

Inside every person who has been abused, is a deeply hurting, fragile child who really wondered if they would survive. Gradually, we will feel safe enough to face and feel the losses, which may include: safety; innocence; virginity; trust; childhood; choice; purity; imagination; family; honesty; will; beauty; belonging; openness; the relationship; being ordinary... whatever our hearts show us. We will need to clear space in our lives for this, as the process will sap our energy. Time and a trusted counsellor who is experienced in this area are also important – as is the presence of safe, ordinary people in our lives who can give us space to change and space to be.

Key stages we will need to work through

It is a bit like a set of Russian dolls where the outer ones are the largest and look impressive, but it is only the little one at the centre of them all that is solid. We might wish that we were more substantial than that by now, but it is that little one that God wants to take and start back into life again. We need to find that extremely vulnerable little one at the core of the issues and invite God to extend comfort and grace to us there, as we also extend grace to ourselves. We invite Him to empower us to say what we need to say and process with Him out of our powerlessness into appropriate strength.

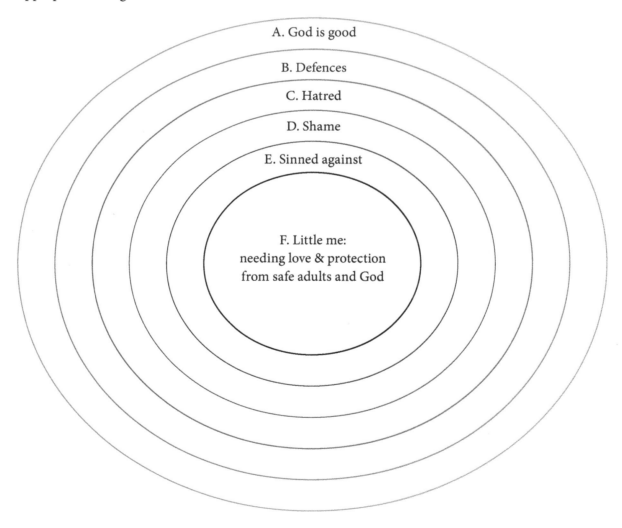

A. God is good

B. Defences

C. Hatred

D. Shame

E. Sinned against

F. Little me:
needing love & protection
from safe adults and God

a. God is 'good'

We need to be honest with God about any misconceptions we have about Him and where we have tarred Him with the same brush as our assailant. We will need to dare to confess to Him such things as: we feel that He too is abusive; that He runs out on us; that He lets us down; that He is helpless when it really matters; that He can't be trusted, etc. As we clear out these very real feelings we can move towards a place where we feel He is trustworthy enough to proceed; there is no other sufficient Comforter actually.

b. Acknowledge our defences

Our defences are the ways in which we have walled off from others, or from life itself, in order to stay alive or maintain any sense of self. We must come to see them as understandable and necessary at the time (they enabled us to survive in our defencelessness) but that they are no longer useful for us, or right in God's eyes.

We need to repent of these defences and be prepared to dismantle them with Him. We start by handing them over to Him. They may include: defensive detachments; independence; anger; rage; pain; passivity; fear; withdrawal or living in victim mode. We also invite Him to be a sure defence for us and to build up clear boundaries and empowerment within us.

c. Acknowledging hatred within towards others

We will need to acknowledge any hatred we harbour towards the assailant; others of the same sex as the assailant; others in the same position; ourselves and those who failed to defend us (this list can include God, our parents and siblings). It is possible for hatred to consume us – it may mean that we wish they were dead or if we had the opportunity we would kill them.

This hatred is very frightening and can often be destabilising for 'good' Christians. Therefore, acknowledging it can be a great relief. We will then need to go on and confess the hatred as specifically as we can, including any rage and revenge and murder that is in our hearts. All of these things are completely understandable given the abuse we have suffered, but they end up destroying us as people and actually increasing the already damaging legacy of abuse.

When we have confessed the hatred and our need of it as part of our defence and strength, we can then go on to repent of it and release it to God.

d. Acknowledging the shame, 'I am bad' / 'I must have deserved it'

When we have suffered abuse someone has broken our boundaries and put their sin and shame into us so intensely that we can have made it our own. We are left feeling, 'I am bad'; 'I am disloyal'; 'I must have been bad or asked for it'; 'I will never be worthy like everyone else' or 'I am different'. These were often the only conclusions we could come to in our defencelessness. They are lies that can stay with us and come to define us – leaving a profound sense of intrinsic worthlessness and deep self-hatred inside.

We need to understand what has happened, and confess these views of ourselves to God. They are familiar 'old clothes' for some of us, and may be hard to let go of, almost part of the defence system.

They keep us in despair and 'acedia' or hopelessness. We must exchange them at the Cross, release them into God's hands and wait for His affirming words instead. Then we must choose to believe what God says about us and ask Him to help us do so.

The shame itself can cover us like a cloak or shroud. We can feel dirty and different in every fibre of our being. Sometimes feeling it is written on us for all to see. As we come before the Lord with the shame, we must allow Him to lift it off us and into the Cross, to pull it out of every cell and cleanse and soothe us through and through. We must wait for the washing and 'perfuming' of us to know real cleansing forever.

Where the shame has led to feelings of self-destruction, these must be owned and repented of too. These feelings are understandable, but again, they are not right or good to have in our lives and the deep wounds underneath will need healing.

e. Acknowledging the sin against me

We need to accept that we are not being disloyal or judgmental in saying that we have been sinned against, even if a family member or a parent committed the abuse. God knows all about it already and is longing for us to feel able to share it with Him. It will always have been present as a hidden agenda between Him and us anyway as it will have been within our families.

A key part of this area is to take the time to unpack the true extent of the sin and its full consequences for us, and maybe for others. This will include our own private hurts, however trivial they may seem to anyone else. It will include pain and losses, ways we have been disabled in life by the trauma, loss of trust, isolation and abandonment. It may even involve the loss of our childhood or our real sense of self.

This unpacking can often be a very profound and painful process. We may need to repeat the process as and when more ramifications come to mind. It is safe to feel our pain at the Cross in the knowledge that anything we release into the Cross does not have to be felt again; it won't be sent back to us, but we may need to face and feel deeper layers of it. Anything that we want to release can be spoken or written down and handed over to the Lord, the Righteous Judge.

f. Acknowledging the need for love – allowing the Lord to become our defence

Inside each one of us is a genuine, inbuilt need for nurture and intimacy. However, to receive this we must become dependant and, in a sense, vulnerable. This is nearly impossible for those who have had to defend themselves against the assaults of abuse.

This need for nurture and intimacy can pose a real problem for us: we may despise it, suppress it, hate it, mistrust it or indulge it. It can feel too dangerous, troublesome or simply too unfamiliar to allow to the surface. The last thing we want is for someone to be nice to us or for us to need them. We are perfectly all right as we are. To receive is too risky. It means:

- Being known
- Having needs that I choose not to meet only using resources within myself
- Not being perfect
- Feeling the pain of the longed for nurture and intimacy
- No longer living alone.

We will only be able to move into this place if we are sure that the Lord is a true and sufficient resting place, that He is good and will receive us just as we are. He can then become our defence – giving us room to move and live and feel, unlike our makeshift walls that bound us up and walled us in without keeping us safe at all. Gradually, we can rebuild our relationship with God on the basis of grace and intimacy – not duty or detachment. We will need help and time to do this.

g. Reclaiming our true selves back from the abuser

We will need to claim back our whole self as well as our ability to choose – we will need to choose life rather than be a victim. We also need to own those parts of us that were taken and robbed, for example: our physical bodies; our mouths and genitalia; our right to our gender; our minds; our thought life and dreams; our future; our relationships; our imaginations and our sexuality. If we have been abused at school by someone of the same sex, then we may think that our participation means we are gay.

For those of us who were sexually abused, there is also the dimension of the assailant using us for their sinful sexual practices and, be it unwittingly, in their worship of Molech/Baal (Leviticus 18:21). Therefore, we need to renounce Baal in this extra way and choose to come off the altar they made to him. We will need special prayer with an experienced counsellor to release physical bodily memories.

We may also need to renounce the spirit of death if we felt threatened to this extent. Some of us may have been left feeling dead and may need to intentionally choose life again and give ourselves permission to live. At times, we can plateau in this as we are surprised at reaching particular milestones that we never thought would be ours to experience. This can cause a real crisis in confidence, rather than the joy that other people expect.

A word about forgiveness

Forgiveness is NOT:

- Forgetting, denying or minimising
- Excusing
- Explaining away
- Blaming yourself
- Tolerating injustice
- Reconciliation.

Forgiveness IS:

- Facing the facts
- Feeling the hurt
- Confronting our hate
- Releasing the person who wronged us to God.

We will explore forgiveness more in chapter 21. We need to resist anyone who wants us to forgive too quickly, or says that we can simply forget what happened to us.

Being an abuser ourselves

Many of us will need to come to terms with the fact that we may have passed the abuse on to others who seemed to be more vulnerable than us. We may have done this in our family through rage, manipulation, passive aggression or by being a continual victim in self-pity.

We may have passed the abuse on to ourselves when we have allowed ourselves to continue in self-destructive behaviour. Or we may have passed it on outside the family by being a bully or being predatory in our sexual behaviour. Our hearts will know if any of these apply to us. We will also need to repent before God of any of our behaviour and allow Him to cleanse and forgive us. In receiving this forgiveness into our hearts we can lay down this defence and need Him fully instead, as our Saviour and Friend.

We will also need to forgive ourselves and this can be a tough call. This may be for being an abuser ourselves or it may be more subtle: forgiving ourselves for being picked off; for being so vulnerable or powerless; for being pole-axed and silent, or for allowing ourselves to be robbed of so much. God will enable us to do this and comfort us in our grief.

Restoration

An essential part of ministry in this area is cutting ourselves off from all unhealthy ties with our abusers, including any sexual soul ties. We reclaim ourselves as belonging to Christ and not being available to anyone else. We can be washed clean and allow ourselves a new ownership of every part of our being and body. We were bought with a price and are infinitely precious. We hand over to God all our old identities such as victim, hopeless, outcast etc and allow Him to take them and replace them with our true identity and worth in Him. We will need to make room for this in our hearts and practise the presence of life and of this change. If we revert back to old ways of thinking we can regroup and invite God to hold us in our new dignity and our true self.

A difficult piece of work that needs to be done is to grieve the losses, especially when they hit us in waves or we feel inconsolable. We can do this by taking ourselves to a safe place and hopefully letting the tears flow. For some of us, crying again is a miracle. We need to let God in – that can mean inviting Him behind the walls we have built and naming each individual brick that we have used to wall ourselves off from life. These may include, saying "No, I'm fine thanks", "No one has suffered like me", "How trivial everyone is", "How dare they enjoy themselves like that", "I liked being the parent to my brothers and sisters – they needed me."

A prayer

O Lord, I never thought the world could be so unjust and cruel; that I could feel such fear and confusion or that I should be so alone. Please help me to allow You into this part of my life, to feel safe enough to let go of my independence and receive the comfort and healing that I need from You. May I proceed at a pace that is manageable and feels safe. Also help me to trust others to be with me in this. May I know Jesus taking all that happened to me into Himself that I may be relieved of all the weight and horror of it and know healing and restoration of who I really am in You.

In Jesus' precious name,

Amen

NOTES

NOTES

CHAPTER 17 – SHAME

Have mercy upon us O Lord, have mercy on us, for we have had more than enough of contempt. Our soul has had more than enough of the scorn of those who are at ease, of the contempt of the proud

(PSALM 123:3–4)

Some of us are living in toxic shame. It fills our first thoughts when we wake up in the morning, "What will I encounter today? Will I have the energy or wit to stave off shame today? Will I succumb and will the day be just another episode of self-contempt and shaming?" We assume that God is also ashamed of us and that He probably doesn't like us any better than we like ourselves.

If we are not as consciously aware of the shame we carry, we may just worry about keeping up appearances. We may live with a protective veneer of defensiveness or narcissism, blame shifting on to others and needing to be right.

We are not ashamed to admit that we cannot mend the carburetor in our car, or the ball-cock in our loo when it breaks. We have to take our car to a garage and call in a plumber. We share freely that we take the cat to the vet and visit the dentist. None of them has ever berated us for not being able to fix these things ourselves – so why are we so ashamed of needing a Saviour and of admitting to fundamental flaws or normal wear and tear in life? The answer is usually shame. Where are we proud? This is usually the flipside of shame.

Of course, shame, fear and feeling naked are the first uncomfortable feelings that Man experienced after the Fall. We can take a definition of shame from the events of the Fall:

- It is the awareness of my fallenness and the memory of my lack of glory, of not being in that place of being fearfully and wonderfully made and God's splendour being visible through me
- It is the fear of this being seen or 'found out'
- It is feeling uncovered, naked, vulnerable and not in control
- It is what we try to hide by contempt
- It is feeling powerless and not being as God
- It is being alone when I know I am made for relationship
- It means having no mastery over our lives

- It means my 'I am' is not enough
- It means we live out of our orphan hearts.

Also:

- Feeling appropriate shame when we have done wrong is guilt and should lead us to confession
- It can be part of a culture operating on honour, shame and revenge
- It can lead to jealousy or envy or counting ourselves out of ordinary favour or blessing
- Family shame can be passed down.

Shame is such a key part of the Fall. Isaiah 53 reminds us that Jesus came to bear our shame, become the victim and be despised for us. This means that God understands the prevalence of shame and is expecting us to need to come to Him with it – simply because we live in a fallen world. God always sees the good in us.

Roots of shame

Shame is resident within most of us: body, mind and soul. Some of us are wrapped in a blanket of shame, allowing it to define us. We have settled for it and think it is normal. Shame sits in our hearts, clouds our perceptions, acts as the arbiter in our decisions and makes itself heard as we assess our bodies. It feeds off comparison and when we anticipate it coming our way, we long to take cover.

Anxiety is often about the anticipation of shame, as well as being about powerlessness and pain. As shame takes hold, we find that it paralyses us and traps our grief and disappointment or the shock of a trauma behind it. It is one of the ways we cope with the primal wounds of rejection, non-attachment, betrayal and intense aloneness: by turning these moments back on to ourselves and saying, 'It must be me' and, 'It must be my fault'.

Our infant self always expected that our parents would respond to their natural instincts and love us and meet all our needs. When this did not happen – sometimes to an abusive degree – we are left in a place of total shame about ourselves and our presence on earth. We cannot bite the hand that we expected to feed us, so we assume it must be something intrinsically wrong with us. We come to believe that at our core we must be unlovable, despicable, unattractive and a lost cause. We begin to feel that we are entirely alone and we no longer have any expectations of care or attention. As we view the world through these lenses, we find a self-fulfilling prophecy at work – we are right. Life is, more often than not, a round of rejection and isolation. Self-pity and self-hatred have become core dynamics in our hearts, and shame somehow numbs their pain and confirms our perceptions.

Shame also denies us our right to mind. We are supposed to protest – to claim what is due to us – but shame questions our right to do so. Some of us were made to feel even more shame if we made a childhood protest or sought to be heard. We may have been deliberately naughty to prove everyone's fears about us.

Anything that begins to smell of rejection, disappointment, betrayal, challenge, a repeated trauma, isolation or exclusion will trigger the anticipation of shame. Our instinctive reaction is then to avoid it. It is vitally important, and significant for our healing, to access these places in our hearts as they can dictate a great deal of our behaviours and perceptions.

And, of course, shame wrecks our relationships with God, with ourselves and with others.

It shows in how we walk through life and how we work. We may develop complex ways of sabotaging good and avoiding detection, of maintaining vows, staying detached and keeping within our fortress – using up precious energy that could go into life. When these start to give way, we may seek relief in addictions and 'treats', which only add to our shame!

What kind of shame am I carrying? Where do I carry it and what triggers it?

Sense of being

Mother

Our first source of shame can be from our attachment, or lack of it, with our mothers.

For some of us who have almost no sense of being, or who feel very insubstantial, simply being asked to be present will be a threat. For example, being asked to make a decision or offer an opinion may make us angry and defensive. We are ashamed of our flimsiness and afraid of being found out; we are worried that more is expected of us than we can give. The primal perceived rejection by our mothers will have broken our hearts and left us feeling infantile and afraid.

If our parents, for whatever reason, were more preoccupied with themselves or life than with us, if they didn't – or couldn't – understand us, or had nothing to give us, we will not have dared to entrust ourselves to them. Instead, we create an unassailable place of safety inside us and hope that this will be sufficient to launch us into life. We will have tried to attach and connect to our parents in many ways, but in our hearts we will have known that there was no point of entry. We will have then resigned ourselves to isolation and independence. To move into healing, this will first need to be expressed to God and He will need to be given a chance to show Himself as different and dependable, before we will dare to allow anyone else in. Occasionally, someone else will prove themselves to be constant in such a way that we begin to let hope rise and move beyond the betrayal.

Without a sense of being, we can absorb other people's sadness and shame and add it to our own – even feeling condemnation and guilt that we cannot fix them.

Father

We needed our fathers to believe in us and for us to identify with him as a worthy human being. We may have felt that there was nothing of true worth in our father and identified with that for ourselves, or that he set himself up as so worthy that we could not compete. We may have been left in no man's land without a vision of there being anywhere we could go for comfort and encouragement.

Siblings

Our siblings may have shamed us in small ways day-by-day, until we came to believe that we had no intrinsic worth. Or, they may have been so abusive towards us that we did not have any dignity or safety within our own home. Our homes may have been a jungle of orphan behaviour, and we always lost out.

Peers

At the point of entry into our peer group, we may already have been on the back foot, unsure of our place or worth and without any clear sense of our identity. This may have been noticed straight away by certain groups and led to bullying. We may have been ill-suited to life with a particular group and have suffered the disgrace of always being picked last for teams or for not playing an instrument well enough, or being too clever. School-age peers usually show little mercy to those who are perceived to be different or outside the group.

Trauma

Trauma leaves us with a split between our right and left brains and we are left remembering it or holding it unchecked and unprocessed in our bodies and hearts. This is why we can often recall the physical circumstances of a traumatic event so clearly – they are not stored as mere facts in our brains, but as a whole person experience. For example, we will recall the weather, the textures, the colours, the smells or the sounds and these can trigger the anticipation of a recurrence years after the event.

The shame of being powerless lives on. This is, of course, painfully true of any situations of abuse of any kind. In this instance, we have been the object of someone else acting out their shame and anger and, usually, they will seek to dump it on us as part of the abuse. We will know it doesn't really belong to us, but we carry it all the same. We will need to identify this and lift it off on to God. We may need some specific trauma therapy.

Later rejection

For some of us, the areas of shame are more specific, because they were caused by wounds inflicted later on in life after we had developed a sense of self. For example, we may have developed shame because of our size. We can be equally wary of revisiting these occasions because they are overwhelming, they seem too trivial, they are still ill-defined or are too embarrassing or 'silly' to share. The effect of them being retained by us in our bodies and perceptions is the same as in an earlier trauma and they are better out than in. It is best to own them amongst safe, confidential people and leave them at the Cross to receive specific healing for them from Jesus.

Outworking of shame

- Overt
- Covert
- Both
- Displaced.

Some of us live out our shame by staying in victim mode, sometimes without even wanting to change!

Overt

Negative behaviour and perceptions, cycles of failure, depression, deadness, self-pity, sabotaging good, self-hatred, negative narcissism, eating disorders, self-harming, addiction etc.

In what ways is my shame most evident?

Covert

We may not be aware of our shame because we have developed behaviours that seek to hide it. We may be driven and successful, we may be funny and very likeable, we may have elaborate stratagems for not being tested and found wanting – avoidance tactics, control, chaos, narcissistic behaviour, co-dependency, staying in our comfort zone etc.

How do I seek to hide my shame?

Both

Usually we flip between the two: in some circumstances we can function well, in others the threat is too intense and we are found out, in others our automatic cover-ups click into place and we make it through.

Displaced

Addictions are activities through which we seek to numb the pain of anticipated shame and displace it. In sexual addiction we seek to displace the shame on to another person. In addictions to pornography, food, alcohol and work, the displacement is on to an object. Being abusive or a perpetrator of abuse is also an attempt to displace our shame and self-hatred and anger on to another. Usually, it is the shame and self-hatred visited on us earlier in our lives. We move from the powerlessness of victim to the apparent power of perpetrator. With addictions, we can often anticipate the cycle kicking in and will be desperate to justify the ensuing behaviour. A convenient way is to pick a fight or observe a serious flaw in a partner or spouse so that the self-pity and blame shifting can provide a reason for the next round of the addictive behaviour.

How do I/have I displaced my shame on to others, e.g. a victim, my spouse, my siblings, my children, at work?

When we are plagued by shame – overtly or covertly – we have no grasp of grace, or even a need for it. We cannot believe that grace includes us – in fact, we can usually make a very strong case for it not applying in our case. We may feel ambivalent about receiving it anyway. There is a sense in which we long for grace – yet it can also be a threat to our secrets and our independence. We will need trust to receive it from God.

Paul, writing to the early church at Corinth says this: "We destroy arguments and every lofty opinion raised against the knowledge of God and take every thought captive to obey Christ" (2 Corinthians 10:3–5). The Scripture reminds us that we make fortresses against God and experiencing Him for ourselves. We come up with "lofty opinions" about people and life to confirm our perceptions and maintain these walls. We can take a position for ourselves and contend with the truth of who God is and indulge in fallen ideas. These are the thoughts then that we must take captive in obedience to Christ.

Yet, if we can stop this inner protest long enough to quieten our hearts, we will feel our primal need for God and for His blessing and allow His grace to rise in us. If we can endure even more of God's presence, or that of a safe attentive person, hope of change will come. We will feel the barrenness in our souls and the truth that grace is our only hope. Our self-hatred and prideful independence now become obstacles that can be offered to God, rather than defences. We all need Christ to bear our shame.

Does shame still sit in my body? if so, where?

What triggers it?

What areas of shame can I identify in my life? Can I put them into words?

Splitting

For some of us, the weight of shame has been too much to bear, so we have split it off into an uncomfortable or unmanageable part of ourselves and live in denial. We may then cultivate a front that parades as a very good person in the hope that we can compensate or deny the 'bad' part of ourselves. This split into good/bad is very hard to acknowledge and can have taken years to form. Those of us who have split in this way usually need professional help to dismantle the toxic shame, allow it to be a part of us and work it through.

Ministry

Shame needs to be renounced. It is not ours to carry. It belongs to Christ on the Cross. We need to intentionally name shame for what it is and pass it over to God to take for us. In exchange, we can make room for and receive our inheritance of honour and blessing and security from God.

We might want to write a letter to God outlining our shame and bring it to the Cross. We will need to wait while we allow Jesus to bear it for us and wait again to receive back our true honour and comfort and peace right into our whole being. We then allow this to replace the shame. We may need to repeat this exercise as more surfaces.

See to it that no one misses out on the grace of God

(HEBREWS 12:15)

This verse comes towards the end of the letter to the Hebrews. It reminds us that we must help each other and make sure that no one misses out on the grace of God. It is a letter written to Christians steeped in the knowledge of the Bible. They understood who Jesus was as Son, Great High Priest and the Passover Lamb. They understood the whole sacrificial system, the tabernacle and the old and new covenants. They appreciated the power of the blood of Jesus, the strength and purpose of the greats of the faith – some of their own church had even been martyred. Yet, here is a call to holiness and a plea not to miss out on the grace of God. From this verse we see that length of service or biblical knowledge does not guarantee that we are living in the good of the grace of God. Hebrews 4:16 talks of us finding grace to help us in our time of need. Yet, that is often the very moment we resist and try to manage on our own.

In our shame, we can tend to isolate ourselves and count ourselves out of being a useful member of the body of Christ. This means that no one is close enough to know where we are in our journey, let alone what we might be missing out on – let alone grace! It is possible to miss out on the grace of God and this can lead to self-pity and bitterness. As we then spread this around, it breeds discontent with God and sin in the life of the church.

Once we are at odds with God, we lose the reality of His comfort and presence and our sense of sin. Our self-pity can then justify anything, and soon, we are seeking consolation in sinful sexual behaviours or instant gratification, like Esau, in food, drink, pornography or any other addiction.

Despising our birthright as sons and daughters of the Living God and feeling we can manage without His blessing, like Esau, we seek to save ourselves through others or things. This can happen in practice or it can be in fantasy and fester away in our hearts. Either way it is a very slippery slope that begins with feeling we are missing out on the grace of God.

In the parable of the prodigal son, one of the reasons the father is looking for the son is so that he can run to meet him. This is regardless of the humiliation of a stately gentleman lifting his robes and quickening his step that society would have felt at the time. The scene would have played out in front of the whole community, who knew of the son's disrespect towards his father, they would have been ready to lynch the son should he ever dare to show his face there again. But the father made sure that he reached him first and so dictated very clearly the terms of his return – the father took on the humiliation so that the son could come home with dignity.

Jesus has taken the path of total humiliation to secure our return to the Father's house. He will be with us as we make our way to the Cross and He will meet us there with His resurrection and healing.

What things about myself do I find easiest or hardest to share with others?

A prayer

Dear Lord,

Thank you for carrying the weight of the Cross, taking the pain of total humiliation and bearing all my sin and shame. Please help me not to miss out on Your grace.

*I realise it's not right for me to carry shame. Reveal to me what shame looks like in my life – **now take a moment to wait on the Lord as He reveals any shame in your life.***

Forgive me Lord for all the ways I have sought to hide and outwork my shame. I ask you to wash and cleanse me by the power of your Spirit.

I renounce shame and release it to You. In exchange, I receive your inheritance of honour, blessing, security, comfort and peace into my whole being.

Thank You for always seeing the good in me. Help me to come into agreement with this and to know my true worth in Christ.

Amen

Shame exercise

Which three people have caused you to feel most shame?	*What are the three most shameful things that other people have done to you?*
Which three things are you most ashamed about?	*What are the three most shameful things you have done?*

NOTES

CHAPTER 18 – TEMPTATION AND THE STRENGTHENING OF THE WILL

Temptation is not sin but our shame tries to tell us that it is. Temptation is only an invitation to sin – it wants us:

- To stay present to our wounds rather than to God
- To stay in an orphan place
- To resist the offer of comfort from God
- To behave as if God is not interested, understanding, present or redemptive
- To deny that we are gloriously made in the image of God
- To feel we have nothing left to lose because we are so shameful
- To think that holiness is merely the absence of naughtiness
- To give ourselves a treat because no one else does.

Like Eve, we succumb to temptation when we lose sight of God's goodness and grace, and question what He has said.

We never have to repent of being tempted.

We only need to turn to God. Just as the first temptation started with doubting God's goodness and wisdom, "Did God really say...?" so we are tempted in the same way. More often than not, we give in to temptation when we are tired, hungry, angry or in pain and we feel we deserve a treat or comfort that God won't allow. So, we take matters into our own hands. We adopt a short-term solution (i.e. instant gratification) that will usually leave us feeling worse. We may withdraw from God and not allow Him to help us objectify what is happening and turn to Him for help. A key to resisting temptation is to see it for what it is: owning both our legitimate needs and our illegitimate ways of meeting them. Our genuine needs must be honoured and explored because our temptations come out of our wounded areas and our places of isolation and detachment. Then we can know progress in our deepest places of temptation. For example, if we did not receive consistent, appropriate touch as a child this need may become eroticised and we may be tempted into sexual sin. However, this underlying need is legitimate and needs to be acknowledged and addressed in a non-sexual way. A pattern of staying isolated at this point of need and managing it alone, for example through masturbation, will not address the underlying wounds and will ultimately be counter-productive.

We also come to realise that we do not need to split off our tempted place but rather realise that we are one person that God loves all the time – not a bad me and a good me. Once we have found the relief of this we realise how good it is to be integrated and how dangerous it is to disconnect from God. He is the one who understands what is going on inside and invites us to come at this exact time when we cannot save ourselves and need the comfort that no one else can give us. If we stay connected we feel alive not numbed out. If we do disconnect we need to come back as soon as we can, rather than allow the days of shame to build up.

We cannot run on empty.

We need to honour our own legitimate needs and talk with others to work out the best way to get them met. This will mean sharing and being known and also monitoring our hearts. If we have neglected ourselves or got stressed then we may need to reach out to another and be accountable for the emptiness and our vulnerability to temptation. White-knuckling it never works. Being connected does.

Living in an isolated place means we are more open to temptation.

What are your legitimate needs? Are you trying to meet them in illegitimate ways, e.g. seeking validation through performance?

Can you think of people you can share these needs with, to work out the best way to get them met?

Temptation comes from three main sources: the world, the flesh and the devil. It does not come from God, though He allows it to happen. God is not part of the problem but our best solution.

The world

'The world' here means the unredeemed, godless culture in which we live, which idolises money, sex and power and elevates self-sufficiency, greed, lust, injustice, the misuse of resources, consumerism, deceit, etc.

Jesus assures us that once we are in Him and in His Kingdom, we are no longer "of this world" (John 15:19). He invites us to recover our true worth and glory, our sustenance from Him, our unique value and our personal security so that we can be objective about our context. We are not duped, and we can be alert to our vulnerabilities and to the seduction that is being played out. We are to function in community and be known (again see Hebrews 12:15) so we can share in our understanding of the 'world' and be prepared to face the temptations it brings.

The flesh

If we see the world as the external pressure then the flesh is the internal pressure of a fallen world. The flesh is made up of our internal drives and unmet needs. These needs can present themselves with such validity and urgency that it can feel that if we don't meet them we will die!

The flesh trades on fear. It comes into play when we doubt God's provision and feel that we must look after ourselves or reward our self-pity with a treat. James 1:14 uses the word "entice", and indeed the bait is something we legitimately need – but we are fishing in the wrong pond!

We need to remember, that we have choice and value and that we can practise exercising our objectivity, choice and responsibility. We can walk away from the temptation. We must evaluate our drives and desires, sort them out and take authority over them. Again, we must not be too proud to call for help at any point in the process because we are encouraged in this life, "not to walk according to the flesh but according to the spirit" (Romans 8:4). And the spirit thrives in fellowship.

We may also need to decide whose side we want to be on, such as victim or beloved, because temptation will continue if we keep a foot in both camps. We can honour ourselves by using temptation to learn more about the places where we still need more of God's love or where we need a better lifestyle. We must be particularly alert when we are **H**ungry, **A**ngry, **L**onely or **T**ired and **HALT**. We are the only people who can make the necessary changes in our life – anything else is just advice.

The devil

The devil's role is to rob God of His glory by robbing us of ours. He also wants to rob us of our living relationship with God and of our fellowship with each other. He wants to take the effects of the Fall – that make us feel vulnerable and doubt God's presence or goodness – and exploit them.

Jesus was genuinely hungry after He finished His forty-day fast in the desert. For many reasons we all have significant genuine hungers left from our childhood and we can succumb to destructive and short-term ways of meeting them. For example, we may have a sense that we will never find real comfort or that we have always been overlooked and can only trust ourselves. This hunger can manifest itself physically and it's hard for us to see how God can meet it. The good news is that God can meet all our needs at the Cross. We remember from John 10:10 that "the thief came only to steal, kill and destroy", yet Jesus came "that we may have life and have it in abundance". As we start to trust ourselves and others they can be part of the solution to meeting our unmet needs.

Because we have not received the levels of nurture and connection that God planned, we will feel 'comfortless' inside and will be tempted to seek comfort outside of God's plans for us. We are afraid of the extent of the pain or isolation and we may even feel that we will die. As we are harmed by life, we are tempted to look after and save ourselves. It is important that we know the ways in which we are vulnerable and feel we can bring these, without shame, to God and to other people.

When the devil tempted Jesus he went for His identity; he will do that with us. As we recall our true identity in Christ and of being made in God's image we can use this to resist doubt and temptation. Jesus did nothing to assert or affirm Himself in His own eyes or in those of others. He only did the will of the Father and allowed the Father to ultimately glorify Him. We must do the same. Because of our lack of affirmation and firm identity we are vulnerable to seeking it through sex, money, work, buying expensive cars, even being a victim. We are eternally loved by God, even if we were short-changed in parental love. The Father's love was sufficient for Jesus, and so it is also enough for us.

So, how do we cope with temptation?

- See temptation for what it is – temptation
- See the world, for what it is – it is not the Kingdom of God
- See the flesh for what it is: my fallen humanity like everyone else's
- See the devil for who he is: the father of lies and the destroyer of the brethren
- Recall that this pain will not actually kill us!
- Take authority over our senses. For example, we can look but not linger. We can learn to heed the danger signs
- Admit when we are being duped
- Be humble enough to own up to what is happening - however far down the line we have gone.

The following prayer by Thomas á Kempis (from *The Imitation of Christ*, 1413) explains it very well.

Christ, addressing the soul, says to us:

> *My son/daughter, I am the Lord, who gives strength in time of trouble.*
> *Come to me when the struggle goes hard with you.*
>
> *Your slowness in turning to prayer is the greatest obstacle to receiving my heavenly comfort. For, when you should earnestly seek Me, you turn first to many other comforts, and hope to restore yourself by worldly means. It is only when these things have failed that you remember that I am the saviour of all who put their trust in Me, and that apart from Me, there can be no effective help, no sound counsel, no lasting remedy.*
>
> *Amen*

The process

- Recognise when we are being tempted and what feelings precede it: self-pity, anger, fear, hunger, loneliness, tiredness, isolation, anxiety
- Invite the Lord in as quickly as we can. Call out to Him, be powerless, tell Him where we are!
- Make contact with a Christian friend
- Remove ourselves from the situation as soon as possible. This may involve: turning off the computer, leaving the building, hanging up a phone call. We can do these things without fear of looking stupid or rude, they are for self-protection
- Recognise that the action is an avoidance mechanism: avoiding shame, pain, loneliness etc. It is self-medication but using a harmful drug that leaves us feeling worse. There are many layers of pain here, but we can survive them with God's presence. It is better to allow the pain to surface and go into Christ on the Cross, than suppress it so that it has to be felt again

- Don't agree with self-pity or excuses. Quite often we say that we 'deserve' the treat of sin, but afterwards we know it leaves us feeling far from blessed

- Every time we win ground or resist a stage in temptation we have made progress. So, we need to feel this encouragement and put it in the bank for next time

- This process is the opposite to the law of diminishing returns that we are stuck in. Every insight and resistance is valid and builds strength

- Don't give up halfway through a bout! We can lose the ground we have made by the above actions. It is even more encouraging when we keep objectivity and are not duped by self-pity and do not dwell on the temptation but allow ourselves to be known and move on

- If we do lose a round, there will be plenty more that we can win – especially if we regroup and get back to God in repentance and humility

- Remind ourselves of our true glory and purpose: to live for the praise of His glory. This perspective helps us to recognise the emptiness of what the world, the flesh or the devil offer us compared with God's dignity and glory, which others need to see and experience in, and through, us

- Temptation doesn't have to lead to sin. This realisation can be a real point of strengthening for our faith and our relationships. Jesus understands: Hebrews 4:15 assures us of that

- We may need to admit that temptation is coming so thick and fast that we are in the throes of addiction. Coming out of denial and facing this is a vital first step.

Our wills

Our will is a very interesting part of us as we can use it for good or for harm. Many of us have developed a pattern of responses that mean our will gives way at exactly the point when we need it to remain strong. Or our will becomes stubborn and detached, just when we want to be flexible or even sacrificial. If our will is defunct we will live out of passivity and despair and feel pathetic. We may galvanise our will merely to protect ourselves and maintain our facade of competence or faith. We may have had our will beaten out or taken from us by an abuser, leaving us as a victim who has no voice or opinion or power.

So, we need a will that is tuned in to the Father. We must ask God to give us an adult will that responds to each occasion and will persevere, even at cost, sometimes genuinely laying down something that really matters, for the sake of goodness and justice and our personal holiness.

We will not want to tune our will into God's until we have experienced His grace and mercy towards us and start to believe He is good.

We will not want to tune our will into life until we believe we are worthy and we embrace our authority and true strength of character of being made in His image. We are not called to be nice and accommodating but to be empowered and blessed.

We can then find a deep resolve to hold firm in the face of temptation and not flip into:

- Self-pity or rebellion/passive aggression/I am in control
- The self-deception of deserving a treat
- Self or relational destruction.

God promises to be with us in our times of need. He can also forgive and restore.

A prayer

Lord, I come to You now, choosing to stand in my true worth before You.

I bring You all the ways in which I am tempted to sin against You and manage my inner pain in destructive ways. I give all my self-pity and hardness of heart to You.

I ask You to redeem my imagination, so that I can see Your Kingdom and my place in it more clearly. I ask that I may see the deception of sin for what it really is.

I ask that You will deepen my trust in You as the good Father that I have always wanted. I ask that You will encourage me, in my heart, to agree that Your ways and will are good, and that sin will only damage and hurt me and others.

I ask that You will take my heart and my will and redeem them, so that I become sensitive to the ways of Your heart and respond to Your voice. Give me a dynamic and lively will that honours Your glory and expresses Your love and salvation moment by moment.

I ask this in Jesus' precious name,

Amen

NOTES

CHAPTER 19 – THE CROSS AND CONFESSION OF OUR SIN

We will start by looking at the nature of sin, whether it is by us or against us, and explore how the Cross is the only source of forgiveness and healing.

Then we will look at our own sin and our need, both for confession to God and forgiveness towards ourselves, so that we can move on and not go through a cycle of repentance and self-pity or despair. We will look at forgiving others later in Chapter 21.

Confession is a test case for how well we have separated out our earthly father from our heavenly Father. It is about coming to the compassionate understanding Father, before whom we have really sinned, and who prepared the Cross for us so that we can be open and sorry. We can dare to own up and take responsibility because He has proved His benevolence and mercy and because we have a great high priest – Jesus Christ the Righteous.

As we imagine the gracious reception we will receive, the welcome because we are coming in our need, we see Jesus and find even more mercy than when He took Israel by the hand and led them out of Egypt. He wants to lead us by the hand out of our Egypt.

Before reading any further, please read Isaiah 53.

The nature of sin

We suffer oppression and sometimes we allow it to remain in our lives. In life we often cannot find the comfort we need and in our desire for this we sin, thinking this will ease the pain and meet our need. However, when we sin we join the oppressors (of ourselves and those we have sinned against). Yet God promises comfort to us even then. This is an equally desolate place, but God understands and brings His comfort to us here too. God's compassion ensures that He does not ever leave us stuck or alone.

Whoever is the sinner, we know that sin always causes damage. For there to be any resolution we will have to reckon fully with the nature and extent of the sin – theirs and ours. Sin hurts us, and it hurts those we sin against. It affects how we see life and all our relationships: with God, with ourselves and with everyone else.

We can define sin as:

- Not living as God intends us to
- Not believing the truth of how God defines us and knowing our intrinsic worth as His image bearers
- Seeking comfort and solutions to our pain or aloneness outside of God
- Not being like Christ and giving ourselves and someone else that experience
- Not living out His glory – as human beings fearfully and wonderfully made in His image
- Not treating someone else as fearfully and wonderfully made in the image of God.

This allows for sin to be something we actually do, or fail to do, something we do in fantasy, or something we do 'virtually'. It can be more pervasive: such as an attitude or mindset – pride, revenge, passivity, forgetfulness, sulking, self-obsession. Hebrews 9:7 assures us that He covers even our unintentional sins.

God knows us through and through and wants us to be holy in our inmost beings, not whitewashed sepulchres or hypocrites.

Which do I want in my life: the appearance of holiness or holiness itself?

Who would be aware of the difference?

We can sin ourselves, or be sinned against by others, by:

Commission

Something we/they do, say, or think. It can be a slander, an inference, a judgment, a look or a cuss. It can be subtle or blatant, a joke or apparently trivial or it can be real abuse. We may even have allowed it to happen, but it is still SIN. It can be physical, emotional, spiritual or psychological.

Omission

Something we/they didn't do or say through neglect, carelessness, deprivation, ignorance or weakness. These can be:

- Intentional or unintentional
- Noticed or unnoticed by either party
- As a one-off
- Sporadic, habitual, continuous or repeated.

Sins of omission can involve someone alive or dead, a third-party known or unknown to us, or they can be passed down the generations. Our families will have sinned against us in any/all of these ways, and the effect of this will be to leave us wounded. Some of us have never cleared out our regrets at what we failed to do or do well.

We need the Cross to be the place of redemption – to get our rightful inheritance of peace, joy and wholeness back and to become the person we are meant to be.

The Lord's prayer

God invites us to forgive others as we are forgiven. So it is very important for us to build up a bank of forgiveness for our own sins before God and be ready to release this grace later to others. They are intertwined. We do not forgive on empty but from full, from God's grace to us first.

Both the modern and traditional versions of the Lord's Prayer are useful here: they describe trespasses and debts! When we ask God to "forgive us our trespasses" and tell Him that we intend to forgive others theirs, we are covering all the ways and times that we/they have crossed the line and acted contrary to God's written law and the spirit of His law in our hearts. It's almost as if we/they have trespassed outside the Kingdom of God into the Kingdom of this world and done things our/their way instead of God's – with all the inherent danger and damage that this brings. Sin is not doing the works of the Father.

We can start to get in touch with the ways our parents may have trespassed against us by imagining what God wanted for us from our family. Or, we can invite God to take all the unhelpful or destructive memories and images so that we can dare to imagine again and experience goodness. We ask Him to restore our imagination (to feel and see all that He wanted for us), knowing that the Comforter will really be there to comfort us as the pain of the contrast becomes acute in our hearts.

These sins of omission are debts that we are asked to forgive. God knows our rightful inheritance and this becomes ours again in Christ. When we were not given the comfort or security we needed we have not received what was our due at a primal level – and so we have a debtor to forgive. A response to not receiving at a primal level can be to withhold from others. For example, we may withhold our affection, forgiveness and commitment. When we do this, in a way we are doing no better than our debtors and we leave people wounded in the same way that we are.

What love debts do I have to forgive?

Where/how am I withholding the good of who I am from others?

When we confess the sin of walling off, fearing a recurrence of shame or disappointment, from a parent or another, we are acknowledging that we are withholding the goodness of who we are from them. The reasons for our detachment may be understandable, but it robs us of truly being ourselves and becoming even more so. The elder son in Luke 15 withheld his whole person from his father and would not enter into his son-ship or allow the father to bless or honour him as the son he delighted in. We can do this with our own parents and with God. We leave people impoverished by withholding ourselves or through our lack of giving, just like the elder son.

We have seen the link between our position as sinners before God and other people's position as sinners before each other and before us. Forgiveness needs to flow in all directions! Until we forgive, we will tend to visit on to others what has been visited on us, even if this is unintentional and subconscious.

Forgiving others as we have been forgiven

We will only be able to forgive others from our hearts if we are experiencing God's grace there for ourselves. (Another approach, of course, is to be in God's presence and invite Him to bless us and fill us with His goodness and life – and be prepared to store it in our hearts in a new way.)

As we read on, we can recall any unconfessed sins that still bother us, however long ago they were committed. Now is the chance to let our hearts speak and receive all the grace and cleansing we need. Of course, we can also confess our more recent sins and allow the truth of how we have sinned against God in these different ways to really shake us so that the value of His grace can impact our hearts. We are confessing all the ways and times we have not been like Christ, or thought and behaved as someone less than a son or daughter of God, or when we have treated someone else that way. We are confessing our orphan behaviour.

We need to note when we find it most difficult to confess. It can be hard to face our own sin and separate it out from that of others. We may want to blame shift on to God or others, but we will only find freedom when we take responsibility for ourselves. God's kindness is there to lead us to repentance, so again it is important to allow ourselves to receive His grace and not to resist it.

God's forgiveness is redemptive and through the Cross He forgives the sin, cleanses our conscience, takes away the sin and dies with it for us, bears our guilt and sorrow over it, carries the wounds and restores our whole being. He does so for our 'simple' sins but also, more especially, for our apparently 'unforgivable' sins. He longs to cleanse us from ALL our unrighteousness.

How do I find owning up and confessing? Who is my safe person for this? Do I believe God forgives?

As we let the specifics of His intention of blessing unfold, we need to ask God to be with us so that:

- We are not overwhelmed by the extent to which we have been sinned against and do not use this as an excuse not to confess our own sins

- We do not rationalise so that we can allow ourselves to feel the injustices and own our responses

- We can allow ourselves to feel the conflict – the moments when words and actions or tone of voice didn't match up; the times when we were left confused and angry

- We can forgive these sins of commission.

Taking responsibility

Some of us find it hard to take responsibility, either because we carried too much as children or because we have never taken responsibility for anything in our lives! Some of us can go through the motions of repentance easily, but find it hard to connect to the reality of our sin in our hearts. As we wait on God, the full weight of what we are dealing with can click into place. Then, like David, we can become truly sorry and extremely grateful for His forgiveness of us, realising that it is all of grace. We will then have this grace in our own hearts to extend to others and want them to benefit from such a release from guilt.

Interestingly, many of our sins are in response to sins against us: our defences, our sulking, our self-pity, our lies, our self-hatred, our bitterness, our need to please, our licence or our need to control etc. Whatever their roots, our sins need to be dealt with by confession and repentance: the receiving of forgiveness, a clean conscience and the removal of guilt. God is not counting our sins, even if we are. He simply wants to get down to the root causes and forgive them and restore us.

How do I find taking responsibility? Where is it easy and where is it difficult for me?

Confession and grieving over our sins before God

Our true glory

As we wait in God's presence and allow Him to show us our true glory and the freedom and creative/redemptive possibilities of who we really are, we may find ourselves grieving for that loss of glory. This grieving process will help us engage with the ways we have participated in our lack of glory. Coming clean with God becomes a relief, and the clarity of our sin and the joy of being forgiven and cleansed can be thrilling.

Our confession leads us on to repentance, where we allow God to find us in our place of powerlessness where we cannot save ourselves. We give our sin and sinfulness over to Jesus to bear it for us on the Cross. He then gives us back our true righteousness in Him.

Confession activates the power of the Cross to us

When we realise we have sinned, many of us are waiting for disapproval or extermination from God. But, He knows that many of our sins are reactions to earlier woundings and are our vain attempt to defend ourselves from further hurt. The possibility and joy of a new righteousness, beyond our usual experience, enables us to endure the death of our sinful ways. We can take the unrighteous specifics of our lives and allow ourselves to share in His death, and therefore, His resurrection.

Confession brings us a new vision of the Kingdom of God

Saying things honestly and in line with God's ways means we nail the lies of:

- Excuses, such as, 'I deserved a treat'
- Pride, such as, 'What would people think?'
- Hopelessness: 'This is all I am'
- Trivialising and saying, 'It doesn't matter'
- Being overwhelmed for example, thinking our sin is unforgivable
- Our own lies that muddy the waters and keep us in passivity or shame.

Confession brings me back into the light and therefore fellowship

When I am not afraid to be known as a sinner, as well as a saint, I can come out of isolation and aloneness and bring other people out of theirs.

Confession stops me being a hypocrite

When I am not pretending to be more righteous than I really am, I am not just keeping up appearances. It also starts to heal up any split I may have created between my good boy/girl and my bad boy/girl.

Confession acknowledges God's power over sin not mine

Confession keeps me in the place of being the creature, not the Creator nor my own saviour. It keeps me participating in God's grace and mercy and this fuels my devotion of, and love and delight in, God. I grow in being a son or daughter, not a slave who lives to appease his master.

Confession opens up the way to healing

Confession relieves me of trying to be perfect in my own strength, of having false expectations of others and, from James 5 we see that, it builds the community of faith. It heals my distorted thinking and gives me an ongoing reality-check in my life.

So, we may well need to take some time before God to identify our own sins that are yet to be forgiven. This will be hugely beneficial for us and also for those we need to forgive! As we share what we are doing with other safe people we will know a deep release from shame.

All sin is damaging, so it is only right to have a law to cover damage limitation – we cannot do whatever we like to God's glorious Creation.

We may need to confess (this is not an exhaustive list!):

- Betraying trust
- Being harsh and not expressing the kindness of God
- Being passive and not living out the intentions of God
- Being in denial
- Being greedy
- Slandering others
- Lying
- Being vengeful or hard of heart
- Comparing ourselves with others
- Self-pity
- Hate
- Cynicism
- Sarcasm
- Drunkenness, addictive behaviours
- Sexual sin
- Self-hatred
- Engaging in power play
- Blame-shifting.

Hebrews 9:14 says, "how much more will the blood of Christ who through the eternal Spirit offered Himself without blemish to God, purify our conscience from *dead* works to serve the *living* God". We must wait for the full valeting service of seeing our sins covered, the guilt taken away and our consciences cleansed. This breaks our cycles of sin and shame. We may even be holding on to our guilt as a penance as if we could make a contribution to this great salvation.

How do we confess?

- Come into God's presence and recall at least one real experience of His grace to us – there will be one!

- Enjoy recognising and feeling grace – for what it is – undeserved and very lovely

- Ask God to show us our sins and help us own them specifically (writing them on a piece of paper to pin on the cross and/or in your journal)

- Go quietly over them asking God to show any patterns, for example, of control, avoidance, drama, detachment or roots of pride, fear, self preservation, etc

- Confess them to God, agreeing that this was not the best for someone so fearfully and wonderfully made. These are the love debts towards God, ourselves and others

- Wait until we become aware of His understanding and compassion, grace, mercy and forgiveness, even in the light of what we have just shared with Him

- Receive all the above into our heart, just for us at this time, treasuring the grace and forgiveness and the relief that we feel, letting it all clunk down and become a part of us. (This is the grace that we will use to forgive others their debts towards us). (This is what Matthew 18:23-35 is all about. The servant had never really taken responsibility for his debt so when he was released from it, it did not impact his heart.)

- We know that if we confess our sins, real ones, God is faithful and just to forgive us, take the guilt of them Himself on the Cross, cleanse us of the unrighteousness, remove the sin from us, comfort us where we are hurt and renew us where we need to be changed more into His likeness

- We can then express our gratitude to God. As the relief sets in, gratitude will flow and we can ask Him to show us how he wants to break the patterns and heal up the roots of these sins in our lives

- Ideally, we should do this with someone else listening in as this really helps to pierce the shame. We can then reciprocate to them! Also, we can stay in this rhythm of being known and forgiven by having a small accountability group who do this together regularly. We will then be in the habit of keeping short accounts.

Generational prayer and family review

During this session, we will have a time of generational prayer, during which we will thank God for all that was good that has come to us through our family. The process of recalling the good can be very encouraging. However, some of us may not be able to get in touch with any good until we have reached a place of objectivity and grace, by starting to own the negative things about our family before God. Then we can face the fact that our family is as fallen as anyone else's and bring to the Lord those sins that needs repentance, forgiveness and redemption.

As we refer back to our family story, what are the themes? E.g. money, faith, shame...?

Introduction

- Much of our pain, confusion and issues stem from our place in our family of origin. Each of our parents was brought up in a fallen home, as were their parents before them – all the way back to Adam and Eve! It is small wonder that despite their best efforts our family circumstances will have been less than perfect; they will have left their mark. Describing our grandparents can often be a good pointer to our parents' issues, and therefore to ours

- There will also have been generational patterns, and even curses, that will have influenced the normal run of life and established a bias towards certain behaviour in the family line, such as marital unfaithfulness, money issues or alcoholism

- Many of our defences and behaviours will have been developed within our family of origin to avoid or handle the pain or disappointment we felt – some are acknowledged, some unconscious

- We can sometimes begin to own more of our own stuff by reviewing our family patterns, imagining what life must have been like and how it might have been for us back then at that age. This objectivity can help us come out of denial and enable us no longer to allow ourselves to be defined by their brokenness or our reactions to it. It can help us disengage the false or needy self and decide to be our true adult selves in life. Ephesians 4:22 talks of "putting off the old self and the lusts that spring from delusion" (KJV). We are deluded if we think our families have left us unscathed, or if we think it is all their fault

- As we recognise the deficits and behaviours for what they were, we can begin to come to the all loving, eternal and almighty God, the Redeemer with the package of who we are and appeal to the higher One who alone can deliver us from the weight of our history and being defined by it.

Jesus' family

- Looking at Jesus' family tree reveals a motley crew! For example, Judah sleeps with his daughter-in-law, who gives birth to twins, including Perez (Genesis 38). We see that Solomon is the son of David and Bathsheba, not the son of one of David's other wives (2 Samuel 12:24)

- We can take heart that Jesus was not ashamed to have forebears who were not perfect; He will certainly not expect ours to be

- His primary concern is that we allow Him to redeem what is not right so that we are no longer restricted by our family history. Instead, He wants us to enter into our full adulthood and becoming in Him.

Biblical basis for asking God's forgiveness for our families

- In Nehemiah 1:6, Nehemiah says to God, "I confess the sins that I and my father's house have committed against you. We have acted very wickedly towards you" The use of the word "confess" here seems to be an owning of the facts before God, an acknowledgement that some of what has happened in Nehemiah's family line is sin against the holy God of Israel

- So, acting in our capacity as a member of the royal priesthood we then plead the blood of Christ on their/our behalf, and ask God to cover this sin and redeem the effects of it in my life and not hold it against them/me. (We own it as sin, but not repenting of something personally that we haven't done.)

- We also know that all time is present to God because He exists outside our earthly time. Therefore, all our family events are present to Him. He can therefore forgive and release or redeem us from anything in the past on the same basis as He forgives us in our present.

Forgiving our family

- God meant for us to be born and raised in families, as they were a relational unit that would model Him – as Father, Son and Holy Spirit – best to us. They should have left us with a good heritage of Christ-likeness from which to launch out into life

- Our parents were supposed to have brought us into a secure and joyful covenant relationship with the full support of an extended family and a real faith in Him, which was passed on to us clearly and appropriately

- We are asked to forgive those who sin against us, whether they ask for it or not. So, as we become aware of the ways in which our family has failed to deliver God's ways to us, we must name and speak out the sin and its consequences and go on to forgive it, even if it is in the past for us

- In so far as our parents have not modelled God's ways for us they have failed us, wronged us and sinned against us. We will need to own this in all its various ways and pronounce our forgiveness before God to our family. For some of us, this will mean forgiving heinous sin, for others, very serious deficits, neglect and irresponsibility

- Our entire family history is present to God, so any significant event, occasion or wounding can be made present to us by the Holy Spirit for healing. Sins can be forgiven; wounds healed; shame lifted; sorrows and griefs borne by Christ; allegiances broken; curses revoked; wrath and rage put on to Jesus the Lamb; broken hearts mended; enmity reversed; misogyny redeemed; the effects of all other sin redeemed; the roots of despair and affliction or infirmity lifted; crowns of righteousness replacing our places of emptiness and ashes; restoration of what never was, and life instead of a hold of death

- There are real decisions to be made here: if we become aware of there being worship of foreign gods in our family line we need to be clear about this and renounce them: 1 Kings 18:21, Judges 2:10, Judges 6:25, Leviticus 18:21, Matthew 6:24. Is there worship of Baal, Molech, Masonry, Mammon, etc?

Coming out of denial

Our family issues can leave us passive and dispirited, but as we know the resources of the Cross are there for us we can dare to own the stuff in our past. Also as we place the Cross behind us – that is, between us and the former generations of our family – we are safe and they no longer have access to us or the power to hurt us.

We can be in denial or be passive about our family issues because of:

- A broken will

- Deep early despair and hopelessness (this is 'acedia' – the worldly sorrow described in 2 Corinthians 7:10 that keeps us present to an ongoing sense of death and of not really being alive)

- Repressed rage (this is extremely disabling, yet it can be convenient. We may need to face how angry we are if we are to engage properly in the healing process. We need to be prepared to separate out our real self from the family version and realign our adult will with God's. Then we can start to be assertive enough to own the issues and work with God to clear it up through repentance and the giving and receiving of forgiveness. It's ok to hurt at the Cross, because we know there will be restoration.)

The process

- As we review our family tree, we will see patterns emerging that can be prayed through specifically. For example there may be lines of contention between the men and the women; lines of misogyny; sexual sin; relational breakdown; lines of spiritual independence or isolation or rebellion or passivity; money issues; adultery, premature death etc.

- These patterns can be owned before God as sin and we can ask God to have mercy on our family and forgive 'the sins of my father/mother's household against Him'

- We can then start to name the effects they have had on us, such as, making us insecure, ashamed of ourselves or our gender, neglected etc. We can then pronounce forgiveness back down our family line for what they have robbed us of, or for the damage it has caused. We forgive them in the name of Jesus for their deliberate or unwitting sin, and ask Him to cleanse the family from this unrighteousness and redeem its effects

- We then own before God where we have bought into the family pattern or have further sinned against Him in defensiveness or survival or bitterness etc. We can then ask Him to forgive us and cleanse us and redeem us. It is not inevitable that we will follow the family line.

When we have dealt with the obvious patterns we can then move through each generation, starting at the fourth one back from us. We ask God to show us any specific issues or sins, confess them as sins before a Holy God; ask God's forgiveness and mercy for them; forgive them ourselves for not laying the right foundations for us, and then lay them to rest putting the Cross between them and the future family. We can then go through the generations to the third, second and first until the present day.

The prayer

Dear God,

Like Nehemiah, I name before You, the sins that I and my father's and my mother's houses have committed against You. We have acted wickedly and not honoured You as the Lord our God. I ask Your forgiveness, I ask for the blood of Jesus to cleanse us from this sin and the guilt and consequences of it.

I ask You to redeem the effects of it in my life and the life of my family as we seek to follow You. Please restore me, take all curses into yourself and bless me as Your own son/ daughter to live for the praise of Your glory.

In Jesus' name,

Amen

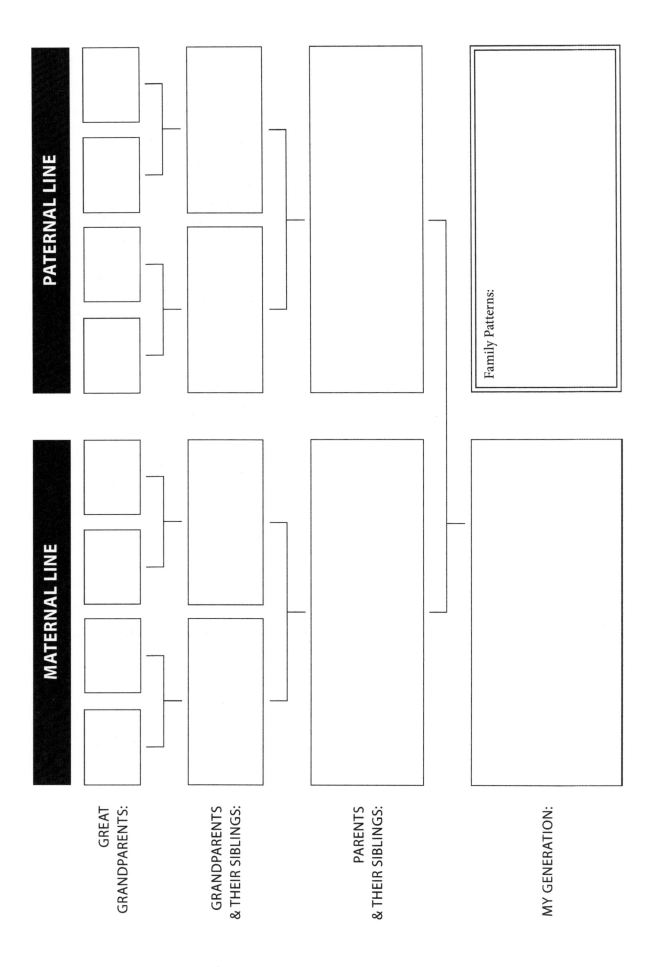

PATERNAL LINE

MATERNAL LINE

Family Patterns:

GREAT
GRANDPARENTS:

GRANDPARENTS
& THEIR SIBLINGS:

PARENTS
& THEIR SIBLINGS:

MY GENERATION:

NOTES

CHAPTER 20 – RENOUNCING IDOLS

Those who cling to worthless idols forfeit the grace that could be theirs

(JONAH 2:8)

The images are false and there is no breath in them;
they are worthless, a work of delusion

(JEREMIAH 51:17-18)

An idol is something or someone that we use to replace God in our lives: to give us meaning; to ease our pain; to give us value in others' eyes; to absorb our attention and divert us from intimacy with God; to complete us, or to hide our shame. An idol can be a possession; our job; an institution; a person; a fantasy or something we do not yet possess, but long for as the answer to our needs. An idol can also be our identity, e.g. our sexuality, profession, or being a victim or perfect, or it can even be our ministry or position in church. We may be using it as a survival mechanism or as our hiding place. We will need to ask God to reveal to us anything that has become an idol in our lives.

They went after false idols and became false

(2 KINGS 17:15)

They served their idols, which became a snare to them

(PSALM 106:35)

All worshippers of images are put to shame;
who make their boast in worthless idols

(PSALM 97:7)

He feeds on ashes; a deluded heart has led him astray; he cannot deliver himself
or say: "Is not this thing in my right hand [my dominant/lead hand] a lie?"

(ISAIAH 44:20) (ESV)

This is a people plundered and looted;
they are trapped in holes and hidden in prisons

(ISAIAH 42:22)

But they themselves go into captivity

(ISAIAH 46:2)

If he cries to it, it does not answer or save him from his troubles

(ISAIAH 46:7)

Why do we seek after idols?

For many of us, our hearts live in tension: between the truth about God and the impact of a fallen world in our lives. The intensity of the Fall, which we have experienced physically and emotionally, can seem to outweigh our experience or heart knowledge of the unseen God. All too often we decide against God and allow ourselves to be disappointed in Him – we say He has been found wanting. We may well have put Him to the test and bargained with Him, and then we feel we are justified in seeking comfort elsewhere or feeling hard done-by.

In Daniel 3:16–18, Daniel and his companions refused to bow down to the idols and stated that God would save them. However, they went on to say to Nebuchadnezzar that even if He did not rescue them they would still not bow down (never mind that they would be dead by then!)

Grasping this is essential. God is not here to do what we tell Him to do. As we submit in love and obedience to God, refusing to entertain self-pity or idols, our whole lives will be aware of the Kingdom of God, rather than the kingdoms of this world. We will recover the perspective of God's truth and the power of the Cross with which to stand firm. We cannot have a foot in both camps. In Joshua 24:15 we are invited, "to choose this day whom we will serve".

We may have no expectation of being included in God's plan of good for our lives. We need to review our lives and see where we have allowed doubts and cynicism to creep in. These will have shifted our focus from God on to ourselves and we will then have sought solutions in idols. The impact and injustice of the Fall will be with us until we reach heaven, but we can hold it in an open hand to God knowing that He has sent the Comforter to help and that He is eternally just.

What are my doubts and how am I cynical?

Our spirituality and our sexuality are inextricably linked

In placing His Spirit within us and through His incarnation, God is clearly reminding us of the relationship between the physical and the spiritual. We are living in both realms – we cannot act out in the flesh without this affecting our spiritual nature, because our bodies are the "temple of the Holy Spirit" (1 Corinthians 6:19–20). The condition of our spirit and our relationship with God both reflect and determine our actions. Our worship is definitely not just for Sundays, rather it's the offering of our whole selves to God, including our sexuality.

This is, of course, why pagan gods, such as Baal and Ashtoreth, demand to be worshipped through sexual rites. As the people of Israel performed acts of debauchery and sexual immorality on the high places and under the trees, they were not only defiling their true selves but also graphically acting out their spiritual adultery before God and the surrounding nations.

> *...pull down the altar of Baal that your father has and cut down the Asherah that is beside it and build an altar to the Lord your God*
>
> *(JUDGES 6:25–26)*

One of the core aspects of the glory of our bearing the image of God is that we are made male and female. It follows that this is also a sure-fire way to desecrate the glory of that image in us, which deeply offends and hurts God. When we defy God's commands and are enticed into a belief that we know better than God, Satan must be at work. He is both receiving worship through acts of sinful sexual practice and also ensuring that the image of God is defiled. When we engage in this behaviour, or turn to cynicism or outright rebellion, soon afterwards our desire for God will wane. The Old Testament is an account, rather than a fable, so we can expect these deities to be seeking followers through every age and culture to the present day and beyond.

If our fathers committed sexual sin, like Gideon's father did, then we may have taken on their idols. We will need to take them down before God and stand up for our own righteousness. Our fathers may have introduced us to sexual sin via pornography. If this is the case, we will need to cut off that spiritual tie; forgive them for a very real sin against us, and invite God to be our loving appropriate Father.

Psalm 121 is about the subject of idols. It is a 'psalm of ascent' and essentially the pilgrims are saying, "As I look up at the high places en route to Jerusalem and see the altars to Baal and Ashtoreth, where does my help come from? I am staying with the Lord God of Israel. He does not slumber like the baals on Mount Carmel with Elijah. I am not worshipping the gods of the sun and the moon who burn you. The Lord God keeps my life safe, He keeps me from spiritual adultery and is mine for ever".

What/who are my idols?

What need do they serve?

Why and how do I hold on to them?

In what ways am I rationalising my behaviour despite God's love for me?

Dare I burn my boats and trust God to meet these deep needs?

The grip of addiction

Rather like the legend of Prometheus, our technology can often have more far-reaching effects on our lives than we are able to imagine or control. It seems as if the possibilities and opportunities for sexual sin, and for it to reach the critical level of becoming our 'right' and 'normal' practice within the culture, have been taken to un-dreamt of levels by television and the internet. Spiritually, despite our sophistication in so many areas, when we commit sinful sexual acts, such as adultery, pornography or casual encounters, we are as deeply into the worship of pagan gods as the Israelites – even if it is from the comfort of our own homes!

We are usually doing this unwittingly – as Christians or as non-Christians. As Christians we need to repent not only of any/all our sinful sexual practices, but also renounce the worship of these pagan gods. This is an essential and powerful part of our discipleship journey.

The prominence of sexual sin in our culture can also help to explain the grip of so much addiction: the promise of satisfaction of a sexual act; the subtle belief that sexual satisfaction is our right; the filling of our imaginations with sexual images, and the deadening, for some people, of their desire for God. Sexual sin promises so much, but the reality is that it actually gives us very little while demanding more and more of our time and energy. It is definitely the law of diminishing returns. At times, we know we are not just dealing with our own flesh and blood, but with principalities and powers. Certainly people struggling with sexual addiction soon realise that they are dealing with something much bigger than their own desire.

This deadening of our hearts is one reason why we are less and less able to offer ourselves to each other with any true intimacy or confidence. An increase of shame and a waning ability to trust another or ourselves and to be vulnerable or known, again fuels the need for a quick fix. We are also seeking to find a means for some sort of 'satisfying' connection without the need for sustaining a relationship or the fear of further hurt, shame or disappointment. 1 John 1 reminds us that when we are known and living lives in the open before God and each other, we then have fellowship with Him and with each other. If we are indulging in secret sin then we will be unable to connect authentically and will continue to feel alone.

Am I looking for meaning or comfort or life outside of God? If so, where?

The problem of lust

Lust could be defined as desiring a sexual interaction without an appropriate relationship and covenant being in place. It is wanting to devour and take and assumes rights where there are none.

We share our common humanity with Adam and Eve. As they – and we – sought the knowledge of what is good and evil in the garden, we should not be surprised at the results. God established the sexual union of a man and woman in a committed, covenant relationship with the capacity to be life-giving and to strengthen our humanity and personhood, as well as to be a comfort and a means of restoration. Without His safeguards in place, sexual intimacy can become a deeply destructive experience – reducing fellow human beings to objects of lust and fantasy and giving false and hideous opportunities to exert power and damage each other at the core of our beings. This licence can cause great heartache and anxiety to those who may then feel deprived or inadequate if their lives are chaste.

We also know that, given our fallen nature, there is no guarantee that what happens in the marriage bed will be God's intention for us either. The church can be naive here – presuming that nothing can be amiss and so leaving couples to suffer in silence. Jesus said that any unfaithfulness, even in fantasy, is adultery (Matthew 5:28).

A sexualised culture

When a culture becomes obsessed with sexual activity, those for whom this is not a possibility (for example, because they are single for whatever reason), are left feeling cheated and deprived – even as Christians. A rights-based culture can encroach on our desire for holiness and righteousness and will challenge our experience of true freedom. This is not God's intention for us either. We are to find the grace in Him to be abstinent in our hearts and in practice – or celibate if that is our call – regardless of sexual orientation.

Our worship is the offering of our lives to God. We will all have areas of mystery and struggle that will either cause us to press into God's grace all the more, or cause us to turn our faces away from Him. For some, this struggle will be in the area of our sexuality, for others it will be something quite different.

In this area, some have found a rest position from which to live. They know they really are a sexual being. Yet, despite not being able to express this in an active sexual relationship, they do not experience lust or an eroticising of their needs that causes them to sin – whether in fantasy or practice.

Others may have access to a sexual relationship within marriage, but find that they have deep unmet – and often primal – needs, which have become eroticised and they are unable to remain faithful or pure. They may sin in fantasy or in practice: making sinful demands on their partner, or looking outside that relationship to fulfil their lust through illicit sexual activity.

Christians are not immune from these pressures. This is why Jesus reminded us that "everyone who looks at a woman lustfully has already committed adultery with her in his heart" and that if our "right [dominant] eye causes us to sin, tear it out and throw it away" (Matthew 5:28–29). Jesus is saying: don't let lust run the show. We know that the sexual and the spiritual are powerfully linked and we do not want to offer God the worship of a life that includes besetting sins. We are to be righteous in the expression of our sexuality, whether we are single or married. Within our culture, so many areas of life have become sexualised and therefore involve us in spiritual adultery. God is not interested in the mere appearance of holiness in our lives, but in holiness itself.

Narcissism

Many of us find that we can be posers, adopting an affected persona, especially if we are feeling unsure of ourselves. In narcissism this goes beyond being a coping mechanism and becomes a posture or lifestyle. Narcissism is the idolising of the self – where we are self-absorbed and live with a profound sense of entitlement, to the exclusion of others. This is usually because we have very little sense of self and well-being and are living out of a place of anxiety and rejection – defending ourselves against the next assault. We cannot be generous or known. We need to self-reference often enough for the attention to keep us alive – even if the attention we receive is negative. Because we have nowhere to hold blessing and goodness, each bit of attention will only have a short shelf life and we will need to provoke more and more. There is often an idealised persona presented to the world, which is a defence against further rejection. Because only God is perfect, it is trying to be like God. The attention we crave is akin to worship and we live off it rather than God. We are in deep need – emotionally and spiritually. Once you notice narcissism in someone it's clear that it is a lifestyle for them.

Am I narcissistic? Am I prepared to check this out with those who know me well?

Relational idolatry

Relational idolatry is the idolisation of another person – looking to them to save us, make us feel alive or stay alive. It can actually be someone from our past, present or future. They can be transient, as in sexual addiction, or longer-term, when we can obsess about the person or even lose our own identity in theirs. This is also akin to worship and we live off the idolised person, rather than God.

In both narcissism and relational idolatry we are asking a fellow creature to tell us who we are and sustain us. It is fuelled by fantasy and denial. We are unable to trust God with our lives.

In a marriage it is possible to look to our spouse to give us affirmation, meaning and life beyond what is healthy. We are looking to them to be God. For singles, we can idolise marriage as the only source of fulfilment and life.

Do I idolise anyone or ask people to idolise me?

Renouncing idols

Here we are putting Exodus Chapter 20 into practice. As we renounce idols we need to name before God anything or anyone that we have used as an idol. The list will include anything or anyone that we have used in the place of God as a source of meaning, power, comfort, superiority, worship or strength etc. It can even be our spouse – as men ask women, instead of God, to encourage and enable them or vice versa.

We will need to name anyone or anything that we have used to satisfy our needs or drives outside of God's conditions of covenant, respect, love and order. The list will include people – whatever the means of contact – such as: prostitution, chat rooms, dating apps, photographs, images, any non-covenant sexual contact (ongoing or casual), anyone to whom we have been acting as a saviour, jobs, circumstances, money, power, fame, perfectionism, etc.

We can also foster this behaviour in others and may need to repent of encouraging others to idolise us.

We come before God acknowledging:

- That He does not tolerate rivals
- That He wants the best for us and that idols cannot deliver what we are looking for
- That He understands the destructive nature of idols and sin better than we do!
- That the Cross holds the power to overcome the draw of these things
- That He is not asking us to renounce anything without offering us the power and comfort to do so, and a better life-giving alternative.

It is essential that we take time to be specific and comprehensive in our repentance. Nothing is too trivial nor too pervasive to be included and for us to know real freedom.

We also encourage you to bring to the Cross and destroy everything that might tie you into that person still, or to a behaviour, such as, clothes, books, letters, jewellery, photographs, etc.
As you ask God for His perspective He will show you what you need to include. It does not matter what their monetary value is – the important thing is establishing our spiritual freedom and cleansing.

From whom do I need to separate out? What do I need to destroy and why?

Breaking soul ties

Given that our sexuality and our spirituality are inextricably linked, we will have created a soul tie with anyone with whom we have made sexual contact outside of God's conditions, that is outside the covenant of marriage, but it will also include any abuse within marriage. We are tied to them and they to us in a negative way. These ties need to be specifically broken. This also applies to anyone who sexually abused us. We need to release ourselves from being wrongly tied to them and claim back our physical bodies, our minds, our personhood and our whole humanity as rightfully ours. We give ourselves permission to live our own life before God and repent of any wrong use of power, compliance or victim mode.

Please make a list of all the people (ever!) that come in this category for you and we will pray with you before God to break these connections. It doesn't matter:

- How long ago
- How many
- Whether you remember all their names exactly
- Whether it was anonymous
- Whether you were a victim or an initiator
- Whether it was opposite sex or same-sex
- Whether it was committed or casual
- Whether you or they are famous!

Why have I used these people like this and/or allowed them to use me?

Prayer for breaking one-flesh unions

Lord, I come into Your holy presence to confess the one-flesh unions and emotional attachments I have had to people. I want to name each one before You now...

As I cut myself free, I ask that You will cut me off from them now forever. Take the darkness out of my soul and find and heal the wounds and hurt underneath.

Forgive me where I have been predatory.

I am so sorry Lord, for using someone made in Your image for my own ends. Find that place of deprivation and entitlement that persists in me. Take it on to Your Cross, so You can heal the deep wounds inside. Comfort and complete me so that I no longer need to look to my fellow creatures for what can only come from You.

Also Lord, release me from being a victim and staying a victim. Unbind me and set me free I pray. Heal the abuse.

Forgive me Lord for all the ways I have sought to self medicate my pain and hide my shame in another. I ask You to cleanse me now and restore me to my true glory in You and with my true self turn to You first as Comforter and Redeemer.

Amen

You will need to read out the names of each person on your list of one-flesh unions and soul ties. Take the sword of the Spirit and cut yourself free from them all. Release them to God. Ask Him to heal up both the wounds underneath the need, and the wounds caused by the tie. We may have extra pockets of being a victim or of shame or anger left in us from the interaction itself. We ask God to attach us whole-heartedly to Him in a new way, and wait while we see what He is doing.

We will then be washed and blessed and anointed for a new sense of being, sanctified in Him.

NOTES

CHAPTER 21 – THE CROSS AND FORGIVING OTHERS

At this point on the course, we are doing the forgiving. We recall that to err is human but to forgive is divine. Forgiveness is indeed a divine work in our lives – it is bringing the Kingdom of God to earth into a place of real sin that has hurt us, and possibly left us doubting the very heart of God. It is a core principle of life in God's Kingdom that transcends culture. We live in the Father's house so we are to do things His way.

In Charlotte Brontë's classic novel *Wuthering Heights*, one of the main characters, Heathcliffe, wants revenge on Hindley, who has hurt him deeply:

'I'm trying to settle how to pay Hindley back. I don't care how long I wait, if only I can do it at last. I hope he doesn't die before I do.'

'For shame, Heathcliffe – it is for God to punish wicked people; we should learn to forgive.'

'No. God won't have the satisfaction that I shall – I only wish I knew the best way. Let me alone and I'll plan it out: while I am thinking of that I don't feel the pain.'

In our fallen nature, we want to justify our position and defend ourselves against further hurt. We want to maintain, not break down, our walls of hostility. But God wants us to do the works of His Kingdom to the extent that we will forgive the 'unforgiveable' in others and in ourselves as He has forgiven it in us. He wants to release us from the most trivial and the most heinous damage and treat the wounds underneath so they don't go any deeper.

What is forgiveness?

Before reading any further, please read Matthew 18:21–35.

We could say that forgiveness is relinquishing our 'right' to be judge and jury and handing the offender over to God, who alone is the Righteous Judge. Forgiveness is asking God not to count this sin against the person who has hurt us, but instead to allow it to be covered by the work of the Cross. We are asking the King to forgive the debt that a fellow debtor owes us. It is writing out a cheque of pardon from the account of pardon that we have received ourselves from God. This account is always in credit. Our forgiveness by God and the ongoing work of the Holy Spirit in our lives is a stream of living water that is always available. God is no person's debtor. It is also rising into our true nature in Christ and being empowered to be real and specific and no longer a victim.

It is doing the works of the Father, of the Kingdom, not just singing or talking about it. In worship we may sing that we want to be like Jesus, and this is the opportunity to put that into practice – to bring the radical ways and heart of God into the detail of our lives and be released from ongoing resentment, rage, depression etc. that comes out of unforgiveness. We cannot just follow Christ on the easy bits that we do in our own strength – when He has provided all we need to live beyond that place and bring in His Kingdom.

Forgiveness is going the Way of the Cross so that we die to our desire for revenge and our powerlessness to inflict an adequate punishment into their lives. We then rise without them – not satisfied because we have taken revenge, but because we are free to live our lives according to our hearts, and not theirs.

In this session, we will be looking at the need to process in our hearts all the ways we have been sinned against before God and each other, and ultimately to forgive the offenders before God. (We are not talking about discussing this with the offender at this stage.)

Forgiveness is seeing to it that no one misses out on the grace of God (Hebrews 12:15) even if we feel they don't deserve it!

Why does God command us to forgive?

- All God's commands are for our good and the good of our community
- It is a live and domestic demonstration of the radical and supernatural nature of the Kingdom of God working in our hearts. It is doing the greater works
- It makes use of the Cross so Christ's work is not wasted
- It is the 'family business': it is part of being made in His image
- It is an opportunity to be full of grace and truth like Jesus, even to our enemies. It is grace after the truth of the sin has been fully acknowledged
- It fulfils the command to love our neighbours and our enemies
- God's Kingdom is about liberality of Spirit and not about things being weighed and measured – although God has said that the measure we give will be the measure we get
- It is having the mindset of Christ towards somebody. It is being a new creation
- It is the way we keep ourselves from being like the Pharisees – white-washed sepulchres or hypocrites – living by appearances. We may give the impression of being a mature Christian adult on the outside but inside we can be like a spoilt, bitter child, plotting someone's imminent destruction!
- We may not feel like forgiving, so we wonder if it would be hypocritical to forgive. But Jesus commands us to embark on the process as an act of obedience – and this will involve us in even more uncomfortable feelings. We cannot use our feelings as an excuse not to face the true extent of the sin against us or not to engage in the process of forgiveness
- It is the way we discover if we are living with a heart of flesh or a heart of stone. A heart of flesh feels pain and powerlessness and knows that it is overwhelmed and needs God. It is a place of humility and intimacy that doesn't have all the answers, but does have the living God. A heart of stone feels very little!

- It is the way to face, and then process, the ongoing impact of the Fall in our lives, rather than trying to rationalise or deny it
- We are giving someone a priceless gift that the world cannot give – full of the love and glory of Jesus.

Why is it conditional?

- God cannot endorse hypocrisy
- He does not put us in the embarrassing position of asking something from Him that we are not prepared to give to others. He does not want us only to want blessing and forgiveness for ourselves and not be a channel of it to others
- Much of our own sin can be caused by unforgiveness and can be hiding under the wound of another's sin against us. As we look at this we can get to the full extent of the wounds and our sin patterns.

What if we don't forgive?

- We deny the power of the Cross
- A shadow is cast over our relationship with God, ourselves and others (more than just over the offender)
- We deny ourselves the opportunity of maturing into more degrees of glory
- We are not facing the power/extent of the Fall in our life, nor choosing to participate in redemption
- We are both cut off from, and tied into the offender
- We extend our unforgiveness to others and can become cut off from them too
- We stay as hurt children, justifying self-pity and denying the opportunity of reconciliation
- Cynicism, malice, envy, rage, self-righteousness, pride (at least we are not like them – oh no!) can take hold
- We become like the object of our unforgiveness (as cold, or as scheming)
- We waste time and energy and use our imagination unhelpfully
- We keep our hearts hard.

Why do we hold out?

- One day they will realise what they have done wrong and say sorry
- They will change and come and love us and we won't have jeopardised the relationship
- God will give them their come-uppance and we won't have to
- We may be waiting until we feel forgiveness towards them. This day may never come!

What if we do forgive?

- We will alter the status quo
- We may be blowing the situation out of all proportion and if we start looking at it we may find it was worse than we thought, or less than we thought
- We will lose our power and superiority over them
- We will lose the sense that it was unforgivable
- It is as if they go free without punishment. They go before God, the Righteous Judge, and then the concern is that He may be too nice or too harsh
- We will no longer be able to justify our behaviours
- We might fall apart without our anger to hold us together
- We will reveal the pain of our wound. As we obsess we are keeping control and hoping our revenge will cover the pain.

What are we doing when we forgive?

- We are validating God's truth and 'take' on life; we are recognising the Fall for what it is: unjust, daily, domestic, pervasive etc.
- We are acknowledging our need of God in our lives to deal with something much bigger than our own resources can manage
- We are calling sin by its proper name
- We are getting into the rhythm of the Lord's Prayer – that daily we will both receive and give forgiveness
- We are not leaving the damage caused by people using their free will to hurt us to go unresolved by falsely denying what has happened
- We are respecting our hearts and wanting to keep them cleansed and open to God
- We are allowing our broken hearts to be revealed and then healed
- We are allowing ourselves to be sinners who are also in need of grace
- We are allowing ourselves to be saints who do the works of the Kingdom
- We are respecting ourselves as individuals who should not be treated like this.

Biblical words for 'forgive'

Nasa (Hebrew) = to have a weight lifted off   Aphiemi (Greek) = to let go or send away

Exaleipho (Greek) = cancelling   Salach (Hebrew) = to let go or lift up

Kaphar (Hebrew) = to wipe off a stain or to clean someone's face

How does God forgive?

- He welcomes us and wants us to pour out our hearts to Him (Psalm 51, 62)
- He does not deal with us according to our sins and forgives all our iniquities (Psalm 103)
- He blots out our sins for His own sake and does not remember our sins (Isaiah 43)
- He was wounded for our transgressions and crushed for our iniquities (Isaiah 53)
- He forgives us the whole debt that we really did owe (Matthew 18:21–35)
- He does not sentence us to a lifetime of paying it off
- He asks us to feel the full weight of the debt, and therefore the full relief of the forgiveness.

How does He want us/enable us to forgive others for real sins?

- He wants us to come to Him just as we are – in confusion, in rage, in defeat, whatever is going on
- We need to ask for help to admit that we are powerless over the person
- We allow this to move us deeper into God, rather than allowing it to be an excuse to shy away
- He reminds us of the Cross, of the cycle of dying to self so we can rise free and alive as our real self.

Steps in forgiving those who have sinned against us

1. Come before the Lord and recruit the Trinity (the Father or Jesus or the Holy Spirit) to be our empowerment and advocate and a guide through this
2. Own the hurt inside
3. Be prepared for it to reveal a sin against you
4. Commission: an act, a word, an inference, a slander, an attitude, a judgment, a one-off, habitual Omission: carelessness, thoughtlessness, neglect, deprivation, ignorance, weakness
5. Define the sin as fully as possible
6. Unpack its consequences, such as: it robbed me of trusting my family, I lost my confidence in my appearance, I couldn't join in etc.
7. Own the losses and the cost to you and grieve them
8. Ask the questions you want to of God, especially if it was in the past or in your childhood. You may not get the answer you want — but it will start to ease the pain and bring you closer to God
9. Come before God with the whole package. It's sometimes helpful to state it out loud or to write it down
10. Know that without minimising or condoning the sin, Jesus forgives the person from the Cross, while at the same time wanting to comfort and heal you of its destructive consequences. When you are ready/able seek, before God, to release your own forgiveness to the assailant as clearly and extensively as you can e.g. naming the sin, telling them what it was like for you and what it has meant etc.
11. Release the person into the hands of God the Righteous Judge. He alone knows where to apportion blame, mercy etc. This can be either a relief or a tussle, but may be the moment when we allow God to comfort us most – as we let go. In doing this, we are renouncing our own desire/need to be the Judge and pronounce the sentence. This alone is God's role
12. Allow God to comfort us. We grieve the might-have-beens, the real losses and the damage

13. Then we ask God to show us our sinful reactions and the patterns that have resulted from being sinned against in this way, such as: defensive detachment, hatred, fear, shame etc.

14. We own these and repent of them and seek His forgiveness

15. We may need to repeat this process even for the same sin as further consequences of it become apparent to us

16. We are not able to forget as God does because we are only human. We will remember what happened but hopefully now the sting will have been taken out of it

17. Ultimately our prayer can be that God will bless the offender and use this to establish or deepen their walk with God through the power of the Cross in their lives.

Forgiving ourselves

We will need to forgive ourselves for all the sins that came as a consequence of the damage. This can be difficult. Also, we will need to forgive ourselves for allowing ourselves to be sinned against in this way. 'How could I have let them do this to me? Why didn't I cry out?' Whatever it is we will need to release ourselves from any self-blame, shame, feeling stupid or complicity and allow God to wipe our faces and hearts clean.

The ongoing process

We need to be ready to see our own sinful reactions to being sinned against, and by confession, begin to clean up the wounds underneath. If we are going to involve the offender, we can only do so after much prayer, asking God for wisdom and guidance and seeking the counsel of others. This will include when, where and how. We must also check out our motives and hearts before we do so, otherwise we will not go with humility.

We are all sinners before God. Although God does not have a hierarchy of sin, we do. We can easily feel that those who have hurt us have sinned in a worse way than us. So we do not go to them to:

- Make them feel bad
- Prove we have power over them
- Show our piety or that we are better than them.

Also, we do not go until our wounds are healed and have stopped hurting. We must go by following the guidance of Scripture. We may not be well received or understood, they may not know what we are talking about, they may be defensive or aggressive, they may crumble in remorse and self-pity, they may even be abusive towards us. So, we will need to be very wise and careful.

Lord, forgive us our sins as we forgive those who sin against us. Thank you.

Amen

The Cross (Isaiah chapter 53)

It is only at the Cross that our broken hearts can be bound up and healed. At the Cross the cycle of self-pity, detachment, revenge or isolation is broken and the effects of this sin can be dealt with. The cycle has to be atoned for, the guilt of it taken away and the consequences of it in our lives redeemed. This is both for us as sinners and for the ways we have been sinned against. As well as sin bringing death and cutting us off from God, Isaiah chapter 53 gives us a graphic account of sin's effects in our world, and therefore on us:

- Marring the image of God in us and robbing us of our real beauty and honour as people
- Despising ourselves, rejection, abandonment, self-hatred – going from pillar to post
- Suffering and sorrow – no joy or relief in our lives
- Sickness and distress, grief, anger and shame
- Wrongdoing, rebellion, corruption and sexual sins
- Punishment, fear and oppression
- Guilt and false guilt.

As we come to the Cross we can begin by naming the deficits or sinful ways of our families. This will set us on the path to healing. As we start to distinguish between a wound, a grief, a sorrow, a sin against us or a sin by us, we can process them properly at the Cross. We will find it to be the place of exchange and healing that we need – receiving comfort for pain, consolation for sorrow, hope for disappointment, peace for rage, belonging for rejection etc.

A few points as we end this section

- It is vital that we call abuse by its proper name so that we can acknowledge the full extent of the trauma
- Shame robs us of living life to the full and dictates our behaviour and perceptions more than we realise
- When we are tempted we have not yet sinned
- We are both sinned against and sinners – so will need to receive forgiveness for ourselves and release it to others
- Those who cling to worthless idols forfeit the grace that could be theirs (Jonah 2:8)
- To err is human, to forgive is divine – it really is!

NOTES

NOTES

III

SECTION 4 - SEXUALITY AND RELATIONSHIPS

So God created man in his own image,
in the image of God he created him;
male and female he created them

(GENESIS 1:27)

CHAPTER 22 – GENDER AND SEXUALITY

We have already considered the inter-relationship between our sexuality and our spirituality. We have also identified the slide into sexual sin that can occur when we are carrying shame and needing grace, when our hearts are in pain, or when we have a wrong sense of entitlement. This can be in fantasy or in action.

So, in this chapter, we will look in more detail at sexuality itself, in its many forms.

Sexuality may be viewed as including our spirituality, sex, gender and orientation. From our sexuality flows the direction towards which we look for apparent – or actual – completion and connection in an emotional, spiritual and bodily way. Our sexuality is about where and with whom we want to be known in our nakedness, and to whom we want to give blessing and trust through the expression of all that we are.

Genetic **sex** is determined at conception and in most people is either XX (woman) or XY (man). Various hormonal interactions during development in the womb affect how our body and sexual organs develop. These interactions also affect brain development usually resulting in an increase in the verbal areas of women and visual areas in men. At birth we are assigned our sex according to how our genitals appear as either male or female. Some individuals are born with variations in sex characteristics including chromosomes, gonads, sex hormones, or genitals that are not typically male or female. These individuals are called 'intersex'.

In today's culture, when not applied to biological sex, the term **"gender"** is used to describe the characteristics that are attributed to, and differentiate between, our concept of masculinity and femininity. The term also covers gender roles, that can differ between cultures, and gender identity - our individual sense of our own gender and how secure we feel as a gendered being of a determined sex.

"Orientation", applies to the direction of our romantic attractions which develop as we grow up and may be fluid. The only fixed part of these aspects is our genetic makeup, which will not change after conception. All other aspects may be influenced by the environment we grow up in including the chemicals within that environment.

Therefore, our expression of sexuality, our sense of gender and orientation, and how we express them, may be influenced by many relational factors.

These might include:

- Our family attitudes and story
- Our upbringing
- Our place in the family and our siblings
- Our role models, or lack of them
- Our sense of self and of well-being
- Our personality and our will
- Our perceptions and choices
- Our theology
- Our culture and our reaction to it
- How well our needs were understood and met
- How well we were trained not to expect instant gratification for our needs
- How we were wounded and how we reacted
- How well we were able to take our place in our same gender peer group
- How good relationships were with our opposite gender peer group.

It is vital that we allow ourselves to be our own unique version of a man or a woman with many different aspects of God's image making us who we are. We are not to conform to cultural stereotypes, nor to compare ourselves with others.

We could say that sexuality is an acceptance of being a gender person and allowing this to be expressed in righteousness and care. Taking a biblical point of view, it is also about respecting other people and not using them as objects – both in practice and in fantasy. It will also mean that the only possibility for a full sexual union is within the covenant relationship of marriage between one man and one woman. As a single person we can feel fully accepted and fulfilled as a man or a woman, in spite of abstaining from sexual relationships.

We need a real sense of our own personhood and to feel solid in ourselves in order to allow something as dynamic and demanding as our sexuality to have full expression in who we are. A secure sense of self enables us to give rather than just take from others.

Similarly, if we feel insecure in our gender and have not really joined our same gender peer group, then we can feel seriously lacking as a whole person, as our gender is an integral part of how we see ourselves as people. We need gender security to have a solid sense of self. If we still feel vulnerable and needy, our sexuality can become a liability for us and not a blessing for another.

As Romans 8:23–24 describes, we are carrying the unmet needs of our orphan state. Sadly, these unmet needs will have had a profound effect on our sexuality. We are literally groaning with pain, anxiety and insecurity because we have not been cared for and filled up as God intended. Many of our immoral and desperate behaviours are just ways to ease, manage, cover up, deny and press through the pain of the Fall that we share with all creation.

Many of us are living so far from wholeness in the area of sexuality that we need a radical overhaul of our perceptions, feelings and behaviour. This means welcoming God openly into our physical bodies and minds to heal and redeem us in all our orphan places. We must take courage and name the ways we are living under the Fall and invite God to move us into a place of peace and blessing where we are no longer needy or demanding of others, but ready to serve and give. This will take us outside our comfort zones.

For example, for men: if we have viewed women with disdain or fear; detached from them; wanted to punish them, or lived in a passive place of non-communication or indifference, then there is a journey of grace to be travelled. This will take us through the healing of these fallen responses, including the underlying wounds, and into the middle ground of peaceful co-existence. We will need to leave our parents behind and bring closure to any ongoing unhealthy relating to them. Then, out on the other side, we will start to see women as equally valuable and complementary to us as men. Rather than just needing women on a new level, we will be ready to serve and bless them: even laying down our lives in blessing to them, as Christ laid down His life for us. This transformation is wonderful, costly, cherishing and honouring and it results from deep repentance and a more healed heart. Our love and laying down of ourselves for women is the polar opposite of blame-shifting or disdain or fear. It is a life-giving journey through new terrain that is only possible with God.

For women: if we have viewed men as unnecessary; pathetic; frightening; beyond our comprehension; powerful; arbitrary, or in any way that does not match how God sees them, we too will have a journey to make. If we have bent into men, looked to them to tell us who we are or viewed them as a source of life for us, then this will need to be addressed. Again, the way ahead involves naming our negative perceptions and behaviour before God and looking to Him for healing. We then allow God to reach deep into our wounds and perceptions to bring about restoration and change. We too will need to leave our immature reactions with God and break free from our unhealthy connections to our parents. As we pass through the middle ground of truce or reconciliation, we need to keep going into a new place of respect and need and receiving – allowing God to name us and resource us. God will take us to new places of vulnerability and receptivity that may well be the polar opposite of our former stance of control or fear. We can take our full rightful place alongside men, giving what is uniquely ours to our relationships with them.

God wants us to live out these radical transformations from our fallen state as counter to our culture. As we allow a new palpable respect and ease with each other to become evident, then we demonstrate the power of the gospel to each other and the world. This is the reversal of the curse of the Fall into blessing.

God's original purpose

In creation, God made us in His image, male and female. He gave us the desire to give, the capacity for intimacy and a yearning to know and be known, both by Him and each other. Like Him, we are also spirit, meaning we can commune and live far beyond the realms of our flesh and instinct. At the time of creation, the mystery of being made male and female meant that we could recognise each other as equal fellow human beings, while having the challenge of relating to someone different. Making us male and female was also the way that God ordained that we should become one flesh.

Such a climactic and glorious union and communion needed to be honoured and protected by a covenant relationship. Within this safeguard, the complementarity of men and women could be explored fully in day-to-day living, and the sexual union would both strengthen and express the commitment and exclusivity of the covenant. This faithfulness isn't an annoying constraint.

Instead it is the appropriate and natural desire of two people who, being made in the image of a holy and life-giving God, enjoy their trust and delight in each other.

Our sexual union is also the means through which we share in the wonder of procreation. Again, God wanted to protect this awesome act within a covenant – expressing the commitment, stability and ongoing presence of Himself to us. We then pass this on to our children.

In His wisdom, God the Creator knew how powerful this experience would be for us. He knew our need for a covenant, but He also went further to use it as a symbol, not only of our relationship with Him, but also as a picture of His relationship with us.

Israel was to be a faithful bride to her Creator. Christ's love for the church and a husband's love for his wife are both expressions of this commitment and joyous devotion – even to the point of laying down His life. But, as Paul says in Ephesians 5:32, "This is a profound mystery". God sets Christ's love for the church in the context of a man and a woman both leaving their father and mother and becoming united as one flesh. With our love and worship of God, and His love and passion for us being symbolised in this way, we are to honour the sacredness of this covenant union.

The following material covers a range of relational aspects, not all of which may be relevant for your situation at this point.

Singleness

In a highly explicit and sexualised society we may feel that it is especially difficult to be single. We need to remember that Jesus was teaching during Roman times, in the land of false gods who's worship was entwined with sexual practices. Jesus' call to sexual purity was as radical for His contemporaries as it is for us. Of course, Jesus Himself was single. He calls us to bring the powerful prophetic impact of celibacy and abstinence to a lost and hurting world. This is another image of the contrast between the Kingdom of God and the ways of the world. As the dire consequences of sexual 'freedom' and a permissive society become increasingly apparent, so the wisdom of God's ways will hit home. We think of the tragedy of so much teenage sexual experience and pregnancy, of sexually transmitted diseases and the resulting infertility, of the shame and worthlessness that many feel and the lack of intimacy and numbness that we can descend into.

We must be careful not to make a spouse, a relationship or the ideal of marriage into an idol.

In singleness and celibacy we experience the discipline of submitting our desires for sexual intimacy and passion, and orgasm, to God. We forgo the intimate companionship of another, perhaps into old age. We may feel that we have not been desired and sought out and chosen; we will potentially not have children of our own. We will experience aloneness and a lack of sharing day-by-day and in the larger moments of life; we will never know what it was like to be married. These losses apply whatever our orientation. But those who are married may experience pain of their own: disappointment, control, childlessness, lack of emotional space, abuse or unfaithfulness. For many, marriage is not a picnic. Those who are married may find themselves single again later in life, if they outlive their spouse or divorce.

In abstinence or celibacy, we are living out the truth that sexuality and spirituality are inextricably linked. We live out the promise that there is a higher love to be sought and known by everyone, and that there is a love to be experienced that transcends any sexual pleasure. By forgoing instant gratification, we stay in the grace of God. As we channel our devotion towards the Lord and press deeply into His incarnational presence, He can meet us with a deep fulfilment and the promise of life. The sexual union is only a transient earthly expression of our union with God. It will be superseded by intimacies and ecstasies far beyond all we can ask or imagine, and these will be eternal. God is able to put fire in our hearts and enable us to have a foretaste of this that many marrieds never find.

For those who move on from singleness into marriage, the value of abstinence up until this point provides a strong foundation for marriage. The discipline of pre-marital abstinence relieves the couple of the pressure of comparison and helps to establish faithfulness.

It is hard too for those of us who are widowed or divorced, and we will also need to find that higher calling and resist the temptation to see ourselves as a special case. God is faithful, and we may well be the means of bringing deeper and wholesome relationships into the body of Christ that can bless many other single people.

Marriage

Marriage is an opportunity for the radical ways of Christ to be lived out. Husbands are called to lay down their lives for their wives as Christ laid down His, and to love her as their own body. Wives are called to respond and receive this (to submit to this love), and to allow themselves to be honoured and cherished. For those of us with control issues this can be very hard.

Most of us who are married will have had a few sessions of marriage preparation, discussing who will put out the bins or make the tea in the morning, but we will have received very little guidance on our sexual relationship in the marriage bed. Once we returned from our honeymoon we were left to it – with no one even checking how it went. But we will have brought all our baggage into the marriage.

In marriage, we have entered into a covenant relationship before God. If we encounter disappointment or difficulties early on, we need to own these, seek good counsel and commit to do all we can to resolve them. It does not help to detach, become cynical or to punish each other.

Two becoming one will throw up many issues:

- Commitment
- Trust
- Personal space
- Being relaxed and intimate
- Feeling 'this is it', especially if we got off to a difficult start
- Our mother and father issues
- Comparison
- Misogyny
- Objectifying women and not relating to them as real people
- Fear of men because of past abuse or victim mode, etc.

We must not be too proud to seek help when we need it. Allowing ourselves to be mentored by an older couple in a useful and frank way will be invaluable. If there has been a history of sexual sin or relational difficulties in either, or both, parties then this is even more necessary.

a. Coming clean

Ideally before we got married we should have had the opportunity to brief each other openly, about our past life and experiences; the opportunity to tell our story. This may reveal earlier sexual sin. This should be done with wisdom and care as it could well be make or break time. We will hopefully demonstrate an understanding of our behaviour and a realistic assessment of where we are now. Our prospective spouse should have been allowed to ask for clarification and been able to ascertain whether there was denial, or a minimising of any sin. Each could then decide how to reach a workable level of trust in the marriage and whether any agreements needed to be made for future disclosure. We can never assume that we will keep each other in the picture. Shame and rationalising of our behaviour can easily set in.

If this sharing has never happened then it may be important to do this, either in private or with a wise and trusted third party present. If there are difficult disclosures to make then it is wise to involve someone else sooner rather than later, and perhaps for each to have separate conversations with the third party before all meeting together.

b. Getting clean

If there is past or present sin, then a time of confession and repentance is essential. This needs to be done, not to shame, but to cleanse and rebuild trust. Explicit giving and receiving of forgiveness and perhaps a sharing of Holy Communion will be needed. If trust is shaky, then it may be necessary to ask if there is anything else that needs to be shared and a system of accountability set up.

c. Ongoing accountability

If it is the husband who has been acting out or sinning in fantasy (such as through the use of pornography) then this can skew the marriage relationship with the wife being put into a mothering/care-taking role or being seen as a constraint. It is wise to agree that the husband has external accountability. This is not easy but moves past the wife's dilemma that the husband must share everything/but if he does anything again he is out! The church should ideally be part of the process. Equally the wife may need to be accountable. It is vital that each party's needs are taken fully into account and regularly reviewed in this process.

d. Relationship issues

These may not involve sinful behaviour on anyone's part but can cause huge pain as we transfer past hurts on to each other. We can stir up old scenarios of fear and shame. We can get stuck in blame-shifting and detachment. Again, we will usually need help to identify what is happening and which parts of the difficulty belong to each person.

e. Being out of balance

Some of us who have been married for some time may have got out of balance with each other.

One may have pursued more healing than the other and may see very clearly what could/should be happening in the relationship. This can be very painful and frustrating for both husband and wife. We are not to sit in judgment, but to attend to our own journey with God. He can use this as a way of deepening our fellowship with Him and of us growing in grace, patience and kindness. As we resist the temptation to become proud or resentful we can pray for the other person and seek new and better ways to bless them. Abusive relationships will need good counsel and care.

It is possible that some of us have even given up on our marriage in our hearts, and are just going through the motions. We will need to face this despair and offer our hearts to God to be comforted and softened. The way ahead will be complex, but we can know His guidance and comfort in the midst of it.

Love and lust

We must make the distinction between love and lust and between intimacy and bodily connection. Love and intimacy are about giving and being known. They should bring renewal and peace and stability. There is a kindness and preferring of the other that wants good for them. This can be expressed in all kinds of relationships. Love and intimacy come out of a place of plenty and of allowing one's self to be filled by God.

Lust and bodily connection are about taking and using. There is a desperation that ends in shame and leaves us unsatisfied and disorientated – even angry – because we are in the law of diminishing returns and neither side has anything fulfilling to give. Again, we can use people in many ways long before it reaches a sexual union. (Think through how you may be using people for your own ends. You may want to write your thoughts on a 'notes' page.)

Attractions

For some, our sexual attractions may not cause us any concern. For others, it can be an aspect of our lives that is filled with tension, frustration and pain. This tension may be due to our attractions conflicting with our understanding of what the Bible teaches about sex and relationships or because of moral and legal reasons.

We may have become aware of our attractions from an early age or in our teenage years, or they may even have manifested later in our lives. Research shows that our attractions can be fluid over a lifetime.

During our life journey we may have experienced some of the following:

- Hiding our sexual attractions due to a fear of people's reactions and judgement
- Fear of being open and 'coming out'
- Feeling different and misunderstood
- Rejection or fear of rejection by family, peers, church and community
- A sense of shame due to our attractions or actions; present or past
- Being ridiculed, shamed or bullied
- Feeling excluded from groups
- Isolation and loneliness

- Frustration if we choose not to act on our attractions e.g. towards the same sex
- Inner conflict if we are married, love our spouse and want to stay faithful despite experiencing attractions to others - of either gender
- Sadness and grief if we have pictured ourselves being married and having a family yet this feels unattainable
- Frustration when Christians quote Scripture without showing empathy and understanding
- Fear of being labelled or seen as a special case
- Angry with God as He seems unfair
- Fear of God's disapproval.

Whatever our experience has been, each one of us has our own unique story and will need the Holy Spirit to guide us in a personal and individual way.

Many of our wounds have happened through relationships and the Body of Christ is the primary place God has provided for us to receive comfort, acceptance and dignity.

We need to belong and find a safe church family/community where we can experience love, belonging and friendship. As for all of us, there is a journey of connecting at a deeper level in a variety of friendships with both men and women.

Our attractions are only one aspect of our personhood and we need to keep it in balance with other parts of ourselves. We need to explore ways to express ourselves through a variety of activities that give us life and fulfilment such as: music, nature, study, worship and prayer, hobbies, volunteering and joining interest groups.

Taking our place with peers will be especially important for us if we have been isolated or felt rejected in the past.

God is our Creator and He knows us intimately. He invites us to come as we are and pour out our hearts in His presence. Here we can receive affirmation and acceptance and know our true worth and value. We can fully know that our identity is in Christ and have our hearts strengthened so that we can become rooted and established in the Father's love.

I pray that out of his glorious riches he may strengthen you with power through his Spirit in your inner being,
so that Christ may dwell in your hearts through faith.
And I pray that you, being rooted and established in love, may have power,
together with all the Lord's holy people, to grasp how wide and long and high and deep is the love of Christ,
and to know this love that surpasses knowledge -
that you may be filled to the measure of all the fullness of God.
(EPHESIANS 3:16-19)

Promiscuity

We may well need to face the addictive quality of this and read on! Promiscuity has at its root the avoidance of intimacy; the risk of rejection; a fear of committing to a relationship and wanting a quick fix of comfort, attention, pain relief, rebellion or 'return' without any investment. It has become endemic in the culture as people become less confident of their own worth and their capacity to do relationships. People are more isolated and in need of comfort and connection but are unable to dare to commit to an ongoing relationship or to be known. Because we are looking for something profound that we cannot receive from trivial sex, we will be in a cycle of disappointment and hurt – particularly for women. Every time we give ourselves we lose some of our self-respect and personhood, yet we receive none of the security and love we yearn for in return. This is why the breaking of each one-flesh union before God is so important because it enables us to reclaim the fragmented self which we have left behind in each sexual relationship.

The consequences of anonymous encounters, one-night stands, sexual addiction, drugs, sado-masochism, group sex etc. can all be faced with God's compassion and grace. We can come to understand what it has been about for us and make a fresh start – receiving forgiveness, cleansing and support.

Fantasy and masturbation

As with all our issues around sexuality, this is about our heart. Who is the object of our devotion and who is our source of life? One of the problems here is that the underlying issues may have gone unacknowledged for a long time. We may be dealing with deeply rooted anxiety and genital pain, with profound emptiness and sexual tension because this has become eroticised. Our pain-relieving or pleasure-giving strategy may have become established and then compulsive, before we had any hope of any other remedy.

The compulsion becomes an obsession and, for some, the need and the stimuli literally fill our day and we can get very little else done or make any meaningful relationships. Only our fantasy life feels valid. It is adultery in the heart. The rest of life seems boring and having an orgasm is our only chance of feeling alive and temporarily stopping the obsession.

The irony is, of course, that the intimacy and connection that we crave becomes increasingly elusive as we become more and more numb and obsessed with our needs. The shame builds and we can become even more isolated.

As we have seen, the pleasure and purpose of an orgasm is reserved for a covenant heterosexual marriage with the foundation of intimacy, commitment and relationship in the context of giving as well as receiving. Biologically, it is not a solo activity. Through masturbation, we are taking a shortcut, instead of putting in the effort of building relationship and committing for life. For those who are married, it is a place of retreat and self-preservation rather than persevering into renewed communication and union.

Although masturbation may have begun by bringing us relief, it soon becomes our master. It can lead us into a fantasy-based life or a shame-based life, both of which are robbery. We are made for life in all its abundance. The good news is that there is a path to freedom. Like everything else, it starts with naming the problem for what it is and sharing with a trusted person.

Frigidity

We may feel that our sexuality has become unsafe or we lack the emotional capacity for it to be expressed. Contributing factors include: overworking, stress, anxiety, tiredness, depression, fear of rejection and intimacy, poor body image or feeling undesirable.

Where there is a history of abuse or other distressing circumstances, we may well have frozen into a hurt, confused, silent place that we have tried to detach from. We will need to own this split and the fact that we are stuck and invite God into the terror and confusion. This can be a reaction to abuse, the behaviour of our siblings or peers, a fear of adulthood and a detachment from our sexuality. A lack of sense of being can rob us of our confidence and subject us to comparison and fear of rejection.

Am I dealing with any of these aspects? If so, how do they manifest?

Addictions

An addiction is a pathological relationship with a mood-altering experience.

This relationship can be with anything that we use to make us feel 'better' – less anxious, less vulnerable, less likely to be rejected, less afraid, or more powerful, more alive, more 'connected', not different, not left out, not ashamed. We can use addictions to ease our boredom or to fill up the in-between gaps in life.

Many 'everyday' addictions are tolerated, or even endorsed, by society or church. They can be: work;

playing computer games; using social media; appeasing; rescuing others; shopping; peacemaking; exercise or running (to displace feelings); eating; watching TV; reading romantic novels (to try to feel something). Others are regarded as more problematic: drinking; gambling; eating disorders or self-harming. These are non-sexualised addictions, but at their root they are ways of displacing bad feelings or feeling nothing.

Do I have any addictive coping mechanisms? If so, what are they?

In addiction there is:

• Difficulty taking responsibility

• Crisis in trust

• Numbing down

• A sense of being different and a victim to it all

• Cycle of failure

• Lots of pain

• A fear of the gaps in life when we confront ourselves and our emptiness

• A need to replace one addiction with another.

We will need to trace back in our lives to identify when and where we have detached from the real. Or we may have never attached to life at a primal level and we will need healing for this.

In addiction, we seek an illusion of control, power, love, connection, adequacy and comfort. These deficits are from our primal wounds and family relationships (or lack of them), and our isolation, usually at puberty.

Our primal wounds and our isolation both cut us off from any godly and good human contact. This is the very thing that would find us in our isolation and succeed in bringing us the comfort and connection that we desperately need. As we get drawn into addictive behaviours, we embark on the journey of diminishing returns and become more withdrawn from real relationships, for fear of being found out or rejected.

Because none of our attempts to ease our pain really meet our unmet needs, we feel emptier than ever. We then either try to get out and fail, or go further in, hoping that more will satisfy us. It's like being hungry and going to wash the car and wondering why that hasn't eased our hunger.

Sexual addiction

In sexual addictions there is:

- Fear of rejection
- Very little sense inside of a real person who is as valid as anyone else
- Withdrawal from real human contact
- A seeking to bond to something undemanding so we can say: 'I am in control here, as long as I have this I am not alone'
- A transitory illusory connection with an object, not a real person.

When we have exposed ourselves to sexually explicit imagery (through pornography, fantasy or with people), we have opened up our God-given imagination to ungodly images. This is particularly true for men who remember visually – and so the imprint goes into the system and soon our brain chemistry starts to change. As we try to manage our consciences, we may well have repressed what we know to be right and inadvertently caused a huge build up of sexual and emotional pressure.

So, in sexual addiction, why is it that there is pain that is too much to bear and needs to be repressed at such a huge cost to everyone? Every sinful activity destroys someone else as well as us: every image needs to be posed for, every video produced, every phone call taken, every track covered up.

In sexual addiction we are also seeking connection without relational risk. It allows us to avoid the cost of being known and of knowing someone else 'warts and all'! It is the ultimate 'trying to get something for nothing' on which our society thrives. When we have become this numb and cut off from our true feelings, only a sexual encounter has the possibility of being climactic enough to be felt. In our weakness, sex is power.

The cycle of addiction

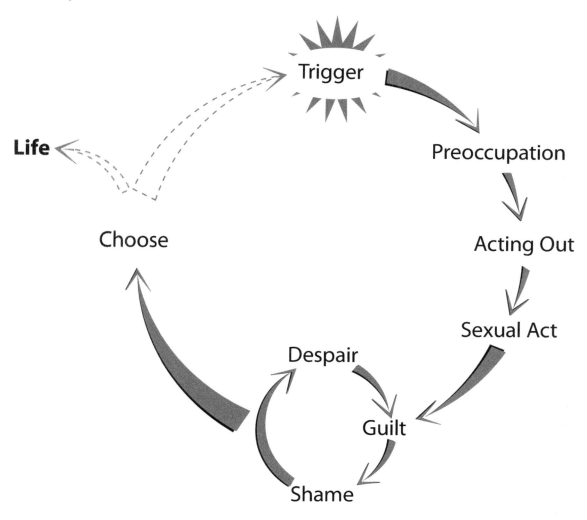

Trigger: External: stimuli through our senses e.g. imagery, a song, a person or a place. Internal: our emotional state e.g. rejection, stress, lonely, empty, bored, shame, anger or unresolved conflict.

Preoccupation: Pressure builds over a long or short period of time, obsessive thoughts, distorted thinking, rationalising, fantasising, planning, scheming, taking steps, ritualisation.

Acting out: Going ahead, ignoring consequences, detaching and splitting off.

Sexual act: Any act that usually ends in orgasm.

Guilt/shame/despair: We feel pain and guilt when we 'wake up' and realise we have fallen again. For a moment the denial is shattered and we feel remorse as we recognise our double life. Despair follows when we still feel empty inside, trapped, powerless and out of control. Condemnation and self-contempt builds. Shame increases which only confirms and adds to the shame already in our heart.

Content above based on material from the following book: Patrick Carnes, Contrary to Love - Helping the Sexual Addict, (Hazelden Foundation, Minnesota, 1994).

Choose:
There are two options:

1. **Stay in denial** and go on needing more. This leads to further isolation and the infliction of more sin and pain on to ourselves, as well as others.

2. **Face the pain** and to own that this area of our life is out of control. We admit that we need help and that we want to stop the compulsive behaviour. We allow God to find our underlying wounds and, with Him, face the pain we have been seeking to avoid. We must be ready to believe that grace can include us and that we can come into a place of trust before God.

The point of making this decision is the crisis that everyone needs to reach. Both are painful options. One keeps us in the addictive cycle, leading to more pain, shame and isolation. The other, despite the challenge of facing the addiction and the pain in our hearts, ultimately leads to more life and connection with ourselves, God and others.

Please read Appendix C: Finding grace in sexual sin and addiction.

Review of sexuality

Healthy sexuality comes as we live out the fruit of the Spirit with each other. This creates genuine intimacy, care and connection within safe boundaries.

Key issues

"Male and female He created them" (1 Genesis 1:27). This was God's blessing for us but we may have difficulties enjoying our gender and living it out well.

"Therefore a man shall leave his father and mother and make a covenant with his wife and the two shall become one flesh" (Genesis 2:24). So we need to leave if we are ever to cleave! If we have stayed as an orphan, we will not have felt accompanied enough to leave our mother and father well. Or, we may have detached from them into a place of isolation.

We have not left our father and mother properly because:

- We never really connected in the first place, so we stay holding on
- We have had our relationship prematurely ruptured, for example through death or going to boarding school
- We have defensively detached
- Our father has never drawn us away from our mother and released us into adulthood
- We have never gone into adulthood
- We still need their accompanying in an unhealthy way, such as financial dependence
- We have not processed issues of the heart
- We have not drawn new boundaries to define and defend our new relationship.

We have not attached well (if we are married) or allowed ourselves healthy, safe relationships (if we are single) because:

- We do not have a sense of being to give
- We cannot trust
- We still have infantile rage and the need to control
- We are at odds with our own gender or that of others
- We are stuck in comparison with others
- We are disappointed and withhold
- We have too much shame
- We live in desperation and have no heart to give
- We are unable to relax
- We experience perfectionism and control
- We have unresolved attachment issues.

So, all of us will have some areas of our sexuality that we need to bring to God, because we are as fallen in this part of our lives as any other. Our culture has idolised sex and has taken us away from God's original purpose. Our testimony in this area is always prophetic and proclaims God's glory and the full extent of His salvation.

A prayer

> *Lord, we offer You our whole being, including our sexuality. We are so sorry for the ways in which Your good gift has become a liability for us; where we have been tainted by, or participated in, our sexualised culture. Forgive us where we have hardened our hearts and indulged in self-pity or rage or passivity.*
>
> *We ask that You will enable us no longer to be conformed the pattern of this world, but to be transformed by the renewal of our minds, so that we may prove for ourselves that Your will, O Lord, is good and acceptable and perfect. We ask that we may present our bodies to You as a living sacrifice. Cleanse us through and through, that we may now be set apart for You and be alive to Your will.*
>
> *We ask this through the Cross of Jesus, our Saviour.*
>
> *Amen*

NOTES

CHAPTER 23 – BEING SONS AND DAUGHTERS OF GOD, PART 1

Our hearts

We are made in the image of God and His nature transcends our gender. This means we will each have a unique blend of what we call the masculine and feminine. Gender is therefore not about sex, but about glory. It is our unique version of being a man or woman that brings glory to God, even when it is still a work in progress.

The feminine in us all - both men and women

As the Bride of Christ, all of us need to be comfortable with being feminine in relation to God and value the feminine aspects of our nature:

- To receive without shame
- To be intimate without fear
- To value and respect our hearts
- To rightly use our imaginations.

During the course so far, we have already thought about God's attributes, but let's just mention a few again here. He is: majestic; beautiful; tender; warrior; persevering; creative; merciful; wise; loving; just; powerful; almighty; mysterious; delightful; fatherly; motherly; strong, compassionate and so on.

Some of these aspects of God's nature fall more obviously into those of a man or a woman, but many others are shared because of our common humanity. We are totally equal in God's plan as image bearers. It may be that the word 'helpmeet', or whatever word is in the translation of the Bible that you use, jars for us as women. It can feel as if we have been relegated to being just a helper, the stagehand, the also ran. We remember from the Creation chapter that the word 'helpmeet' expressed mutuality, complementarity and common life in God.

But it is not a question of men being the true image bearers and women adding a few niceties. Nothing could be farther from the truth. Women are as essential as men in revealing the image of God on earth. The word 'helpmeet' can also be translated as life giver or lifesaver. At last, we are bone of his bone. We are co-heirs – in Christ there is no competition. Women are just as honourable, substantial and essential as conveyors of God's image as men. We deny half the human race their glory, their dignity and their place in God's creation if we disagree with this. Our humanity and our being men and women together is the best way that God has to show His image and glory. He always makes the best, and that includes each of us. We are here to display His splendour to the whole of creation.

Whatever our history, we must all rise into this complementarity with confidence, humility and authority. Otherwise we will not honour or live out the differences between men and women, nor will we enjoy who we are in Christ. Many of us have not had any glory or complementarity modelled for us. We may not be able to think of a single 'good enough' role model. We are also living in a culture that breeds confusion and rebellion.

Keeping an open heart to God – The Angel Gabriel and Mary (Luke 1)

In the first chapter of Luke's Gospel we read that the angel Gabriel visits Mary at home on an ordinary day. He uses her name and calls her "O favoured one". From this we see that God wants to bless us in our everyday lives and that His presence is not meant to shame us, but to honour us and to bring us favour – the favour many of us are yearning for, but have never known.

God invites us not to be afraid. God knows that He is awesome and terrifying, as well as tender and true. He knows many of us have issues with authority and find it hard to believe in benevolent strength and in favour, not shame. It is often this fear that makes us resist God and say: "Not now, not today. I need you but I want to resist you and keep my independence."

Receiving His Living Word

God wants us to receive His word of life in us, actually, again and again, and to allow it to develop into life and salvation within us. This is not an abstract concept – He wants it to develop within the flesh and blood of our lives. We are to allow Kingdom life to be birthed in us and through us.

When God sent the angel Gabriel to Mary she listened and responded, which is another way of receiving. How much more do we need to listen so that we can actually receive living words from God? This is in secret at first, and it then becomes apparent: God's restoring of our gender is like this. As we allow His living word a home within us, and we nurture it and allow it to grow into whatever He wills, our restoration will become apparent and glorious and alive. So we must nurture and bless what God is doing and allow it to come to pass.

Mary was entrusted with Jesus and made a home for Him. We are to do that too and make a home for Him in our lives, whatever change this means in us. Many of us hardly know what this part of us even looks like, but we are to want more. This may mean we change beyond recognition but this is nothing to be ashamed of.

The power of the Holy Spirit

Again, we are not too proud to need a Saviour. The angel Gabriel said to Mary, "The power of the Holy Spirit will come upon you". Of course, this is how God will work His healing in us. Mary had probably prayed many times for salvation to come to God's people, Israel. We too may have prayed many times for healing for ourselves and for God's Kingdom. And here, she was being part of the answer. But she could not manage it by herself. She had to receive from God and then collaborate with Him. Her life was at risk – sometimes the challenge will feel immense for us too.

We need others

Mary may have felt very alone (What would Joseph and her society say?) But God had already provided Elizabeth to be there for her. So too can we trust that God will provide the right companions we need on the journey. We will also need to be known and receive from each other.

Our imaginations

We need real imagination to believe God's promises for us and to allow Him to transform us into more "degrees of glory" (2 Corinthians 3:18). Where our imagination is filled with ourselves, pornography, self-hatred, fantasy or even nothing, we will need God's cleansing. Part of despising the feminine is to despise the prophetic and the heart.

So our imaginations, our hearts, our capacity and desire to receive before God all need to be reviewed and made right. After all, we are coming, "To Him who is able to do immeasurably more than all we can ask or imagine, according to the power at work within us" (Ephesians 3:20).

We are in the Kingdom of God rather than the kingdom of this world (where what you see is what you get, even if you get plenty of fantasy!) In God's Kingdom we live in reality.

We wait for the redemption of our bodies. For in this hope we were saved. Now hope that is seen is not hope. For who hopes for what he sees?
But if we hope for what we do not see, we wait for it with patience

(ROMANS 8:23–25)

Hope of redemption, of salvation and of being something more that we can imagine is not magical or wishful thinking, but it is not of this world. It is 'other' and we need to offer our hearts and imaginations to God, for more and more salvation, so we can live in that place of peace and glory and hope and humility.

The feminine quality, before God, for both men and women, is acceptance:

• Of my heart and of intimacy

• That I need to receive everything, including life

• That I need to listen

• That I need to still my heart, voice and thoughts

- That there is more to life than I can see
- That I need my imagination to apprehend it all
- That God comes not to shame me, but to draw me to Himself and give me His favour.

Being a daughter of God

(Primarily for daughters, but also applies to sons)

Introduction

So, how do we feel about being a woman? Is it a blessing, a threat, a great unknown? We may have rightly resisted the stereotypes offered by our culture, or even by our Christian community, but we may have little else in their place. It can be hard to feel at home in the world of women. The emphasis on beauty, delight, being the helpmeet, being relational and valuing the heart can make us feel vulnerable or angry.

This is not God's intention, hence the importance of inner beauty and character. He wants our gender to be a blessing and for us to be comfortable in who we are. It can be like finding a well-cut dress: it may be something we would never look twice at in a shop, but when we try it on we find that there is a unique style to suit each of us that is a good fit. If we have cut ourselves off from our gender, He can find us our rightful place.

Biologically

In general terms, men seem to be more visual and concrete in their thinking and women are more intuitive and imaginative. We have less physical strength than men, but plenty of stamina! We have more hormones evident in our daily lives than men and live with monthly menstrual cycles. We bear children. We are usually more aware and welcoming of our feelings, even dictated to by them, and we often define ourselves by our relationships.

What are the biological truths about women, and what might be some of the areas of God's nature that we especially convey?

What are my key areas of identification as a woman?

Our answers may have included:

His beauty; compassion; mercy; understanding; comfort; wisdom; mystery; grace; delight; involvement; attention to detail; creativity; that life is not just functional; His heart; He is relational – a Trinity; His passion, His Sabbath rest; the rhythms of life; risk, faith…

What other aspects of God's character do we enjoy?

Women are the final crowning glory of creation. But soon after creation we experienced a fallen world; we lapsed in our obedience and reached for the tree.
The consequences of the Fall for women include:

- We become a victim of blame-shifting not covering
- In attacking our radiance, Satan mars God's glory in us
- We despise our beauty, and yet yearn for it, wrestling with self-contempt
- We feel cut off and in contention with men
- Mystery is hard to sustain and if it feels too vulnerable it is given away too easily
- We lose confidence in our discernment and start to value only masculine ways of thinking
- Our passion becomes a liability and is seen as hysteria or being demanding
- We can tolerate pain as our lot.

Instead of helpmeet and co-heir we can become – or be perceived as – controlling and needy. Much of our behaviour will then be concerned with managing this. Also, men's behaviour becomes their reaction to this: how to resist being emasculated, and how to defend against our competence and neediness, which can feel overwhelming for them.

Our woundedness

God's image is marred

Satan was the most beautiful of the angels. He is described as "Lucifer – the bearer of light", but after his rebellion he was banished. In retaliation, he wounded woman who epitomised the beauty of God. In wounding woman, he was deeply wounding God and His glory.

Inner beauty

We can be stuck focusing on externals, stereotypes and in comparison so that we dismiss ourselves as having no beauty of our own. We know we have an inner beauty, but we need room to explore this, express it and be affirmed in it. We may be stuck in a cycle of comparison with others, comparing our appearance, our walk with God, how much we are noticed by church leadership etc.

Eve is cut off from God and Adam

As a relational creature we will suffer the consequences of this cutting off. This explains the desolation and isolation many of us feel inside.

Broken hearts

As women, we live more from our hearts than our physical strength so a broken heart affects the very core of our being. We will be vulnerable to disappointment and rejection with an underlying feeling of being unnoticed and unappreciated. We may feel that we are not worth being with.

Lies

We can find ourselves agreeing with lies about our lack of worth and allow them to determine our life. Our doubts about God can live on.

Adventure

Many of us are deeply frustrated and have not found life to be the adventure God intended. We can feel that our many gifts are unused.

Our voice

In our wounding we may not know how to find our own real voice or how to use it well and be heard by others.

Blessing and place

If we do not feel blessed or that we have a full place, we can feel deeply frustrated, inadequate and ineffectual.

In what ways do I feel wounded?

Misogyny

Misogyny is the devaluing and dishonouring of woman and of this feminine part of our humanity. It first raised its head in the Fall when the serpent caused Eve to question her heart knowledge of God and her relationship with Him. He caused her to want more food and more wisdom and to be enticed by appearance. In her doubt, she self-referenced and felt deprived, laying her imagination and feelings for God aside. Meanwhile Adam remained silent. The blame shifting that ensued and the subsequent consequences of the curse severed this intimacy with God and with each other.

The first expression of misogyny for both men and women is when we question the goodness of God, despise our reliance on Him, and want to be His equal.

The second expression is when we are cynical about our hearts and about intuitive ways of knowing. We settle for being detached and hard-hearted, rather than engaged and committed to life with our whole heart as Jesus was. When we defend ourselves in this way, we are also cutting off from our imagination and from the importance of the unseen and the spiritual – from the mystery of God's wisdom and our ongoing relationship with the Father. Jesus was not ashamed of His intimacy and utter dependence on the Father, nor of only ever doing His will. We often settle for being earthbound and concrete – staying unmoved by life and ashamed of needing a Saviour. We deal with this by accepting our feminine heart within ourselves and in relation to God.

The third is the despising of the feminine in women. Misogyny is also the most blatant expression of hostility between the genders. It is masculine strength pitted against feminine responsiveness. As an outcome of the original curse men toil and become heartless and frustrated by the futility of their labour (Genesis 3:17-19), and women feel the pain of the Fallen world and of childbirth, with a tendency to need men to give them significance and place (Genesis 3:15–16).

Men will have a tendency to want to belittle women, to overpower and dismiss them, feeling that their demands are overwhelming. They can feel they don't understand women and retreat and detach into cynicism or passivity. Men will prefer toil to intimacy and fear control and emasculation.

Women can be made to feel demanding and insignificant, betrayed and alone. They will be deeply frustrated from not fulfilling their full potential in God.

Because of the masculine way not to consider and reflect on situations, men will tend to move on or deflect, not notice or shrug off what has happened. They will blame-shift and push the responsibility on to woman. We see this in Adam (Genesis 3:12) and in Tamar and Amnon (2 Samuel 13). It can come out in fathers telling children to 'ask your mother' or calling the family, 'your children'. We know too that women can compound this by their devaluing of men, or their need to control.

Because the fallen feminine way is to internalise and take things too personally, we can take the blame and withdraw from the conflict resolution that should occur. The sword of enmity[1] stays in all our hearts until we ask God to take it out and move us on into maturity.

In what ways have I experienced misogyny?

---

1. Here, the term 'sword of enmity' is used to describe all the antagonism, contempt, hatred, bitterness, animosity and hostility that we have in our hearts about an issue. We come back to this in Chapter 25 – Reconciliation.

In what ways do I experience this contention between men and women?

How does this wounding occur?

The wounding of misogyny occurs in both men and women and is a wounding in our hearts. It leads to our being cut off from our hearts and living only from our heads – even despising feelings, comfort, intimacy and need.

Absorption

From mothers to daughters

- Doormat or servile
- Not modelling vulnerability or that it is good to receive and have needs
- Anger against men e.g. all men are a waste of space
- Men are putty in your hand, despise them and punish them with your favours
- Men are ogres and are terrifying
- This can be overt or covert.

From fathers to daughters

- Women are objects or trouble e.g. decorative, a pretty face, needy, demanding
- Women are just there for me
- Men rule in this household
- Different rules for sons and daughters
- Not blessing the transition to womanhood
- Victimising and abuse.

From mothers to sons

- Your masculinity threatens me and I despise you. I am afraid to bless you in it and release you to become a man (this can set up hatred of women in sons), I am afraid of you becoming strong and earthy
- I hate men, or men are not kind so, 'If you really love me do not become one'
- Men are different and I do not want to lose you by you becoming different from me, especially if I am using you as a husband and not as a son. I cannot let you go to another woman
- Not modelling vulnerability or that it is good to receive and have needs.

From fathers to sons

- Big/real boys don't cry or have feelings
- Real men are chauvinistic and domineering
- Women are objects
- Too much solidarity – creating a united front against the women
- This is how you should treat women – treat them mean to keep them keen
- Introducing pornography as an initiation
- No sissies or types of son I don't understand here
- Aversion to women
- Denial of being a complement to women.

Where these woundings deny us our hearts and our feelings they set up misogyny. Where they confirm enmity, they set up fear, contempt and confrontation, rather than valuing, complementing or trust. A family line of misogyny can go back generations.

Direct assault

- Physical: abuse, rape, voyeurism, shame at one's body
- Verbal: innuendo, rage, insults, sexualised conversation
- Emotional: false promises, no commitment
- Culture: laws, church practice, objectification
- Spiritual: denying the prophetic, denying women their place in the church, despising heart responses to God.

Reaction

In some men, misogyny is a defence against further wounding or against being discovered as less of a man than they would want.

- You (e.g. mother) despised me, now I will put that onto other women
- I could not/dared not speak against or break away from my mother so I will treat you as I wanted to treat her
- If I don't fend you off and keep my place I will lose control
- I cannot meet your demands so I will belittle you instead
- I do not want you to abandon me as my heart tells me my mother did, so to make sure this does not happen again I will control you and keep you in my sights. Ironically, this can drive the woman away again, leading to a repeat abandonment
- Self-hatred: why do I behave like this? Yet attack is my best form of defence
- I will detach and not reward you with my company or attention.

Early wounding

When we have no sense of being:

- We are not present as a full person so live in shame
- We appear demanding in our neediness and anxiety
- We have no resistance and any attention is better than none
- Men needing women as a surrogate mother and women negating their true worth by giving this
- We are angry at women instead of our mother
- We are angry about our helplessness and our need to receive
- We are unable to do relationship because of anxiety, fear and hardness of heart.

How have I been wounded?

Without a sense of personhood we cannot be confident in our gender; if we are not present to our gender we will not have a clear sense of personhood.

If our mothers were anxious, detached, absent or unsafe we will not have experienced:

- Trust
- Receiving
- Being
- Letting ourselves be loved
- Dependence: the sense that it's OK that I cannot do everything for myself: I can need milk, changing, cuddles, wonder
- A sense of being safe and provided for, or that the world is safe and I can join it.

Until we have peace with ourselves as women and peace with men, we will not embrace the good of the feminine for ourselves or see the creative possibilities of the other. When we are each secure in our gender we inspire complementarity in the other. As we sense respect, we can draw each other out more.

To recap, what is this feminine quality? It is the capacity to be intimate without fear, and to receive without shame. It is being confident and relaxed about who we are and what we can give, defining ourselves positively – not negatively or by comparison:

- To see beyond reason into more ways of knowing
- To receive
- To distil and brood, wait and nurture

- To make room for more and weigh and hold different realities
- Intuition
- It is the valuing of beauty and radiance
- It is giving a right place to the imagination in a non-idolatrous way
- It is about daring to seek freedom and radical ways
- It is about being at rest, being at home with ourselves and being at peace
- It is about allowing space for becoming
- It is being patient and kind, forbearing, gracious
- It is being able to put yourself in another's shoes.

Of course, this needs to be balanced by the masculine for life to be lived. It is also subtle, which is why it is easier to symbolise woman in her physical form. It is also essential for any culture to value the unseen and all that is outlined above. Otherwise, there is no thirst to go beyond the concrete, no acknowledgement of the spiritual, no capacity to imagine more or eternity and no valuing of the heart.

If the feminine is absent then we are reduced to:

- Merely existing
- No outside meaning
- Functionality is valued over beauty
- The survival of the fittest with competitiveness and gaining at others' expense
- No heart for the poor
- Edgy restlessness in the culture, no home building (we see this in new flats being built without kitchens as they aren't needed)
- Loss of heart knowledge, hearing God, understanding the need to be saved
- Only concrete thinking and reason are valued and thought expedient
- Despising affection
- Creating false intimacy and connection, such as through social media, online chat etc.

The thing we need the most we fear the most. So we can defend ourselves against needing to the point of such complete independence and sterility that mutual, real relationships are no longer possible, society no longer has any heart and ultimately breaks down.

What does misogyny look like in men and in women?

In men:

- Avoidance of intimacy
- Misuse of physical strength
- Rage, control/submission, exasperation, lack of respect

- Women as objects from wolf whistles to pornography, dictating how they dress etc.
- Cynicism, dismissiveness
- Lust and sexual addictions
- Anonymous sexual encounters to avoid real human connection
- Sexual abuse
- Laddishness
- Denying a woman her voice and place
- Only valuing masculine ways of thinking: analytical, rational, concrete
- Stubborn, patronising, bigoted
- Denial of feelings and creativity
- Despising the sensitive parts of self and others
- Causing shame.

For men, how have you experienced this and how have you been guilty of misogyny?

In women:

- Self-hatred and despising other women
- Not joining the peer group
- Masculinised competition with men
- Needing to be appreciated by men
- Denial of femininity and feelings
- Dressing to please men
- Fierce independence
- Preferring sons to daughters, and vice versa
- Receiving shame.

For women how have you experienced this and how have you been guilty of misogyny?

To compensate we can develop a false feminine. This can include:

- Over-sentimentalising
- Passivity and manipulation
- Seduction
- Being effete and overtly needy
- People pleasing and appeasing
- Not taking responsibility
- Feeling for everyone else while neglecting our own heart
- Narcissistic dressing.

All this happens in our hearts – we need to clear them out so they are free to feel and respond to life as God intended.

Our hearts can be:

- Empty of life but filled with despair, anxiety, grief, sadness
- Full of mess: other people's sin, anger etc, we have allowed this to be left behind in our hearts as we had no power to resist
- Walled off: through independence, vows we have made, fear, plotting or detachment.

What do we do?

- We ask God to show us our hearts
- We realise how hungry and thirsty we are for connection, intimacy, being known and loved
- We start to pour out our hearts to God
- We are prepared to feel, receive, be known, reach out and connect
- We are ready to see how well defended we have become, and allow our hearts to cry out to God for more life
- We find our true voice and declare our needs before God without shame.

We start to confess the ways we have participated in misogyny ourselves

- Tolerated it
- Acted it out into people's lives
- Lived out of a place of non-being and self-hatred
- Carried it in our hearts after abuse of any kind
- Lived in victim mode
- Lived in cynicism and independence.

We ask God to continue a cleansing, liberating work in our hearts and to restore this capacity to be intimate and be open to receive from God and each other. Later we will pray some prayers together that seek God's forgiveness for misogyny and for the restoration of this capacity in us.

My version of the feminine – for men and women

As homework this week please write out your response to the chapter.

What do you feel are the key formative issues in your family, childhood and later experiences?

What is your experience of misogyny?

How do you find receiving and being intimate?

Prayers for the healing of misogyny and the restoration of the feminine

Women's prayers

1. Corporate confession of the sins of misogyny committed against women

Lord, we come to the foot of Your Cross, to own before You, that we have been dishonoured and devalued and violated for being women.

We have been treated as less than men.

We own before you that we have been used as objects of ridicule, hatred and lust.

We have been taken advantage of and hurt by men using their strength and power wrongfully and abusively – even in an evil way.

We have also been wounded by fellow women.

We name these sins against us before You now...

2. Identification with Christ in His sufferings: Binding away the sins of misogyny into the Cross

Lord we ask You to come in Your holy power to enable us to stand in our true selves before You now. Come Holy Spirit.

Lord, we stand before You to renounce the sin of misogyny and ask You to release us from it now. Take it out of us and into Your Cross.
We refuse to live under the curse of misogyny any longer.
We tolerate it no more.

Come Lord Jesus and free us from this prison of non-becoming and from the darkness and death in our hearts.

Come and take from us: the shame and deception, the rejection, the anger and betrayal, the hatred of ourselves or others, our sense of unworthiness or our need to destroy or maim.

Lord Jesus, we release our wounds into Yours.
We release our victim identity into Yours.

We release the despising and the marring of Your image in us into Your sufferings.

Come, bring us out into Your light and freedom, and into our true identity in You.

Thank you Lord, for Your death and resurrection righting this wrong in us.

Amen

3. Confession of disowning our womanhood

(This includes the ways we have taken on shame and dishonour from others – and ended up hating the good of our own feminine.)

Father, we come before you now, to confess that because of our woundedness, we have agreed with those who have hurt and devalued us and we have come to despise the good of the feminine within ourselves. We too are guilty of misogyny.

Our womanhood has become a liability or a source of shame for us and not the gift and source of blessing you intended it to be. We have also, at times, believed the lie that it is better to be a man. Lord, forgive us for believing these lies and tolerating these wounds within us.

Lord, we ask You to come in Your holy power and enable us to stand in our true selves before You. Free us now to receive Your love and favour.

Free us to receive back the good of our feminine and be reunited with it at the very core of our being. Help us rejoice in our inheritance as women, and to know and bless Your image restored within us.

May we grow in the truth that as women we bear Your image as fully as men, and that You esteem our feminine ways of knowing and being as highly as You esteem the masculine.

We receive Your favour as daughters of the King of Kings.

Amen

4. Forgiving those who have sinned against us

Father, we ask that You will give us the grace to forgive those who have sinned against us. Please cleanse us of fear, hatred, pride or revenge, that we might allow You to be their Judge and Jury and we can walk free with our dignity and honour restored by You.

We ask we may know Your holy protection as we seek to walk forward into life free in You.

In Jesus' name,

Amen

Men's prayers

1. Corporate confession of the sin of misogyny committed against men

Father, we come to the foot of the Cross and own that we too have been hurt.

We have been ridiculed for trusting, for being sensitive or being vulnerable. We have suffered at the hands of others, even our mothers and fathers, as they have passed on to us their misogyny or hatred. We name these sins against us before You now...

2. Prayer of repentance of any misogyny

Father, we confess to You the ways in which we have participated in misogyny: believing the lie that men are superior, that women need us or are to be controlled by us, or that they are there to serve us or make us feel good.

We name our specific sins before You now...

We confess the ways we have believed that to receive or have needs is a sign of weakness and we ask You to heal this perception and fear in us. Give us back our hearts where we are cut off from them and enable us to show a new care and mercy towards ourselves and towards women, especially the women in our lives.

Lord, please show us if we are still carrying any hurt from, or hatred against, our mothers. Enable us to cut ourselves free from them now. Forgive us Lord where we have taken these things out on our wives or other women in our lives. Please forgive us and may we seek their forgiveness before You.

Amen

3. Forgiving those who have sinned against us

Father, we ask that You will give us the grace to forgive those who have sinned against us. Please cleanse us of fear, hatred, pride or revenge, that we might allow You to be their Judge and Jury and we can walk free with our dignity and honour restored by You.

We ask we may know Your holy love as we seek to walk forward into life free in You.

In Jesus' name,
Amen

NOTES

CHAPTER 24 – BEING SONS AND DAUGHTERS OF GOD, PART 2

Our hearts

We need to understand the masculine part of our nature and integrate it into our lives so we can mature in Christ. Like the feminine, this is also a matter of the heart.

It is all about knowing we are a beloved son of the Father and that we are loved with an everlasting love forever. It is being secure and rooted in this whatever happens.

The masculine in us all – both men and women

As God adopts us into our sonship all of us need to be comfortable with being masculine in relation to God and value the masculine aspects of our nature:

- Strength – both physical and in our character
- The ability to persevere and get the job done
- The ability to be objective and not be swayed by feelings or fear
- The ability to have authority and use it well
- The ability to take risks.

Psalm 112 talks about the masculine "part of our hearts", in contrast to the receptivity and openness that we saw in the "feminine part". It talks of the person who "delights" in God's commandments. This means that we have deeply understood the wisdom and purpose of them, and that we know that they fit with who He has made us to be and how to live well. We go on to welcome and celebrate this revelation of God, and make it our own at all costs. We want to do more than defend the truth; we want to delight in it. We are so established in God that we will not be moved from Him.

The Psalm goes on to describe this person's heart as firm, trusting in the Lord, steady and "not afraid of bad news". This is the result of being rooted and grounded in the Father's love so that we are established and can be filled with His strength in our inner being (Ephesians 3). We know that this almighty presence transcends the knowledge and experiences of the world and is eternal and complete in us. This is God's strength to us in the midst of life, even in times of weakness or trouble.

We learn that this person is not afraid and will persevere until they know they have triumphed over their adversaries. He/she lives in an ordered way and manages their affairs well. Part of this is the ability to stay objective and clear in a situation, and not to be swayed by feelings or fear.

This is the masculine presence that our fathers needed to impart into us, so that we could be drawn away from the protection of our mothers to face the world and take our place in it. Our father would have proved himself trustworthy and reliable as he accompanies us and passes us over to the Eternal Father's care, to the Trinity. There is such dignity in this.

Zechariah chapter 3 also describes the stature that we are to have in God. It talks of us being relieved of our filthy rags of shame, of duty and of not feeling enough, and having them replaced by clean, fresh clothes. We are told that as we keep God's commands ("delight in them") we will be given access to the courts of the Lord and authority within them. We will participate in God's redemptive plans for the world and have a fruitful place, which is our territory, and from which we can be a community that entertains and blesses others.

This masculine strength needs to be imparted to us by our fathers and by God the Father, establishing in us the rhythm of receiving and living out His will, as Jesus did. We then become part of it coming to pass and persevere in this. We cannot do this alone, we also need to be known and live in community with others.

The ultimate example of masculinity was Jesus' sacrifice on the Cross. We become true to our heart when we die to the false desires of power and accomplishment. Real masculine authority comes out of weakness. When submitted to the Father through Christ, such weakness produces an anointing of strength and truth.

Indeed, true masculinity has everything to do with strength and truth. When this is set in a soul, it provides a platform from which we can approach life, give it form and persevere through difficulties. It involves discerning truth and committing oneself to it, regardless of the cost. It also liberates the capacity to initiate and give shape to structures that enable truth to flourish – in our relationships, families, churches and out into the world. We can see that it is essential for us all to be able to order our lives, persevere in difficulty and contend with evil and opposition.

Women also need to develop the masculine, just as men need to develop the good of feminine responsiveness. (The masculine cannot fully develop in a man without the co-existence of the feminine.) Each one of us will have a unique way that we reflect these parts of God's nature.

*One thing God has spoken, two things I have heard: that you,
O God, are strong, and that you, O Lord are loving*

(PSALM 62:11–12A)

Let us remind ourselves of God's nature:

Majestic, strong, creative, warrior, benevolent, merciful, upright, with authority, clarity of purpose, persevering in our salvation, sacrificial, a risk-taker, faithful, advocate...

These are all essential qualities for a mature and rounded person – they are different qualities from the feminine.

The false masculine

It is possible to develop a 'false' masculine as a means of compensating for what we instinctively know is lacking. What might it look like?

The false masculine is not balanced by the feminine – it is living from the head and being cut off from the heart. It is living from a place of detachment and defendedness. After the Fall, Adam was reduced to futile toil and striving; in any of us there can be a cynicism and drivenness that is escapist.

Some adult expression of the false masculine, **in either men or women**, can be:

- Work addiction. This happens when our worth is bound up in achieving more and more. We seek favour through our work, usually as a result of a father wound. No amount of approval or recognition is enough, and the cycle continues. Work can also be a distraction from anxiety or loneliness and a deflection of rejection. Deep down we believe that one day we might hear the word of affirmation that we crave

- Being stressed out but having nowhere to go to deal with the stress. This may include bearing huge responsibilities but dealing with them in unhealthy ways. Either we have no one to turn to for help or we don't want to admit we need help. The stress will find outlets in various ways: angry outbursts (which may include violence), withdrawing from real relationships, or an addiction

- Hardness of heart and control

- False strength and a heartless use of authority

- A lack of order and structure in life, leading to stress and chaos

- Over-working to appear noble but with diminishing efficiency

- Passive aggression

- Passivity – this can be through shame, exhaustion, non-engagement, lack of passion and perseverance

- Sexual sin.

In men, some expressions of the false masculine can include:

- **A macho alpha male persona**
- **Peter Pan:** we simply don't want to grow up. We remain in a prolonged state of adolescence. We detach from those whom we fear will shame or overpower us
- **Bent towards father-figures:** instead of rebelling, we can look to father-figures to soothe our father-wound. It's important for the father-figure to keep pointing us to our heavenly Father, and to model the true masculine. Like Christ, they are to call us into our true selves, not make us into their own image

- **Trying to be a father-figure:** some of us seek to father others out of our own emptiness in a desperate attempt to bring some fathering into life. Having others follow us gives a sense of position and affirmation.

So there is something here for all of us! Of not being ashamed, of having passion and vision, of fighting for what is right and just and of having a heart and sharing it. It is about being known. This fits well with the radical nature of the gospel.

The path that we will describe in the next section – 'Being a son of God' – will also resonate with women:

- To be a precious daughter
- To engage in real adventure and make a unique contribution with our wisdom
- To respond to the man's need to be a warrior and allow them to fight and exercise their strength in and of itself, and on behalf of women. Men need to roar and find their full voice
- To respond to being wooed and loved and stay intentional in our relationships
- To exercise authority well
- To be mentored by older women, and eventually to mentor others.

The masculine thrives in relation to the nourishing and honouring feminine. As a man earns a woman's respect, her high regard can encourage him in his masculinity in a unique way. If a woman has been wounded by men, this may be hard for her and vice versa.

How do you feel about the masculine? Can you identify with this part of your personhood?

Being a son of God

(Primarily for sons but also applies to daughters)

Introduction

As we read the stages below, women will be able to identify how they too needed a father's presence in their lives, and where they are stuck or immature. They will also see where they need to encourage and give space to the men in their lives while they progress on their journey.

Society and the church must allow men space to express their strength and voice. So often we reduce masculinity to being 'nice' and lock it up. But we need true masculinity, in our own lives, in the church and in wider society.

One helpful book that clearly identifies the path into more and more sonship is *Fathered by God – Learning What Your Dad Could Never Teach You* by John Eldredge.

Eldredge has identified six stages: Boyhood; Adventure; Warrior; Intimacy; King and Sage. It is not possible to give an exact age for each stage as they overlap and there are aspects of each stage in the others. However, there are times in our lives when one of the stages is more prominent. Ideally we progress and move forward once a foundation has been laid at each stage. We are going to use these stages as a framework.

The stages we are going to describe could be seen both as a map and a field report from someone on their own masculine journey. It is not a formula. A map cannot answer all our questions, but it can act as a very helpful guide.

The material can be helpful for men, for those bringing up boys and those working with men and/or boys.

In our society, most men are either fatherless or unfinished. We could say they are boys in men's bodies. The two main effects of fatherlessness are:

1. A feeling that I am alone in this world (unaccompanied)
2. The feeling that there isn't any room for mistakes – so I had better get things right. This also leaves us with deep questions in our hearts such as, 'Have I got what it takes?' and 'Am I going to be found out?'

Most men have not had anyone to guide them on the masculine journey. But, there is another way. And, there is a Father ready to show us that path and help us along it.

The masculine journey

Masculinity is bestowed. A boy learns who he is and what he is made of from a man (or a group of men). It can't be learned in any other way, especially not from our mothers. We have no rites of passage in our culture, and no core group of men of all ages to join – there is no tribe in which to take our place. We need a process, a journey, an epic story of many experiences woven together, building upon one another in a progression. And on this journey we need a Guide to show us the way.

We aren't meant to try and work life out on our own. Many of us will need to start by admitting that we are fatherless and need help along the journey in many ways. We will have to turn from our independence and all the ways we either charge at life, or withdraw from it in anger and frustration or passivity and despair.

This won't be easy for us. The more we have been used to doing life on our own and on our terms, the harder it will be to turn to God. So much of what we misinterpret as hassles or trials or mistakes on our part are in fact God fathering us, taking us through something repeatedly in order to strengthen us, or heal us, or dismantle something in us that is unholy. It is also His way of showing us what is in our hearts that still needs His healing and redemption. He guides us on this journey.

The hardest, gladdest thing in the world is to cry Father! from a full heart.
The inability to look up to God as our father is the one central wrong
in the whole human affair; the refusal, the one central misery[1]

(GEORGE MACDONALD)

How do I identify with this lack of fathering?

Let's look at each stage in more detail

1. Boyhood stage

This is a time of wonder and exploration – a time of building tree houses, reading comics and keeping tadpoles. This is the stage of being the apple of our father's eye. This stage is primarily a time for affirmation, to know that we are prized, delighted in and that we are the beloved son.

When God created Adam in the Garden of Eden, He set His son in a world that was safe and secure, yet full of mystery and adventure. The true heart of a boy longs for daring adventures and battles – in play and through books.

---

1. George MacDonald, Unspoken Sermons: Series 2, originally published by Longmans, Green & Co, London, 1886, revised into modern English by Jim Mellis, 2014.

A boy is also a warrior. It is for these reasons that films like *Star Wars* are still so popular now. When a boy imagines himself as a character, it is nearly always as a superhero – this is the heart of the warrior emerging. Boyhood is also meant to be a time of receiving gifts from our fathers. This will have an effect on our ability to receive good gifts from our heavenly Father and to believe that He has good gifts for us.

Without the certainty that a boy is the beloved son, he will misinterpret the stages and lessons that are to follow, often feeling instead they are a form of rejection or punishment from God. And as he grows into a man he will move unsteadily through the rest of his life, trying to prove his worth and earn his beloved identity through performance or many other ways.

Did you know that you were a beloved son? if so, how? If not, how did this affect you?

2. Adventure stage

This stage is entered at adolescence (around age 12 or 13) and continues into the late teens/early 20s. It is a time of great adventures and testing, and also a time for hard work and learning. A change starts to take place in a boy's soul at this age – a yearning for real adventure. He has a desire to prove himself and be tested.

The question, 'Do I have what it takes?' begins to present itself in nearly everything the boy-becoming-a-young-man does. This stage is meant to confirm that he does indeed have what it takes.

David was a shepherd before he was a Warrior and a King, and this was his adventure stage. Being a shepherd was a hard job where he had to contend with lions and bears. It was here that David learnt many lessons and proved himself.

The young man on the adventure stage needs to know that life is hard and that there will be testing. (He is largely shielded from this during the Boyhood stage.) Until a man learns to deal with this fact, he will spend days chasing the wrong thing, using his energy trying to make life more comfortable and any challenges will be misconstrued as annoying or as 'attack'. Encouragement and objective truth from a father or father figure are crucial at this stage as a way of processing mistakes, especially as there will be failure.

Nature is also vital as there are lessons that can only be learned by being outside in God's creation (like David being out on the hills with his sheep). It's important to include this in our lifestyle.

Doing things with a group of men is crucial to the masculine journey. Far too much has fallen on the shoulders of the father alone (if he is around). It takes a group of men to bring a boy into the masculine world and to bring young men along into maturity.

What has been our experience of this stage?

How might we revisit it?

Do you have areas of self-doubt or worry that you do not have what it takes to really be a man?

3. Warrior stage

This stage emerges in the teens and lasts well into the 30s. In the Warrior stage a man gets a cause to fight for and hopefully a 'King'. This needs to be our cause but we may need help discerning it. For example, it could be a sport, a career, university, a mission, young people… Whatever it is we will need perseverance and courage at times to follow through and to counter opposition in whatever form it comes, both from within ourselves and from outside.

Passivity can be a real enemy, especially if we feel unaccompanied and it was the example we were given. It also thrives in isolation so this is all the more reason to be known and to belong. For example, Adam did not intervene and challenge Eve in the garden. Passivity is also a way of suppressing passion and to be a Warrior we need to make room for passion and involvement. This is harnessed in discipline but may take us right out of our comfort zone and break new ground in us.

This stage is typically also the time a man enters a relationship with a woman. Although it would often be best for him, and for her, if he lived as a Warrior for a while first. A man in a difficult marriage can persevere only if he finds the Warrior inside.

The two main lessons during this stage are:

1. To know that you as a man are dangerous and powerful, but you are meant to use this for good
2. To know that you will be tested and developed and will need to make room for passion.

Finally, it is important to know that the enemy's first plan is to keep a man out of battle altogether, be it through fear, self-doubt, bad theology or ignorance. If a man does rise up and begin to battle, the enemy's second plan is to bury him in the wrong battles – trying to lure him into battles that aren't his to fight. Again, deep fellowship with other men is key to discerning the right battles for each individual.

How do you feel about being passionate? What are your passions?

How do you feel about being dangerous and powerful?

What are the battles that God is calling you to fight?

4. Intimacy stage – becoming a man after God's heart

Many of us did not learn that we have what it takes during the Adventure stage, and found ourselves as a Warrior without a mission. In this stage, we can end up taking this uncertainty to a woman, hoping to find validation and a reason for living in her. We are meant to offer our strength to a woman, not get it from her.

The Intimacy stage is about becoming a man after God's own heart (1 Samuel 13:14). In aligning our hearts to God in this way, we are best able to show this love to a woman. This stage is not foremost about the woman but, woman is the personification of Beauty, and it often takes her to turn the young man's attention away from adventure and battle. It is the time when a young man discovers the way of the heart – that poetry and passions are far closer to the truth than mere reason. He discovers music and literature, and like the young David, he becomes a romantic and it takes his spiritual life to a new level. Service for God is overshadowed by intimacy *with* God.

Often, God arouses our hearts through His creation and pursues us so that we come to realise that being His beloved son and being intimate with Him is the central issue. As we experience this, we begin to see that God is pursuing us. In this stage we begin to see that intimacy with God, not our battles, is the central issue. Once a man has become one after God's own heart, he is then ready to become a King and rule a Kingdom.

Have we moved from appeasing God or serving Him, to loving Him and being intimate with Him?

How might we experience this shift?

5. King stage

The King stage is the goal of a man's masculine journey: to wield power, influence, and property in His name. It might be said that the goal of masculinity is designed also to prepare us to handle power – God's power – in the right way.

This time of ruling is a tremendous test of character, for the King will use his influence in this for the benefit of others. It is vital that a King knows that his position is not for his own comfort, but is to serve others. A King might be the leader of a pastorate or church group, a middle manager, the chair of a global company or in a senior position of leadership in a church. Maybe we are made the commander over a division - the senior Pastor of a church. It could be any position where we have influence over others and the opportunity to lead with the benevolent and facilitating strength of Jesus.

A key issue in our crisis of leadership in all walks of life today, is precisely the degree of power we allow people to have without the personal formation and character to use it well.

A midlife crisis often occurs when we come into money and influence and use it to go back to recover what we missed as the beloved son (buying ourself toys) or the Adventurer (going off on an adventure or having an affair). We are an undeveloped, uninitiated man. There is a great cost and responsibility to being a King and therefore it is not a position we should take lightly. The test of a good King is asking the question, 'What is life like for the people under my/his authority?' The two main dangers for a King are pride and isolation. A King will have to make decisions that people do not like, but we must be careful not to withdraw from key relationships.

As well as ruling over a Kingdom, ideally the King will draw around him a company of young Warriors; he is now also a 'father' to younger men, while maintaining his own live peer group and his own fathering from God.

What areas of influence do I have?

What is life like for those under me?

Have I withdrawn and do I have any pride at my position?

Am I a servant King?

6. Sage stage

The final stage is the Sage. The sage is the grey-haired father with a wealth of knowledge and experience, whose mission now is to counsel and mentor others.

His Kingdom may shrink – the kids have left home, and he may live in a smaller place. He steps down from his role as chair etc. and his income may shift to savings and investments made while he was King. However, his influence should actually increase!

This is not the time to pack up and detach himself from others. Maybe he becomes an elder at his church or uses his experience on a board. His time is spent mentoring younger men, especially Kings, in the same way that Gandalf mentored Aragon, as Paul mentored Timothy.

Instead of feeling life is over this can become the time of greatest impact. The Sage draws us near to God. He offers a gift of a soul that has lived long with God. He does not need to be heard as a Warrior might, nor does he have to rule as a King might. He offers understanding, kindness and discretion.

The greatest gift we can offer a Sage is the opportunity to sit at his feet and ask him questions. It's important we ask, because in humility the Sage will often not offer until he is invited to do so. We should seek out a Sage, and if one cannot be found, we could seek them in the written word. We need the wisdom of the Holy Spirit coming through a fellow man.

And finally, for any Sages who may feel we are unfinished in the previous stages, God is able to both heal and use us at the same time. It's not too late!

Do I have a Sage in my life? If not, is there anyone I should ask?

My version of the masculine: for men and women

> *Lord, we ask that we will welcome both the feminine and masculine rightly into our lives, that we may become the unique expression of the son or daughter, made in Your image, that You have created us to be. May we welcome Your Holy Spirit and each other into our journey?*
>
> *Amen*

As homework this week please write out your response to the previous chapter. The following questions are for men.

What do you feel are the key formative issues in your family, childhood and later experiences?

What is your experience of fatherlessness and of relating to men?

Where are you on the journey?

With which stage do you identify most?

Prayer 1 – Confession (for men)

Father, we come to You now in our woundedness. We confess the ways we have failed to walk uprightly in our true manhood. We come to lay down at Your feet the many expressions of the false self. Whether we have been striving and overly powerful or have been passive and felt powerless, we lay these things down as the broken masculine, and not as the truth of who we are in You. We lay down where we have lived as an orphan and not a precious son.

(We confess our own sins to the Lord.)

Lord, we ask You now to set in us the truth that You have broken the power of the curse that keeps us in our prideful independence with its passivity or addictive strivings.

We confess pride and independence as sin. We ask You to set us free from our activism and restlessness, and from any despair and hopelessness at our current state.

Lord, find our hearts that are cut off and hurting. Reclaim them and breathe life into us so that we may feel and connect into life again. We ask You to enable us to be truly open with You, reconciled with women and with each other.

We confess to You the deep emptiness and aloneness we have inside. We confess the frustration of having real needs but being unable to ask for or receive Your healing. Lord, You know just how heavy this burden is. We want to break our silence on this.

Release us to own our needs we pray, enable us to cry out to You, the Saviour and to each other.

Lord resurrect your life in us we pray.

Amen

Prayer 2 – Renouncing sin (for men)

Father we ask, that You would enable us to understand and renounce those aspects of our relationship with our earthly father that have clouded our knowledge of You and our ability to be Your son.

Lord, I release to You the brokenness and sins of my father and the ways I have that brokenness or the reaction to it within me. I renounce:

- *His silence*

- *His detachment/passivity and his dependence on me*

- *His inability to bless and affirm me as his son*

- *His rage or the outbursts or abuse and humiliation*

- *His addictions*

- *His arbitrariness*

- *His misogyny...*

... as sin against me, and I take the sword of the Spirit and break any allegiance with these strongholds in my life. I choose to break with these sinful expressions of the false masculine.

I am a new creation in Christ and I claim my full inheritance to a life of righteousness and abundance in Him now.

I ask You Lord to renew my mind that I may know what it is to live by grace and be rooted in Your truth.

Father, we also want to take authority over any dishonour we have experienced from women that has caused us to question the good of our manhood. We come out from under that enmity and confess to You our broken or vengeful reactions to it. We ask that we may be able to bless and honour ourselves as men and be reconciled with the feminine within us and with women.

Lord, You know where we have detached from our need for woman and her complementarity to us; where we have rejected, feared or suppressed our authentic and God given desire for intimacy with her.

Please forgive us for setting ourselves against Your created ways and restore this to us, we pray.

Amen

Prayer 3 – Solidarity with other men

We renounce the lie that we are self-sufficient. We need encouragement and blessing from our brothers.

Teach us, Father, to rightfully rely on each other and to give and receive the protection we need from one another as our true masculine takes form.

Make us like Christ in our ability to call out the best in others and bless it. Enable us to facilitate and press into good relationships that reflect your ways with us, O Lord.

Grant us peace and joy in our manhood that it may be a true blessing to us.

Free us to walk uprightly in the honour and favour you have for us as your sons, and from that place of affirmation and dignity. Use our strength for your glory and praise.

Amen

Prayer 4 – For the women

Lord, we come before You now with our wounding from our fathers and with all the ways that this has clouded the truth about You as the faithful and loving Father. It has also caused us to be unsure about the good of men.

We also come with all the wounding we have received from men in our lives. This has caused us to deny our complementarity and has caused us to despise or disrespect men as our equals.

We confess our fear, detachment, revenge, hatred and confusion about them.

We confess the sinful ways we have felt about them or acted towards them. Please forgive us.

We acknowledge before You now that this has left us at odds with the true masculine within ourselves. We have lost the order and balance that we need to live out our true feminine with purpose and confidence. We ask You to forgive us and enable us to lay down our emnity and be reconciled to all the good of who men can be for us and the good of who we really are in You.

We ask You to protect us. We ask You to open our hearts to each other and use us for your glory.

We pray in Jesus' name.

Amen

NOTES

CHAPTER 25 – RECONCILIATION

As the course comes towards the end, we will seek to identify where we are detached, withdrawn, opposed, angry, contemptuous etc. – we use the term 'sword of enmity' to describe this – and how we can move into lasting reconciliation and relationship.

Reconciliation with God

God is not a man that He should lie (Numbers 23:19). This comes in the Bible where the kings of Moab who worship Baal enlist Balaam to curse the people of Israel. He seeks God three times and each time God says that Balaam is to bless them and not curse them. This infuriates the King of Moab and he leaves; Balaam refused to make God a liar. But for many of us there are times and places when we call God a liar: 'Did God really say…?' We do this either so we can go our own way, or so that we can feel sorry for ourselves.

Some of us have quite a backlog of unfinished business and unresolved issues or grudges with God. The sooner we process these and release them, the better.

We need a reconciliation with God to take place in our hearts because He is not part of the problem – He is our one resting place and solution. The Father, the Son on the Cross and the Holy Spirit are ours for a purpose and every way in which we detach and behave as if we can manage our own salvation, the more proud and distanced we become.

What do our hearts say when we think of coming closer to God? Is it: dread, contempt, cynicism, numbness, delight, anticipation, awe?

- Do I know the incarnate God here with me in my life on earth?
- Do I have a live grace-filled relationship with God? Or am I functioning as a slave, servant, wary friend, dutiful or angry son/daughter towards Him?
- Am I defensively detached from God?
- How do I view Him? As an arbitrary father, distant, demanding, indulgent, interfering etc?

- Have I allowed Jesus to show me the Father's true nature?
- Do I actually live in a vacuum without any imminent presence of God?
- Do my fantasies, whinging, bitterness, sin or aloneness eclipse the goodness and presence of God for me?
- Does anyone wrongly occupy space in my heart (including myself) and eclipse God's presence for me?
- Am I so cut off with a numb heart that I am not really doing any relationships, least of all with God?
- Am I becoming more and more the person God made to be? Or have I plateaued and am merely surviving?

One of the purposes in Christ's coming to earth was to break down this wall of hostility and bring us back to being a child of God again.

Where am I in this? Have I climbed back over the wall? Am I living out in the cold?

When we speak of this sword of enmity being turned on God, it sounds horrific. Yet, this will be a reality for some of us. It is better for us to face this and to put the sword down, than to persist in defiance.

Hebrews 5:7 says that Jesus' prayers were heard because of His reverence for the Father. In the Lord's Prayer we are to pray to the Father whose name is hallowed. So we must keep God in this place of reverence in our hearts and not be presumptuous – however intimate He then invites us to be with Him. However intimate we are, or are used to being, with God, it must always start with reverence.

What is our position with reference to God? Distance, fear, suppressed rage, timidity, OK, good, cynical?

So, we come before God in reverence and then pour out our hearts to Him, acknowledging where we need to repent and bow and move into a new place with Him. This may even involve laying down our sword at the Cross and allowing God to be the Almighty God and for us to be a creature before Him. (At this point, you may want to write a letter of confession and explanation to God to leave at the Cross.)

Reconciliation with myself

We need to be reconciled within ourselves to all the truth that God speaks to us. He says:

- I exist and I have been fearfully and wonderfully made by my Creator Father. This truth transcends the circumstances of my conception as I have been born by the will of God not man (John 1:13)

- I am to know this full well deep in my heart regardless of what the family or my peers thought, or think, of me (Psalm 139:14)

- I am made in the image of Almighty God: Father, Son and Holy Spirit. The great I AM. My value or worth comes from who I am, not from what I do or don't do

- I have made it through to adult life, even if I never expected to, and I need to be reconciled to that. I am both unique and ordinary. Maybe my wounding made me special, maybe my narcissism makes me feel special, but I need to take my place among the common people of God and hear Him gladly, as well as being special to Him (Mark 12:37, Zechariah 2:8).

I am to be reconciled to:

- Being here and having my own unique existence and being a unique and beloved son/daughter of God

- Being a creature and not God

- Having a real intrinsic worth that is not performance related

- Being called to show forth the glory of God just by the quality of who I am.

The sword of enmity turned onto myself results in: self-doubt, self-hatred, self-harming, contempt, narcissism, relational idolatry, rage, cynicism, depression, blame-shifting, not allowing good things to happen to me – self-sabotage, not doing joy and rationalising life into my construct.

How do I feel about myself? Am I holding a sword of enmity or despising any part of myself? If so, we will need to confess this to God and realign our lives with His truth.

What might I need to face about myself? Can I allow God's grace into my life?

(I might need to accept that I am not God and that I am a mere creature. I will need to accept that I am a glorious member of the human race. I need to accept that I am both special and ordinary, and that I can make mistakes and take responsibility for my life under God.)

Reconciliation with having my gender

Some of us find that we can manage the 'person' bit of ourselves, but that we are really ambivalent about the gender bit. It is either such a liability or challenge or non-event, that we would rather live in a no man's land than embrace this core part of our identity. If this applies to us then we will have to make peace, first with having gender, and second with our specific gender. God reveals more of His nature through our gender and we need to make room for this in who we are, and enjoy it and live it. We may feel our gender is deeply flawed through no fault of our own, and we can know that our Father doesn't condemn us, but rather sees where we have been plundered and robbed and wants to restore our full personhood to us.

We also need to renounce stereotypes and comparison, particularly around our gender.

As men, our glory is to live with our full humanity as a beloved son and express the majesty and strength of God in our own unique way.

As women we are called to live, again in our full humanity, as a beloved daughter of God, and express His beauty and compassion, His relational heart and His radiance in our own unique way.

Again, living to a stereotype is a key cause of us not enjoying our gender. Let us ask God to restore our true imagination to us and give us a sense of who we really are. Let us ask Him to show us how to be 'our' kind of man or woman that will really fit in with who we are. This also means us welcoming the masculine and feminine parts within ourselves as equally valid and in our unique balance.

Pause to take stock of how you feel about having a gender, and then how you feel about having your specific gender.

Am I vulnerable to comparison in anything, either constantly or in certain areas? If so, where and why? Is this where I am at odds with God?

Sword of enmity in men

What is it like being a man who is at odds within himself, and with fellow men and with women?

a. Within ourselves

When we are ambivalent about ourselves, we will feel 'less than', vulnerable to feeling emasculated, or hiding these feeling by being macho or narcissistic. We may find that work no longer fulfils us but has become toil or feels futile – leaving us feeling we were never enough. We feel that we are never enough. We may constantly compare ourselves with other men or with our culture's stereotype of who a man is, and we may feel judged. We feel we cannot meet women's expectations of us.

This ambivalence regarding our gender can result in us staying in passivity rather than trying to persevere. Conversely, at work drivenness can set in, fuelled by the fear of failure or an attempt to get affirmation from a father figure. There may also be shame or frustration and a sense that the reward from work is not what we want it to be. For some we may hide in detachment to avoid being found out or to avoid woman's neediness, anger or passive aggression.

b. With other men

The need for each and every man to take his place among men and make good heart connections to others cannot be over-emphasised. Until this happens, the soul is crippled by a deep sense of isolation and vulnerability. God originally set men in tribes where they worked together to provide and defend. Standing alone is not a virtue – it runs counter to creation. Do use your time on the course to explore more ways to find your place among men in an ongoing way.

c. With women

Of course, the sharpest wielding of the sword of enmity is misogyny. This can range from subtle to blatant. The first place misogyny shows itself is in our relationship with God, where we can find it hard to worship and bow down, to receive from God or to confess sin or hurt. It is difficult to acknowledge our need of a Saviour or Comforter and hard to knit into the body of Christ. This relates back to the mother wound: we cannot receive without fear or be known or intimate without shame, because we were not given the chance to do this as children. We may have a fear of, rather than a respect and care for women. This may be shown in passive aggression, cynicism etc.

Some of our misogyny will stem from an internalised, unhelpful relationship with our mothers, which leads us to develop an ambivalence about going there again; we want to punish our mother by punishing other women. This may be especially true for us as we cannot bite the hand that feeds us and we may not have been helped to leave her clutches by our father. The ultimate expression of misogyny is when all women are seen as mother. (Being sent to boarding school at an early age will also have ruined this process as we had a premature rupture of our relationship under the guise of it being a wonderful opportunity. We then could not leave clearly or decisively as a teenager.) Also if we are left inside as a little boy, then we will not be able to relate to these huge adult women who may eat us for dinner! We may have despised our gender, and ourselves, since then.

Pause: Confession time to own where we are: afraid and cannot receive; driven; fearful; immature; in self-hatred and not knit in and known by other men. Then move on to confess our attitude and behaviour to women and our misogyny.

Sword of enmity in women

a. Within ourselves

If our womanhood has not been affirmed then we can be ambivalent about our value and place and be loathe to take it on board. We will not be able step up into our beauty and radiance and instead will go down the road of comparison with other women and with our culture's stereotype of who a woman should be. We are then open to self-hatred and having no voice or presence. We will harden our hearts to being a woman.

When we turn the sword onto ourselves we despise our vulnerabilities; our desire for relationship; our lack of conventional beauty; our intuition and our appreciation of intimacy and connection. We will have a deep lack of self-esteem and self-worth and will feel very alone. There will be no freedom in our hearts, or 'dance' in our lives.

b. With other women

If we are in competition with other women, we can count ourselves out and not join the club, because we have not found our personal version of being a woman and taken our rightful place. Relationships that have gone wrong, or not having enough of them may have demoralised us. We too can see our mother in other women and this can skew relationships making us aloof, or too needy in emotional dependency. Like men, we needed to be affirmed by our fathers and drawn away from our mother's clutches too.

c. With men

As women, we will project our outstanding issues with our fathers on to men. We will make assumptions and despise or punish them in a way we did not dare with our fathers. Sometimes, of course, we may not even realise that this is what is happening. We may have an urge to control where we feel insecure and be wary or afraid of a man's power or competence. Yet we may bend into him asking for significance. If this feels overwhelming for the man, then we will pick up on this and feel rejection.

We will also be extremely uncomfortable under misogyny and control, especially if we succumb to it and only later realise what is going on. A man can then sense this loss of compliance as rejection and danger, and this will need to be worked through. We were not made to experience dominance by men, but rather delight, covering and benevolent strength – union not competition.

Our hearts may wonder if our vast capacity for relationship – for intimacy, for being known and understood and for connection – will ever be met. When this is not fulfilled, we feel even more bereft, isolated and alone. In our emptiness we create little 'affairs of the heart' where, at least in fantasy, we are happy, loved and understood.

Some of us hate this place in our hearts and inbuilt capacity for relationship, because it makes us feel vulnerable, beyond reach, a nuisance, needy, demanding or desolate, when in fact we are just being ourselves. We can flip in and out of control and neediness.

Pause: To confess – owning where we are afraid and cannot receive, where we are fearful, immature or in self-hatred. Move on to name before God our attitude and behaviour as women and our own misogyny: feeling that it is better to be a man. This is the sword of enmity.

Reconciliation inside ourselves

We need to make room for the 'other' within ourselves i.e. women need to know the form and structure and perseverance of the masculine, and men need to be able to receive and feel, have intuition and be known. Without this we are not complete; we may have the sword turned to one or both of these aspects of ourselves.

As we ask God to reveal to us the places where we are living in contention, we can work out why: what is the perceived threat to my safety? We can look in a new way through our adult eyes and make new decisions about how we want to conduct our relationships, and how we want to live out who we really are in Christ. We may also want to ask God to reveal to us how this chapter applies to our relationship history and if there is anyone with whom we need some kind of reconciliation or exchange of forgiveness. There are different approaches depending on the circumstances, but these could include: writing a letter or email, in person or starting with prayer.

In as far as it depends on you, live at peace with everyone

(ROMANS 12:18)

It's well worth spending time with the Lord asking him how this applies to us.

A prayer

Dear Lord,

You live as a Trinity in total love and respect and delight in each other. We are so sorry where we have retreated into defensiveness and contention with You, ourselves and each other. We ask that You will enable us to lay down our swords and pursue reconciliation and relationship. So, bless us Lord as we seek to be reconciled:

To You.

To being an adult person in our own right with a unique balance of the masculine and feminine.

To our own gender and reject the judgments and stereotypes, stepping up into our new creation version, with which You are wanting to bless the world. Enable us to open our hearts and welcome this.

To be a blessing and in good relationship with the opposite gender and be willing and able to give ourselves to their redemption and receive what they give us as part of ours.

We ask this for Your glory and to enjoy Your will.

Amen

NOTES

CHAPTER 26 – STAYING ON THE JOURNEY

The purpose of this course has been discipleship:

- To examine our relationship with God and hopefully to move it into a place of greater openness and intimacy
- To look at our primal relationships with our families and check for any ways which are still adversely affecting us in our relationships with God, ourselves and other people
- To acknowledge that we are gender people and to enjoy that more
- To deal with sin and shame in our own lives, and in the lives of others.

It is, and always will be, a Journey of Grace. We make this journey with our Redeemer Kinsman who pays the price of redeeming us because we are family. Jesus confirms that we have successfully made our way back to the Father and are now His beloved sons and daughters. So we take our place in the Trinity and make the Journey of Grace with, and, in them until we see them face-to-face.

God is exactly who He says He is and who He has shown us He is, in Christ. We need an open relationship with Him as Father, Son and Holy Spirit. He cannot and does not lie. Everything He says about Himself is true and we need to let this sink deep down into the core of our being. He is not part of the problem. We need Him. We need to allow ourselves to be loved and delighted in – even if this feels alien for us.

As we become more Christ-like, we also become more and more the person God created us to be. This redemption is happening.

We are who God says we are: fearfully and wonderfully made in His image, without exception, and we are to know this full well. We each have intrinsic worth and are far more loving, dynamic and gracious than we imagine. We are that wonderful. This is true and we need to let this sink deep down into the core of our being too. We can also move, into those parts of who He is that we are lacking, and find Him building us up into full people. We can move into being creative, having discernment or wisdom, being centred and confident and enjoying grace. His righteousness becomes our right-ness. It is who we are made to be.

The healing process – allowing it to be a journey

Our healing is a process. We are being transformed from one degree of glory to another (2 Corinthians 3:18) and like the growth of any living creature, this will often go unnoticed. At other moments it will involve a profound engagement with God and others. As we become more honest with God, and ourselves, we become more able to need other people appropriately, and use the tools God has given us:

- Of coming as we are
- Waiting in His presence
- Connecting to any feeling
- Validating where we are
- Naming any wounds
- Naming sin (by us or against us)
- Naming confusion, disappointments and causes of grief
- Naming anger, rejection, shame etc. and bringing them to God
- Facing reality in Him: He will keep us alive.

We can then participate in an exchange with God and be enabled to receive what we need from Him: comfort, courage, forgiveness and so on, remembering that sometimes we cannot even express what we are carrying or bringing. This provision is real because Jesus came in the flesh to make it so. God is infinite, unshockable and all knowing, so He can supply the peace, affirmation, comfort, strength, cleansing – or anything else that we need – in full measure.

God is the Giver of Life

As we learn to rest in God's presence, so many things in life start to take care of themselves and we save a lot of the energy that went on fretting or holding ourselves together.

- Finding rest for our souls in God alone is essential
- Receiving ongoing life/being from God can ensure that we are not running on empty or living out of a place of deprivation or need. We will reach the place of fullness or quietness within that we never thought was possible
- As God mends our broken hearts we have a place to store His ongoing gift of life
- Seeking God for His affirmation and advocacy. We need to keep going on this until we start to believe it for ourselves and our old labels or persona are exchanged for God's truth and honour
- We offer God our difficulties to attach and invite Him to heal this and enable us to dare to draw near and attach to Him.

God the Good Shepherd

As we come to an end, it is a good time to review Psalm 23, which we looked at near the beginning of the course:

- Do I now feel more accompanied by God and cared for, as by a shepherd? Where do I graze? With the flock, near the shepherd or off on my own?

- Am I becoming more secure in God's care? Am I more able to just 'be' and dare to be alone, still and quiet both for myself and to practise God's presence?

- Can I sleep any better? Am I seeking God for good rest?

- Do I feel more substantial inside, more the person I feel I was made to be?

- Am I becoming more aware of what righteousness is for me and am I becoming more empowered to recognise it, desire it, choose it and expect it in my life?

- Even though I may have walked through the valley of the shadow of death, am I more prepared to emerge from there now? Have I glimpsed more 'life'? Is God's love and presence more tangible for me? Does His face shine on me, or is it still eclipsed by shadows? Am I choosing life? Have I stopped camping in the shadow of death and moved into the Father's house?

- Am I aware of God's accompanying presence and advocacy for me – His encouragement and strength with me?

- Am I enjoying the feast He has laid for me in His house? The feast has all my favourites and what I need to refresh and nourish me. I am the honoured guest and He does this in front of all my unseen enemies from the past. They can only look on as I enjoy honour and welcome in the courts of God. They haven't won. I am not stuck in isolation, shame and grief. I have chosen life

- He anoints me as His son/daughter, as His chosen, as one who is His priest in the world, to make Him seen and felt

- My cup overflows so I am sure of having a full measure. I have not been cheated. He has not over-looked me or skimped on His joy over me. He is lavish towards me. He toasts me!

- As I bed down in His love, I can know what it is really to live in, not simply be a guest in, His house and be fully enfolded by His goodness and mercy forever.

In Middle Eastern culture, a guest would never choose where they would stay; it was always at the invitation of the community who would give the best place they could. In the same way, God invites us to live with Him in His house and in His community.

God the Trinity invites us to celebrate with Him that we have been adopted fully back into His family as beloved sons and daughters, that Jesus delights in us His brothers and sisters and has shared His full inheritance with us and that we have the Holy Spirit living in us as our comforter and advocate and guarantee. Hallelujah!

Who is among you who [reverently] fears the Lord,
who obeys the voice of His Servant, yet who walks in darkness and deep trouble
and has no shining splendour in his heart? Let him rely on, trust in,
and be confident in the name of the Lord,
and let him lean upon and be supported by his God

(ISAIAH 50:10) (AMP)

Then my soul will rejoice in the Lord and delight in His salvation.
My whole being will exclaim, Who is like you, Lord?
You rescue the poor from those too strong for them,
the poor and needy from those who rob them

(PSALM 35:9, 10)

You have come to know the grace or undeserved favour of God in reality:
deeply, clearly and thoroughly, becoming accurately and intimately acquainted
with it. That you may live and conduct yourselves in a manner worthy of the Lord,
fully pleasing to Him and desiring to please Him in all things, bearing fruit in
every good work and steadily growing and increasing in and by the knowledge
of God [with fuller, deeper and clearer insight, acquaintance and recognition.

(COLOSSIANS 1:6, 10) (AMP)

My salvation and honour depend on God. Find rest O my soul in Him alone

(PSALM 62:7, 5)

The thief comes to steal, kill and destroy.
I came that you may have life and have it abundantly

(JOHN 10:10)

Amen!

NOTES

APPENDIX A
CO-DEPENDENCY VS EMOTIONAL DEPENDENCY

	CO-DEPENDENT	EMOTIONAL DEPENDENT
Presentation	Saint, servant, messiah, safe, dependable until overstretched then panic	Sinner, pain in the neck, chaotic, demanding
Aloneness	Alone inside, terrified, wants friends but fears letting anyone close, rejection, hides aloneness, unaware of the pain inside	Alone inside, terrified, latches on in exclusive relationships, bust up, shows aloneness, desperate not to be abandoned
Control	Over control, fears loss of control, actually is being controlled by another's opinion etc. Sacrifices choice to survive	The emotional attachment is/feels out of control, seeks to control the other, desperate to stay connected, sacrifices choice to survive
Touch and affection	Terrified of it, yet yearns for it	Craves and demands it
Shame	Very fragile self-worth, real or perceived rejection, sense of shame about who I am	Very fragile, feelings of shame and disappointment, incidents of abandonment or rejection
Change	Afraid of change, especially in object of control	Afraid of change and terrified of loss
Sensitivity	Only aware of other's feelings, feels them in preference to their own: may have to face pain, thinks they are very feeling person but often numb or only feeling different types of anger, terrified of criticism – often perfectionist and judgmental	Often only aware of their own feelings, afraid of other people's feelings in case of rejection, can mistake craven need for passion and love
Idolatry	Their competence and control	The object of their affection
Survival	Death through rejection, at some point really feared extinction of self	Death through aloneness, at some point deep abandonment
Sense of self	Very little – laid it down rather than be unacceptable	Very little – and try to get it from relationships

	CO-DEPENDENT	EMOTIONAL DEPENDENT
Fear	Rejection, intimacy or being out of control	Of abandonment and non-being
Trust	Inability to trust – refusing help is safest. It's best to do it themselves	Apparent over-trust of others
Unmet needs	Of nurture, tenderness, affirmation and acceptance	Of belonging, nurture, bonding and affirmation
Boundaries	Very scary so over-set boundaries, but in life unable to say no or make decisions that risk rejection, usually on overload	No boundaries until need to be exclusive, invades the other's boundaries
Self	Feels tiny, unlovable or unacceptable inside. Avoids attention until the martyr phase	Feels unloved but exposes neediness and demands attention and help
Relationships	Control and avoidance of intimacy, mostly in service mode. Set pattern: need me, I know best – how you feel, what you need, when, how! Rescue mode, avoid the true picture. Only their version is valid, manipulative, jealous, passive-aggression if crossed, cannot receive so no reciprocity. They have no needs that anyone else need meet. Advice giving, solution giving	Out of control – also avoidance of intimacy, merely an intense connection. Sometimes eroticised. Set pattern: I need you completely, read and meet my needs, rescue me, fill me, no objectivity – so immersed, manipulative, jealous, all consuming, devoted, only receive, nothing to give

APPENDIX B
ADULT CHILDREN FROM DYSFUNCTIONAL FAMILIES

Living in a strained, chaotic, deprived, abusive, overcrowded, alcoholic, workaholic, overly pious, criminal, or exotic, that is, in a dysfunctional family, can leave us with very little idea of what is normal. We will have probably grown up thinking everyone got everything they asked for, or everyone's Dad gave them a black eye, or only appeared at weekends, or no one had new clothes or personal space, or jetted off on skiing holidays every year or that everyone's Mum cried every day. Whatever it was, we may find we are left with some gaps in reality and some behaviour patterns that aren't shared by many other people. It can help to put things into perspective and make new choices as an adult.

We can subconsciously engineer circumstances as repeat scenarios that have become familiar to us. For example, always having the adrenalin rush of being late; never trying our hardest; choosing the same type of broken person again as a friend or getting out of a relationship before rejection comes. Some of these may ring a bell for us:

- We have to guess at what is 'normal'
- We feel as if we are on the edge of life – as if we missed the briefing and everyone else knows the rules
- We find it hard to make choices or follow anything through to completion
- We have little sense of fun and find it hard to relax and have fun or risk looking foolish
- We take ourselves rather seriously
- We have difficulty letting ourselves be known – real intimacy is frightening because we might be discovered
- We lie when it would be as easy to tell the truth
- We judge ourselves harshly
- We can tend to blame shift and are afraid of taking the consequences of our actions
- We are more comfortable at the extremes: at 1 or 10, or when things are dramatic or tense, as this is our familiar zone
- We can swing between being super-responsible and super-irresponsible
- We constantly need affirmation, reassurance or approval
- We maintain a misplaced loyalty to some people regardless of the evidence
- We lose it or overreact to circumstances where we are not in control
- We can be impulsive and continue a course of action that is not the best – we cannot cut our losses
- We can find it hard to leave our families behind, or we have cut off from them inappropriately.

We may want to change and give ourselves new permission to live from a place where:

- I can make choices beyond mere survival
- I have a right to say 'no' to anything if I don't feel ready or it is unsafe
- My life need not be motivated by fear or guilt
- I can dare to feel and know my feelings are as valid and useful as anyone else's
- I can start to be objective about life and not feel guilty about everything – including being alive
- I can make mistakes and own up to them. I can allow others to make mistakes
- I can mind about things and be upset without apologising. I do not need to smile when I cry
- I can make choices about people: I do not need to continue conversations with people who put me down or make me feel humiliated
- I can and must take responsibility for my lifestyle: my health, my finances, my home, my diet, my recreation. I do not need to settle for less, prove anything or view myself as 'less than' or undeserving
- I can be relaxed, playful and frivolous
- I can take risks and set boundaries and limits
- I can be angry with someone I love. I can learn to handle conflict and keep the relationship
- I know I am as loved by God as everyone else and can become the person God has made me to be.

Thank you, Lord, that I am a new creation in Christ and that I am a beloved child of the Father, fully owned as a co-heir by Jesus and indwelt and loved by the Spirit.

Amen

APPENDIX C
FINDING GRACE IN SEXUAL SIN AND ADDICTIONS

See to it that no one misses out on the grace of God

(HEBREWS 12:15-17)

This call comes towards the end of Paul's letter to the Hebrews. It is a letter written to Christians who were steeped in knowledge of the Bible. They understood who Jesus was as Son, Great High Priest and the Passover Lamb. They understood the whole sacrificial system, the tabernacle and the old and new covenants. They appreciated the power of the blood of Jesus, the strength and purpose of the 'greats' of the faith, and some of their own church had even been martyred. Yet, here we find a call to holiness and a plea not to miss out on the grace of God. This shows us that length of service or biblical knowledge does not guarantee that we are living in the good of the grace of God.

It is possible to 'miss out 'on the grace of God and this can lead to self-pity and bitterness. As we then spread this around, it breeds discontent with God and sin in the life of the church. Once we are at odds with God we lose the reality of His comfort and presence and our sense of sin. Our self-pity can then justify anything, and soon, we are seeking consolation in sinful sexual behaviours or instant gratification, like Esau, in food, drink, pornography or any other addiction.

If we despise our birthright as sons and daughters of the Living God and feel that we can manage without His blessing, we seek to save ourselves through others or through things. This can happen in practice or it can be in fantasy, festering away in our hearts. Either way it is a slippery slope that starts with feeling we are missing out on the grace of God.

The progression is as follows:

A sense of missing out on the grace of God ⇒ Bitterness and self-pity ⇒ Sexual sin and immorality ⇒ Instant gratification ⇒ Despising our birthright in God – to be His sons and daughters ⇒ Feeling we can live without the blessing of God

The kindness of God towards us, even in our sin, is meant to lead us to repentance. His desire for us to be holy comes from His knowledge of us and His love for us. This is the best way for us to live – it works, blesses us and enables us to be a blessing to others. We become fully human, not deprived or naive. It means the nature and glory of God continue to live on earth through us. We are to live out of the dignity and splendour of who He has made us to be.

For the Hebrews, it was their failure to live as residents of Mount Zion (Hebrews 12:22-23), even in the mortal stage of eternal life that was at the root of their sin. They had lost this wonder, and with it, their place among the heavenly host. They had lost sight of the new covenant.

So, if you are in the throes of any kind of sexual sin – check out *where* you live and *how* you live. Are you living out of the knowledge of His love for you?

You are fearfully and wonderfully made - do you know that full well moment by moment?

Do you live in the goodness of God's grace to you, or are you missing out and settling for less or resigning yourself to a place of isolation and self-pity?

The likelihood is that somewhere along the line you feel you've mislaid the grace of God. It can help to go back and find out when and how this happened. As you ask God to find you in this place, you will see the Father running to meet you and welcome you back. We simply need to let the love of God enfold us as we humbly seek to come to the end of our self-sufficiency and isolation.

Jesus has taken the path of total humiliation to secure our return to the Father's house. He will be with us as in humility we make our way to the Cross and He will meet us there with His resurrection and healing. This will be particularly relevant for us if we are suffering the pain of an addiction.

The pains of addiction

Pain of a broken heart

A broken heart manifests itself in a feeling of emptiness deep inside, rather than being full of life and being. We feel completely alone and are aware of not being accompanied through life by a good father and all that this brings – affirmation and benevolent strength. We feel that we are not enough and may always feel left out. Three questions may tug away: Can I feel safe? Is there enough? Am I enough?

Pain of the addictive cycle

We will feel the pain of the underlying need and the grip of the addiction. We feel the release in the early euphoric phase of the cycle: the acting out, followed quickly by the pain of realising our acting out hasn't helped. This is followed by the pain of still being empty and of shame, helplessness and guilt.

The spiritual pain

This is the pain of separation from God and the life, comfort and forgiveness He brings. We are aware of the thirst for God but trying to meet it through sin. We may despair as God seems not to rescue us. We experience the pain of deadening out our humanity and heart and we will even experience this in our ongoing real relationships.

The pain of lust

Lust is the drive to find a substitute for God. It is the opposite of love because it only wants to take, to use and to devour. It is driven, not free and fails to take into account the effect on others. It consumes. There is a hypocrisy and vanity about it.

The pain of false intimacy

This is shutting off to godly ways of knowing. Mutual respect and being known are denied. There is a deep rejection wound that needs to be protected so the only relational contact is sensual and/or in fantasy. Of course, this is deeply frustrating and leaves us lonelier than ever and, if we allow ourselves to realise it, guilty and ashamed.

Relational pain

How do we conduct our everyday relationships with these secrets? We will be detached and unreal, with even our spouse being reduced to a sexual object as sexual fantasy is used, even in our marital sexual relationship. Everyone else is reduced to a sexual object and they will feel it with sexual fantasy being used to engage in any marital sexual activity. There will be anger, blame-shifting and projection of our pain onto others. The tension can be turned into an excuse and quarrels are precipitated to justify the behaviour. The betrayal hurts both parties as well as any children.

The pain of narcissism

This is putting yourself first and of trying to maintain an exterior that can face the world, despite very real crippling self-doubt on the inside. Narcissism requires high maintenance. It even sets itself up against God, knowing better what it needs. The amount of energy needed to keep up the denial and the façade is huge. Glimpses of the fragile sense of self inside are too awful for us to bear.

The pain of shame

This includes despair, guilt and apparently unanswered prayer. This often comes in waves and can be both a means of extra pain or grace to us.

The pain of obsession and compulsion

This is a preoccupation with an object of attachment. An obsession comes with the feeling: 'I have to have this, attach to it or "I will die"'. Eventually these thoughts can fill the mind so completely that ordinary life becomes an intrusion. In a compulsion, the obsessive thoughts have become persistent actions/behaviours. They override logical thinking and the conscience. When we have numbed out on real life and our thoughts are filled with sexual acts they can dominate all our thinking, decisions and life. The pain of our early unhealthy attachments or lack of attachment to our mothers is still unhealed. The desperation we feel is a potent reminder of how lost we are.

What pains do I know in my heart?

The effect of addictions on our relationships

Relationship with God

When we live with addictions, God can feel distant. It can feel as if He is eclipsed by the struggle, or we blame Him and label Him as a hard task-master. If this is the case, then there has probably never been a real understanding of grace as the basis for salvation: that we could never earn His love; that we have been saved from rejection and that God is trustworthy.

A key part of the healing journey is daring to practise His presence, which alone is the healing, comforting presence. God just wants to meet us at the very point of conflict and sin and to meet with us as a whole person, not just with the presentable part of our life (if there still is one). This meeting with God is our only hope for bringing our heart out of numbness and back into life. Our fantasy bubble must burst.

Relationship with oneself

This will be complex:

- There will have to be an inner split for someone made in the image of God to be so at odds with his or her beliefs. We will need to come out of the denial that says: everything is OK really, we just have a minor issue to solve!
- We will need to pray for and find a new, or resumed sense, of the fear of the Lord. From this we can start to come back to God and commune with Him. For example pouring out our heart, even if it is not coherent. As we do so, we should include the blame-shifting and the anger towards God and self. He longs to take it!
- We will need to pray for God to reinstate our conscience, will, choice and ability to take responsibility
- We will need to move on from confession into repentance
- We allow Jesus to understand and be present as Man as well as God . We offer Him our broken hearts so that they can function again, so we can know and see/feel with our hearts, and not just in the flesh
- We choose to acknowledge and lay aside passivity, cynicism and slothfulness
- We will need to eat humble pie.

How is my relationship with God and my relationship with myself?

We need to realise:

- Just how cut off we have allowed ourselves to become and that we have not allowed anyone to "see to it that [we didn't miss] out on the grace of God" (Hebrews 12:15)
- That we are clinging to a worthless idol and therefore missing out on the grace of God (Jonah 2:8)
- That this thing in my right hand is a lie and I am being duped (Isaiah 44:20)
- That however isolated we have been in our behaviours, they will have affected other people and our ability to relate in real-time
- Compulsive masturbation may have become our only type of 'feeling'
- How much we have despised or distanced ourselves from the ordinary stuff of life.

Relationships with others

This will also be complex:

- Coming out of the control of the fantasy and the buzz of illicit connections is difficult, but vital. These things need to be named for what they are
- Real-live relationships will be perceived as risky, boring, threatening, the unknown
- Broken trust, betrayal, the ability to lie and deception will all have taken their toll. Eventually the inner split must be resolved for us to become one person in Christ. This is possible as we grow in our experience of grace from others, and choose to be known and allow this grace to become a part of our life
- We need to enter into the stress and effort of working on ordinary relationships. We will need to join in with ordinary life and allow non-sexualised encounters to have their own worth and benefit. This will be an essential part of our healing
- We need real and straightforward accountability, but who should it be with and how much should our spouse know?
- Allow for our spouse to have their own concerns and needs and to set new boundaries in the relationship and find their own support.

Often there is the dilemma of: "You must now tell me everything so I know you are being open and I can start to trust you again" versus, "If you do anything again then you are out". There is a need for and clear discussions between all parties, as trust can only be built slowly. The next step may be for the spouse to allow someone else to know more than they do while sobriety is recovered.

Is this a key issue for me? Do I need to explore some specific help in this area?

The healing process

We will need to go into the healing process with people who are not afraid to challenge, but with whom there is respect and safety. Truth, dignity and grace are all vital to the process.
We will need to:

- Come out of denial and victim mode

- Take responsibility and surrender any sense of entitlement

- Set up real, honest accountability with peers

- Keep up the process of accountability especially when it's hard – realising that each step will lead to more

- Start to be aware of feelings and dare to come out of the numbness: am I hungry, anxious, angry, lonely or tired? Where do I feel it? Can I allow myself to feel something and not have to numb it out straight away?

- Identify fears and anxieties more and more specifically and allow God and other people to know about them and meet them

- Use extra materials specific to sexual addiction. Soberly and carefully work out your addiction cycle and face the triggers so that when they occur they can be named and dealt with

- Use the basic biblical principles of healing of wounds layer-by-layer and the confession of sin, simply stated without excuses

- Forgive others specifically and allow the hurt they have caused to surface and be grieved

- Offer the inadequacies and mysteries to God for His comfort

- Realise that one set of addictions can just be replaced by another unless the roots and denial are dealt with

- Try to see a fall as 'not progress' while accepting that all is not lost. What can I learn from this? Ask questions such as: Why now and in this way?

- Allow others to see to it that you don't miss out on God's grace. This will involve coming out of isolation and learning to receive without shame

- Play an active part giving who you really are, rather than getting stuck as the problem person

- Stay at the Cross

- Remember, 'Lust promises what it cannot deliver'.

Other vital areas of ministry

- The surrender process

- The Cross and confession

- Choosing to trust and building a new intimacy with God

- Building a disciplined life

- Allowing God to reveal the roots and wounds

- Embracing loss as the way of gain
- Generational prayer
- Spiritual cleansing
- Facing and being healed from the woundings from our mothers, fathers, siblings and peers
- Facing and being healed from abuse
- Forgiving others and myself
- Rebuilding my true self in God
- Redefining normal life as opposed to life through addiction
- Appreciating and living out the simple things of life
- Living in right relationships and accountability.

NOTES